The Internet and Mobile Telecommunications
System of Innovation

The Internet and Mobile Telecommunications System of Innovation

Developments in Equipment, Access and Content

Edited by

Charles Edquist

Linköping University, Sweden

Edward Elgar
Cheltenham, UK•Northampton, MA, USA

Published by
Edward Elgar Publishing Limited
Glensanda House
Montpellier Parade
Cheltenham
Glos GL50 1UA
UK

Edward Elgar Publishing, Inc.
136 West Street
Suite 202
Northampton
Massachusetts 01060
USA

A catalogue record for this book
is available from the British Library

Library of Congress Cataloguing in Publication Data
The Internet and mobile telecommunications system of innovation :
developments in equipment, access, and content / edited by Charles Edquist.
    p. cm.
Includes indexes.
1. Wireless Internet. 2. Wireless communication systems. I. Edquist, Charles, 1947–

TK5103.4885 .I54 2003
004.67'8—dc21   2002037936

ISBN 1 84376 232 3 (cased)
     1 84376 347 8 (paperback)

Printed and bound in Great Britain by MPG Books Ltd, Bodmin, Cornwall

Contents

Figures

Tables

Contributors

Nicoletta Corrocher is Research Fellow at the Centre for Research on Innovation and Internationalization (CESPRI), Bocconi University. Current research areas include economics of information and communication technologies and the Internet, diffusion of ICT in the financial sector, evolution of industrial districts, and emergence of new industries and technologies in high-tech fields.

Bent Dalum is Associate Professor with the IKE Group, Department of Business Studies, Aalborg University. His research focuses on technology and international specialization and regional innovation systems in information and communication technologies.

Charles Edquist is Professor at the Department of Technology and Social Change, Linköping University, Sweden. His main fields of research are economics of innovation and innovation policy. Hommen and Edquist together coordinate the Systems of Innovation Research Programme (SIRP).

Leif Hommen is Associate Professor at the Department of Technology and Social Change, Linköping University, Sweden. His current research concerns the socioeconomic aspects of innovations.

Esa Manninen is a PhD student at the Department of Technology and Social Change, Linköping University, Sweden. His thesis focuses on quantitative employment effects of process and product innovations in the Swedish telecommunications industry.

Gert Villumsen is Associate Professor at the Department of Business Studies, Aalborg University and Research Librarian at Aalborg University Library. His research centres on relations between economic development and technological specialization, with focus on clustering dynamics.

Preface

This book focuses on 'new' areas of the telecommunications sectoral system of innovation, particularly fixed data communications (including the Internet) and mobile telecommunications (including mobile Internet).[1] We largely disregard traditional telecommunications – equipment for fixed telecommunications systems and fixed telecommunications voice services, and concentrate instead on what is emerging and growing, i.e., how the sectoral system of innovation is currently changing and how previously independent systems are converging.

We address both equipment production (material goods) and the production (provision) of intangible service products. This is because innovations in manufacturing and services are *complementary* – service innovations are dependent upon manufacturing innovations, and the reverse is also true. It is hard to imagine a mobile phone call without a mobile handset, and vice versa. And the Internet is useless without content. Such a combined approach, addressing both the production of goods and services, is unusual.

Equipment production includes routers and other kinds of exchanges for the Internet as well as base stations, exchanges and handsets for mobile telecommunications. It might be noted that such equipment is currently constituted not only by hardware, but also by software to a very large extent. Equipment producers such as Cisco and Ericsson employ thousands of software engineers and might therefore be labelled giant software firms.

The provision of Internet service products is often said to be accounted for by so-called 'Internet service providers' (ISPs). However, with this term we normally mean provision of access to the Internet – which is certainly a service product. This means that firms usually known as Internet service providers would be better named Internet access providers (IAPs). This increasingly includes providers of access to mobile telecommunications systems. However, for the Internet to be useful and in demand there must also be content supplied. Other kinds of service products constitute this

---

[1] When we use the term 'telecommunications sectoral system of innovation' we refer to fixed data communications (including the Internet) and mobile telecommunications (including mobile Internet). In chapter 1 we address whether it is useful to talk about *one* system or *several* systems of innovation in this field.

content and other firms than the IAPs often supply it. A proper name for these would be Internet content providers (ICPs).[2] For these reasons we shall be talking about 'equipment production, access provision and content provision' in this book.

The findings reported in this book were part of a Targeted Socioeconomic Research project sponsored by the European Commission/DGXII.[3] It was entitled 'Sectoral Systems in Europe: Innovation, Competitiveness and Growth', or more commonly called by its acronym, ESSY. ESSY was co-ordinated by Franco Malerba at CESPRI, Bocconi University. The ESSY Project is the result of the work of ten research groups in seven European countries. The overall purpose of the project was:

- to build a research methodology which focuses on sectoral systems,
- to understand the functioning and evolution of six major sectoral systems in Europe,
- to study the determinants of the European performance in these six sectors and
- to develop new policy options and implications on this basis.

We used a system perspective to analyse and compare the salient features of six sectoral systems of innovation.[4] System boundaries, demand conditions, links and interactions among firms, non-firm organizations (government, universities and financial organizations) and institutions were analysed. Moreover, patterns of change and coevolution among technology, firms, market structure, demand and European international performance were assessed. We asked whether the factors conducive to European innovative and commercial international leadership, or to European lack of success, were sector specific or pertained to regions or countries. Finally, we aimed to develop policy implications and options for Europe.

Chapter 1 introduces the subject of the sectoral system of innovation in fixed Internet and mobile telecommunications. It discusses conceptual matters related to the systems of innovation approach. It is also partly a synthesis and partly a summary of parts of the rest of the book, in addition to addressing issues not covered in these.

In chapter 2, Bent Dalum and Gert Villumsen analyse the fixed data communication network with some emphasis on the development and

---

[2] Hence IAPs and ICPs constitute ISPs.

[3] We gratefully acknowledge financial contributions from the European Commission and the Swedish Agency for Innovation Systems (VINNOVA).

[4] The six case studies of specific sectoral systems were Services (Retailing, Airports and Medical services), Software, Fixed Data Communications and Mobile Telecommunications, Pharmaceuticals and Biotechnology, Machine Tools, and Chemicals.

production of equipment. Leif Hommen analyses second- and third-generation mobile telecommunications in chapters 3 and 4, and this is followed by Bent Dalum's account of the part of satellite communications that is related to telecommunication networks – both wireless and wired.

Chapters 6 and 7 are devoted to the Internet services industry, fixed and mobile. Nicoletta Corrocher analyses first the sectoral dynamics of the Internet services industry, where services include both access and content; then she provides an account of country-specific trends in the UK, Italy and Sweden. Finally, chapter 8 is devoted to the policy implications for Internet and mobile telecommunications as well as an account of the future of the sectoral system in Europe, the US and Japan.

Charles Edquist
Linköping, 24 June 2002

1. The Fixed Internet and Mobile Telecommunications Sectoral System of Innovation: Equipment, Access and Content

Charles Edquist

1. INTRODUCTION[1]

This chapter introduces the subject of the sectoral system of innovation in fixed Internet and mobile telecommunications. Sections 2 and 3 are mainly conceptual and theoretical discussions of the characteristics, general policy implications and boundaries of the systems of innovation approach. Section 4 deals with Internet and mobile telecommunications: it is part summary, part synthesis, of the following six chapters. Readers more interested in telecommunications and the Internet than conceptual and theoretical issues related to systems of innovation are advised to proceed directly to section 4.[2]

2. SYSTEMS OF INNOVATION (SI)

2.1. Characteristics of the SI Approach

'Systems of innovation' (SI) is a fairly new conceptual framework for the study of innovations. An SI can be defined as including 'all important economic, social, political, organizational, institutional and other factors that influence the development, diffusion and use of innovations' (Edquist 1997:

---

[1] I wish to thank Bent Dalum, Nicoletta Corrocher, Jeffrey Funk, Leif Hommen, Per Högselius, Michael Jensen, Martin Kenney and Gert Villumsen for very useful comments on earlier drafts of this chapter.
[2] Chapter 8 draws together the policy implications of the analysis and discusses the future of the sectoral system of innovation and the relations between Europe, the US and Japan within the system.

14).[3] These factors can be studied in a national, regional or sectoral context. In other words, national, regional and sectoral systems of innovation coexist and complement one another. Initially, a national perspective (e.g., Lundvall 1992; Nelson 1993) dominated the SI approach. Later regional (e.g., Braczyk et al. 1998) and sectoral ones (e.g., Carlsson and Stankiewicz 1995; Breschi and Malerba 1997) were developed and have become more important. These three kinds of SI approaches can be seen as different variants of a generic system of innovation approach, as argued in Edquist (1997: 11–12).

The generic SI approach can be characterized as follows. We know intuitively and empirically that different organizations and institutions are important for innovation processes. Let us therefore, for the time being, consider organizations and institutions to be the main *components* or *elements* of systems of innovation. There is also general agreement on this in the SI literature, although this is sometimes not expressed in a clear and direct manner. Let me specify what organizations and institutions mean here.

Organizations are formal structures that are consciously created and have an explicit purpose (Edquist and Johnson 1997: 47). They are players or actors.[4] Some important organizations in SIs are companies (which can be suppliers, customers or competitors in relation to other companies), universities, venture capital organizations and public innovation policy agencies.

Institutions are sets of common habits, routines, established practices, rules or laws that regulate the relations and interactions between individuals, groups and organizations (Edquist and Johnson 1997: 46). They are the rules of the game. Examples of important institutions in SIs are patent laws and rules influencing the relations between universities and firms.[5]

Although there is general agreement in the literature that 'organizations' and 'institutions' are the main components of SIs, there is no agreement what these terms mean. For example, institutions for Nelson and Rosenberg are basically different kinds of organizations (according to the definition above), but for Lundvall the term institution means the rules of the game (Nelson and Rosenberg 1993: 5, 9–13; Lundvall 1992: 10). Hence, not only is 'institution' used in at least two different senses in the literature but these senses are often confused – even by the same author. The conceptual ambiguity and fuzziness

---

[3] Innovations are defined as new creations of economic significance, primarily carried out by firms. They include product innovations as well as process innovations. Product innovations are new – or better – products (or product varieties) being produced and sold; it is a question of *what* is produced. They include new material goods as well as new intangible services. Process innovations are new ways of producing goods and services; it is a matter of *how* existing products are produced. They may be technological or organizational. For further specifications see Edquist et al. (2001: 10–17)

[4] Although there are other kinds of actors than organizations – e.g. individuals – the terms 'organizations' and 'actors' will be used interchangeably in this chapter.

[5] Obviously, these definitions are of a Northian character (North 1990: 5).

surrounding 'institution' has not been sorted out; it is an unresolved issue (Edquist 1997: 24–6).

Systems of innovation can be quite different from one another, with regard to specialization of production, resources spent on research and development (R&D) and so on. For example, industrial production in the United States is much more specialized in R&D intensive ('high-tech') products than the European Union (EU) (Fagerberg 2001; Edquist and Texier 1996). Further, within the EU, R&D intensities vary greatly between countries. In addition, organizations and institutions constituting components of the systems may be different. For example, research institutes and company-based research departments may be important organizations in one country (e.g., Japan) while research universities may perform a similar function in another (e.g., the United States).[6] Institutions such as laws, norms and values also differ considerably between systems.

In summary, there seems to be general agreement that the main elements in SIs are organizations and institutions. However, the specification of these components certainly varies between systems.

The SI approach emphasizes interdependence. This is based on the understanding that firms normally do not innovate in isolation but interact more or less closely with other organizations, through complex relations that are often characterized by reciprocity and feedback mechanisms in several loops. This interaction between organizations occurs in the context of existing institutions.

Let me now therefore address the *relations* between the main components of SIs. *Interactions between different organizations* are crucial in learning processes that are normally the basis for the development of innovations. These relations may be of a market or non-market kind. Here it could be mentioned that markets only co-ordinate transactions, i.e., items sold and bought. They do not deal with other kinds of relations. Interactive learning processes between organizations, for example, concern exchange of knowledge elements and collaborations that are not easily handled through market transactions. Markets are important in systems of innovation, but other mechanisms – e.g., non-market-based collaboration – which mediate the relations between components in the systems are also important.

The *relations between organizations and institutions* are important for innovations and for the operation of systems of innovation. Organizations are strongly influenced and shaped by institutions; organizations can be said to be 'embedded' in an institutional environment or set of rules, which include the legal system, norms, standards, etc. But institutions are also embedded in organizations. Examples are firm-specific practices with regard to bookkeep-

---

[6] Hence, different organizations may perform the same function in different systems.

ing or concerning the relations between managers and employees; many institutions develop inside firms. Hence, there is a complicated two-way relationship of mutual embeddedness between institutions and organizations, and this influences innovation processes as well as the performance and change of systems of innovation (Edquist and Johnson 1997: 59–60).

Some organizations create institutions. Examples are organizations that set standards and public organizations that formulate and implement rules that we call innovation policy (Edquist and Johnson 1997: 60). Institutions may also be the basis for the creation of organizations, e.g., when a government makes a law that leads to the establishment of an organization.

There may also be important *interactions between different institutions*, e.g., between patent laws and informal rules concerning exchange of information between firms. Institutions of different kinds may support and reinforce one another, but they may also contradict and be in conflict with one another.

The relations between organizations and institutions are very complex and often characterized by reciprocity. This emphasis on the complex relations between components constitutes a major advantage of the SI approach. However, it also constitutes a challenge since our knowledge about these relations is very limited. The relations between two phenomena cannot be satisfactorily investigated if they are not conceptually distinguished from each other. It is therefore important to specify the concepts and to make a clear distinction between organizations and institutions in order to be able to address the relations between them. A precise scientific language is a precondition for empirical work; analytical distinctions and conceptual specificity are essential.

When the innovation concept has been specified (as in footnote 3), a crucial issue is to identify all the important 'factors that influence the development, diffusion and use of innovations', i.e., the factors that define a system of innovation. It is not sufficient to identify the main components of SIs and the relations between them. We must also explicitly address what 'happens' in the systems. What do the organizations do in relation to innovation processes? How do institutions constrain or prevent organizations from doing certain things related to innovation processes and stimulate them to do others? What role do the relations between the components in the systems play for innovation processes? What is the overall function of the system as a whole – constituted by the components and the relations between them? Hence, it is important to move beyond descriptions of components of the systems and the relations between them. An obvious way to do so is to deal with the 'activities' and 'functions' of the systems.

At one level, the most important function – i.e., the 'overall function' – of an SI is, of course, to develop, diffuse and use innovations. At a more specific level it is a question of focusing upon factors that *influence* the development, diffusion and use of innovations. Examples might be the production of economically relevant knowledge through R&D or the financing of innovation development. Hence system 'activities' and the 'specific functions' or 'sub-functions' of systems are more or less the same as determinants of innovation processes or factors influencing them (Edquist 2001c: 9).[7]

For national SIs, country borders normally constitute the geographical boundaries. Regional SIs are simply spatially delimited to a certain subnational geographical area. These spatial boundaries of innovation systems are fairly easy to specify. Other kinds of boundaries (sectoral and functional) will be addressed in section 3, where sectoral SIs are discussed further.

2.2. General Policy Implications of the SI Approach[8]

Here I briefly deal with *general* policy implications of the SI approach. They are general in the sense that they are of a 'sign-post' character. They can serve as rules of thumb and point out relevant issues. However, they are not a sufficient basis for designing specific innovation policies. The general policy issues do not tell a policy maker exactly what to do and how in order to improve the functioning of the system. The SI approach as such cannot provide this, but neither can any other approach or theory.[9]

The following lists general policy implications that have been discussed in more detail elsewhere (Edquist 2001b):

- Organizational actors might need to be created, redesigned or abolished.
- Institutional rules might need to be created, redesigned or abolished.
- Innovation policy should focus not only on the elements of the systems, but also – and perhaps primarily – on the relations between them.

---

[7] The literature has thus far neglected to deal with these sub-functions in systems of innovation in a systematic manner. They were largely ignored in the early literature and have only recently been addressed. Thus, surprisingly, little systematic and detailed research has been done on determinants of innovation. At the same time it is a crucial issue, which should motivate a major effort to increase our knowledge of how to explain innovation (Edquist 2001c: 8, 10). However, one could argue that since Nelson and Winter (1982) there has been a focus on some key functions like 'variety creation' and 'selection' – but these are functions of a fairly general kind.

[8] The discussion in this section is intended to serve as a basis for the discussion of policy implications specific for data communications and mobile telecommunications to be presented in the final chapter of this book.

[9] However, the systems of innovation approach also provides a *framework* of analysis for identifying *specific* policy issues. It is helpful in identifying the 'problems' that need to be the object of policy and in specifying how innovation policies to solve or mitigate these problems could be designed. This discussion is elaborated in Edquist (2001b: 50).

- Innovation policy should ensure that negative lock-in situations are avoided.
- Innovation policy should facilitate changes in the production structure.
- Innovation policy should support structural changes in the direction of production sectors dominated by product innovations rather than process innovations.
- Innovation policy should primarily be proactive, supporting emergence of new product areas and new sectoral systems of innovation.
- Innovation policy should be focused on the early stages in the development of product innovations and new sectoral systems of innovation.

The basis for some of the points above is that the potential for dynamic innovations – and the resulting consequences for productivity growth and employment – varies greatly between sectors of production. For example, annual productivity growth is sometimes 10 to 20 times larger in knowledge-intensive sectors than in other sectors. On this basis it can be argued that the sectoral approach to systems of innovation is central with regard to policy. The changes in and between the sectoral systems of innovation lead to changes in the production structures of national and regional systems – as a *consequence*. Such changes in production structures are crucial for the performance of national and regional innovation systems in terms of productivity growth and employment creation. Sectoral systems of innovation are therefore very important when it comes to understanding dynamics (Edquist et al. 2001).

It could also be added that with globalization, regionalization and the consequent erosion of national boundaries, the sector – just like the region – is becoming a crucial level of intervention for national governments pursuing innovation policy. It therefore becomes important to discuss how different kinds of systems of innovation relate to one another.

3. SECTORAL SYSTEMS OF INNOVATION AND SYSTEM BOUNDARIES

A sectoral system of innovation (SSI) is simply a system of innovation restricted to a certain sector. This means that we must specify what we mean by a sector, and by doing so we immediately enter into a discussion of the boundaries of the (sectoral) systems. The distinction between what is inside and outside the system is crucial, i.e., the issue of the boundaries of systems of innovation cannot be neglected. It is therefore necessary to specify the boundaries if empirical studies of specific SIs – of a national, regional or sectoral kind – are to be carried out. As will be discussed later, one way to identify the (functional) boundaries of SIs is to identify the causes or determinants of innovations. But first we must address different kinds of innovation systems – national, regional and sectoral.

We saw earlier that the specification 'national systems of innovation' is only one among several possibilities. However, there are strong reasons to talk about innovations in terms of national systems. One reason is the fact that the various case studies in Nelson (1993) show that there are sharp differences between various national systems in such attributes as institutional set-up, investment in R&D and performance. For example, the differences in these respects between Denmark and Sweden are remarkable – in spite of the fact that these two small countries in northern Europe are very similar in other respects such as language, culture, standard of living, lifestyle, consumption patterns, size of the public sector, and strength of trade unions (Edquist and Lundvall 1993: 5–6). Another very important reason is that most public policies influencing innovation processes or the economy as a whole are still designed and implemented at the national level.[10] In other words, the importance of national systems of innovation partly has to do with the fact that they capture the importance of the political and policy aspects of processes of innovation. It is not only a matter of geographical delimitation; the state, and the power attached to it, is also important.[11]

Systems of innovation may be supranational, national or subnational (regional, local) – and at the same time they may be sectoral within any of these geographical demarcations. There are many potential permutations. Whether a system of innovation should be spatially or sectorally delimited – or both – depends on the object of study.[12] All the approaches mentioned above may be fruitful – but for different purposes or objects of study. Generally, the variants of the generic SI approach complement rather than exclude one another. This is because it is a limitation to talk about globalization and regionalization without addressing the national level. Therefore, it is useful to consider sectoral and regional systems of innovation in relation to national ones.

There are three senses in which we can identify boundaries of SIs:

1. spatially/geographically;
2. sectorally; and
3. functionally.

---

[10] For very large countries the national SI approach is less relevant than for smaller countries – but institutions such as laws and policies are still mainly national, even in a country like the US.
[11] We shall return to the political and innovation policy aspects in section 5.
[12] An 'industrial complex' or 'cluster' as used by Porter (1990) can be seen as a combination of a sectoral and a regional SI if it is regionally delimited. However, such regional/sectoral systems can also be regarded as parts of a national or international sectoral SI.

To define the spatial boundaries is the easier task, although it also has its problems. These boundaries have to be defined for regional and national SIs, and sometimes also for sectoral ones.[13] The problem of *geographical* boundaries is somewhat more complicated for a regional than for a national SI. One question is which criteria should be used to identify the 'region'.

For a regional SI the specification of the boundaries should not be a question of choosing or using administrative boundaries between regions in a mechanical manner (although this might be useful from the point of view of availability of data). Rather it should be a matter of choosing geographical areas for which the degree of 'coherence' or 'inward orientation' is high with regard to innovation processes.[14] One possible operationalization of this criterion could be a minimum level of localized learning spillovers (between organizations), which is often associated with the importance of transfer of tacit knowledge between (individuals and) organizations. A second one could be localized mobility of skilled workers as carriers of knowledge, i.e., that the local labour market is important. A third possibility could be that a minimum proportion of the innovation-related collaborations among organizations should be with partners within the region. This is a matter of localized networks, i.e., the extent to which learning processes between organizations are interactive within regions.

For a national SI the country borders normally provide the boundaries. However, it could be argued that the criteria for regional SIs are as valid for national ones. In other words, if the degree of coherence or inward orientation is very low, the country might not reasonably be considered to have a national SI.

On what it means to be 'national', Nelson and Rosenberg wrote: 'On the one hand, the concept may be too broad. The system of institutions supporting technical innovation in one field, say pharmaceuticals, may have very little overlap with the system of institutions supporting innovations in another field, say aircraft' (Nelson and Rosenberg 1993: 5).[15] Here they actually argue for a sectoral approach.[16]

Leaving the geographical dimension, we can also talk about 'sectorally' delimited systems of innovation, i.e., systems that include only a part of a regional, national or international system. They are delimited to specific technological fields (generic technologies) or product areas.[17] The 'technological

---

[13] However, in the latter case it is usually in practice a combination of sectoral and national/regional delimitation.

[14] This is also important with regard to policy, since it is difficult to influence a very outward-oriented system from a political level within the region.

[15] It may be noted that they use the term 'institution' in the sense that we have defined 'organization' in section 3 and that they deal only with 'technical' innovations.

[16] Richard Nelson also takes this perspective in Mowery and Nelson (1999).

[17] They can be, but are not necessarily, restricted to one sector of production.

systems' approach belongs to this category (although it did not initially use language associated with systems of innovation). Carlsson and Stankiewicz state that

> The nation-state constitutes a natural boundary of many technological systems. Sometimes, however, it may make sense to talk about a regional or local technological system. ... In yet other cases the technological systems are international, even global. Where the boundaries are drawn depends on the circumstances, e.g., the technological and market requirements, the capabilities of various agents, the degree of interdependence among agents, etc. (Carlsson and Stankiewicz 1995: 49)

According to Breschi and Malerba, 'a Sectoral Innovation System (SIS) can be defined as that system (group) of firms active in developing and making a sector's products and in generating and utilizing a sector's technologies' (Breschi and Malerba 1997: 131). However, it is not self-evident what a sector is, i.e., the *sectoral* boundaries are partly a theoretical construction. There is a degree of arbitrariness here and we have to be pragmatic (but must still specify the boundaries). We shall discuss this with specific reference to the Internet and mobile telecommunications system in section 4.4.

To summarize: specific technologies or product areas are used to define the boundaries of sectoral systems, but they must also normally be geographically delimited.

However, within a delimited geographical area (and perhaps also limited to a technology field or product area), the whole socioeconomic system cannot, of course, be considered to be included in the SI. The question is, then, which parts should be included? This is a matter of defining the *functional* boundaries of SIs. These have to be defined for all kinds of SIs: national, regional and sectoral. And this is more complicated than in the cases of the spatial and sectoral boundaries.

Actually, the founding fathers of the SI approach did not address this problem in a systematic manner (and they did not use the term 'functional'). They did not provide a sharp guide to what exactly should be included in a '(national) system of innovation' (Edquist 1997: 13–15, 27).[18] Nor have the functional boundaries of the systems been defined in an operational way since then.

At the beginning of section 2.1, a system of innovation was defined as including 'all important economic, social, political, organizational, institutional and other factors that influence the development, diffusion and use of innovations'. If the concept of innovations has been specified (e.g., as in footnote 3), and if we know the determinants of their development, diffusion and use, we

---

[18] Nelson and Rosenberg provided 'no sharp guide to just what should be included in the innovation system, and what can be left out' (Nelson and Rosenberg 1993: 5–6). Lundvall claimed that 'a definition of the system of innovation must be kept open and flexible' (Lundvall 1992: 13).

should be able to define the functional boundaries of the SIs. This is one reason why it is so important to identify the functions in SIs and the determinants of innovation processes. Given the satisfactory realization of these tasks we should be able to identify the functional boundaries of SIs, whether they are national, regional or sectoral. Admittedly this is not as easy in practice as in principle and for the time being it is an unresolved problem of a 'catch 22' character (Edquist 1997: 15).

To conclude: all SIs must be functionally delimited; they must be geographically delimited if they are not global; and when we address sectoral systems the boundaries of the SIs must also be sectorally delimited.

4. THE MOBILE TELECOMMUNICATIONS AND FIXED INTERNET SECTORAL SYSTEM OF INNOVATION

4.1. Introduction

Section 4 covers important developments occurring in recent decades in mobile telecommunications and fixed data communications (Internet). It synthesizes other reports produced within the ESSY study of the fixed Internet and mobile telecommunications sectoral system of innovation that are included in this book. It is based on these reports, without always explicitly referring to them. This section also tries to fill in the gaps by covering some important issues that are not dealt with in later chapters. This implies, for example, dealing with the birth of mobile telecommunications as triggered by the NMT (Nordic mobile telephony) standard, i.e., part of the institutional basis for the first generation of mobile telecommunications.

Section 4 addresses some key questions in the ESSY project mentioned in the preface, e.g., the knowledge base of the sectoral system, its organizations and institutions and the boundaries of the (data communications and mobile telecommunications) sectoral system. Public policy, the future of the sectoral system and comparisons with the US and Japan are addressed in chapter 8.

Since the main elements of all systems of innovation – including sectoral ones – are *institutions* and *organizations*, I shall discuss these factors – and changes in them – with regard to data communications and mobile telecommunications. The relations between different kinds of organizations and between institutions and organizations will be a central focus in what follows. Institutions are often created by organizations. At the same time, existing institutions influence organizations as well as the relations between them. I shall try to make a clear distinction between institutions and organizations in order to be able to discuss the relations between them.

In addition there is here a certain emphasis on the *functions* of the sectoral systems of innovation. As argued in section 2.1, it is important to address these, and not only the elements of the systems. The main function of innovation systems is the carrying out of innovations. However, the functions of the SIs also include activities leading to innovations. These secondary functions or sub-functions influence the ability of firms (and other organizations) to carry out innovations. Examples of important functions are knowledge creation (through R&D and in other ways), collaboration in pursuing innovation processes, provision of relevant education, creation of standards, etc.

In section 4.2, the main functions and organizations in the sectoral system(s) are briefly addressed. Section 4.3 focuses on institutions, institutional changes and consequences these changes have for organizations and functions. Different subsections will concentrate on fixed Internet, mobile telecommunications, satellite communications and rate structures. In section 4.4, the boundaries between subsystems and convergence between them are addressed.

4.2. Functions and Organizations in the System(s) and Relations Between Them

As we saw in section 2.1, organizations can be defined as formal structures with an explicit purpose which is consciously created. They may also be called agents, actors or players. Their purpose is to perform certain functions in the system(s). In the fixed Internet and mobile telecommunications sectoral system(s) of innovation (SSI) some of the most important functions are:

- developing equipment (innovation in new equipment, hardware and software);
- conducting R&D relevant to the further development of the system(s);
- providing relevant education and training;
- creating standards and other regulations of importance to the systems(s);
- providing access, e.g., Internet access or mobile telecommunications subscriptions;
- developing new content (introduction of new services, e.g., e-commerce); and
- providing consulting services related to all the above.

The functions of an SSI may refer to the development and diffusion of innovations and how smooth and efficient these processes are. In turn this may be a result or how good the SSI is in creating new knowledge or new combinations of existing (and new) knowledge, in providing education, in creating standards, etc. Other functions could also be mentioned. They might refer to how efficient the financing of product development is, how smoothly new firms are created, how inclined firms in the system are to diversify into new product areas, or how efficiently new markets are created for the new products (goods and services).

On the whole, much more work needs to be done on systems of innovation functions. This is quite similar to studying the determinants of innovation – which in section 3 was also argued to be a useful way to define the (functional) boundaries of the system.

Functions are carried out by organizations (or in some cases by individuals). However, there is not always – or even often – a one-to-one relation between functions and organizations. A certain organization can carry out several functions and one function may be carried out by different kinds of organizations. Below is a list of functions and some corresponding organizations that carry them out:

- The development of equipment, which is increasingly of a software kind, is done by telecommunications and Internet equipment producing firms, such as Siemens, Ericsson, Cisco and Motorola.
- These firms also carry out a large part of the R&D needed for developing new systems. Some R&D is also carried out by public universities and dedicated research organizations.
- Education is of great importance to the sectoral system of innovation and is largely carried out by publicly controlled and funded organizations. However, firms also sponsor further education and provide training. In addition learning-by-using and learning-by-doing take place within organizations.
- There are organizations that create the standards and regulations which are important to decrease the degree of uncertainty for equipment producers and to co-ordinate their relations with various other organizations in the Internet and mobile telecommunications sectoral system of innovation. They have often been of a public character, although private organizations have also been intensely involved in these activities. In addition, there are various industry organizations that have a quasi-public character, but no 'official mandate' from government.
- Access is provided by Internet access providers (IAPs) and mobile system operators. They own (or lease) the physical infrastructure (the network) and in this way provide the backbone of the Internet and mobile telecommunications. This category includes incumbent telecommunications operators, new entrant telecommunications operators,

cable TV operators, alternative network providers and 'pure' Internet access providers.[19]

- The access providers may also – and often do – provide (some) content to be transported by the systems, but there are also pure or specialized content providers which own the content (but do not provide access to the systems). There are general content providers, such as companies running portals, and specialized content providers, like news and financial companies. We call these Internet content providers (ICPs). They include traditional media and publishing companies as well as new firms. Often they derive their revenues from advertising but they are increasingly trying to charge a fee for the provision of content. Their ability to do so increases if their content is highly specialized and/or customized. However, consumers tend to want content to be free of charge. Electronic commerce is offered by new firms working only over the Internet, such as Amazon.com, but increasingly old and established firms are also using the Internet as a new marketing outlet. This includes business-to-consumer as well as business-to-business e-commerce.[20]

- Finally, there are consultancy firms – as in all knowledge-intensive sectors – that offer various services related to the Internet and mobile telecommunications. Examples are web design, web hosting, development of platforms for electronic commerce, etc.

Over the last twenty years, we have seen increased functional differentiation and organizational diversity in the telecommunications SSI (in a wide sense). For example, in the past it was common that (monopolistic) access providers were also regulators. Now separate organizations have been created to perform the regulatory functions.

Digitization or 'digitalization' has provided the technological basis for separating telecommunications and Internet network operations (access provision) from content provision. With the emergence of the fixed Internet – and even earlier with the digitization of fixed telecommunications, it has been possible to make this kind of separation between infrastructure, access and content services. This separation was facilitated when the second generation of mobile telecommunications appeared. Nevertheless, this separation was not fully implemented with the second-generation mobile standards such as GSM (global system for mobile telecommunications), despite the best efforts of the

---

[19] For reasons presented in the Preface to this book, we have chosen not to call these organizations Internet service providers (ISPs) although they certainly provide service products.
[20] E-commerce is dealt with in more detail in Kenney (2001).

European Commission (section 4.3.2.2). This would change with the third generation of mobile telecommunications (section 4.3.2.3).

In telecommunications in the broad sense the set-up and character of organizations has changed tremendously during recent decades.

- Publicly controlled telecommunications operators were transformed into joint-stock companies and privatized so that they were no longer public-sector monopolies (with regulatory power).
- The relations between the most important organizations in the system changed considerably.
- Formerly close ties between 'national champions' in equipment production and monopolistic access providers were progressively loosened.
- Important new organizations emerged in the system, e.g., IAPs and content providing organizations (ICPs).
- Similarly, new regulatory agencies were created, concomitant with privatization of public telephone operators (PTOs).

4.3. Institutional Changes and Consequences for Organizations and Functions

In section 2.1, institutions were defined as sets of common habits, routines, established practices, rules or laws that regulate the relations and interactions between individuals, groups and organizations. Relevant examples in this context are laws concerning deregulation/liberalization, technical standards (particularly relevant for Internet and mobile telecommunications), access tariffs, rules with regard to intellectual property rights (IPRs). The institutions constitute the rules of the game that influence the players – or organizations, e.g., firms – when they are trying to achieve their purposes. However, the relations between institutions and organizations are mutual. Institutions are formed and changed by the actions of (some) organizations. I shall now discuss the relations between institutions, organizations and functions in various parts of the sectoral system.

4.3.1. Fixed Internet
As we shall see in section 4.3.2, an institution – i.e., the NMT 450 mobile telecommunications standard – provided the cradle for the development of mobile telecommunications in Europe. But what provided the cradle for fixed data communications or the Internet?

Fixed telephone lines have existed for more than a century. As mentioned in the introduction to this chapter we shall not deal with fixed voice telecommunications here (except occasionally for reasons of comparison). Instead we begin our story when fixed telephone systems started to carry data as well as voice in their cables. As a precondition for this, fixed networks became digitized. There were two technological breakthroughs that made this digitization possible: packet-switching technologies and the Internet protocol.

In packet-switching technology, 'packets' of information share the network lines (bandwidth) with other packets, optimizing the use of the existing bandwidth. In packet-switched transmission protocols any type of information (voice, data, video, etc.) is broken down into packets, which are sent from one computer to another with no chronological order. A 'header' on each single packet directs the routing from the sender to the receiver; the header contains information about the destination. The packages are sent individually and reassembled to a complete message at the receiving end.

In comparison, in the traditional circuit-switched networks, an end-to-end communication path is established before the communication begins and it stays open during the whole connection. With the conventional telecommunications network, each conversation uses a fixed amount of bandwidth for the duration of the call and the available bandwidth is dedicated to the call even if no information is transmitted (e.g., during silences in a voice conversation.)

In early 1969 the US Department of Defense Advanced Research Projects Agency (DARPA) granted a contract to the Cambridge, Massachusetts based engineering firm Bolt, Beranek and Newman to build the first packet switch (Abbate 2000: 55; Mowery 2001: 8). Hence this was a matter of public technology procurement, i.e., a public agency placed a contract to a firm ordering the development of a technology or an artifact which did not exist at the time of granting the contract but which the partners believed could be developed (Edquist et al. 2000b). The resulting switch was called an interface message processor (IMP), and linked several computers to one another. The result was ARPANET, which was the earliest forerunner to the Internet.

In 1973, two DARPA-funded engineers, Robert Khan and Vinton Cerf, developed an improved data-networking communications protocol that simplified routing, eliminated the need for IMP and allowed physically distinct networks to interconnect with one another. The idea of an open architecture that allowed network-to-network connectivity was a key intellectual advance in their design. Kahn and Cerf called the new protocol transmission control protocol (TCP) and openly published the specification in 1974. Later it was split into two pieces and renamed TCP/IP (transmission control protocol/Internet protocol) (Abbate 2000: ch. 4; Mowery 2001: 9–10). Hence these protocols, which were absolutely central to the development of the Internet, were also developed with the help of military research funds.

The TCP/IP is based upon a distributed architecture, within which the IP and the TCP have separate functions: the TCP handles transmission characteristics, while the IP manages routing and network anomalies. The TCP/IP is embedded in distributed customer hosts that are located at the network periphery, therefore reducing the need for centralized control. The software is located on the servers and on the user hosts, which makes possible Internet connectivity and integrated applications.

As a matter of fact, an increasing part of voice is currently sent over IP networks; users may be unaware that a telephone call or a portion of a call is routed over an IP network. The transmission network is today (partly) common for Internet and voice telephone networks. This convergence has also, of course, influenced the telecommunications and Internet equipment industries.

TCP/IP was rapidly adopted. There were several reasons why. It was highly reliable, and it was an open standard that arrived just as the computing research community began to standardize on a common platform.[21] TCP/IP became an integral part of this standard platform. As a result TCP/IP became the dominant protocol for most networking applications in the early 1990s and is now virtually synonymous with the technical definition of the Internet (Mowery 2001: 10).

One reason why TCP/IP became dominant was the National Science Foundation (NSF) decision to adopt it as the standard on its national university network. Beginning in 1985, any university receiving NSF funding for an Internet connection was required to provide access to all 'qualified users on campus' and use TCP/IP on its network (Kenney: 2002: 14). Again, public action was crucial – this time for the early diffusion of TCP/IP.

Other government organizations in the US were also important for the development of the Internet. In the late 1970s, the NSF and DARPA founded a set of organizations to oversee the standardization of the backbone on TCP/IP. The Internet Configuration Control Board (ICCB) was established in 1979. In 1983, when ARPANET switched over to TCP/IP, the ICCB was reorganized and renamed the Internet Activities Board (IAB). The IAB had two primary sub-groups, the Internet Engineering Task Force (IETF) which managed the Internet's architecture and standard-setting processes, including editing and publishing, and the Internet Research Task Force (IRTF) which focused on longer-term research (Mowery 2001: 12–13).

The Internet is not formally standardized as a public telecommunications network. There is no standardization body such as the ITU (International

---

[21] This platform was the Unix operating system originally put forward by AT&T/Bell labs, but gradually adopted by the main computer firms, initially driven by some of the then newcomers in 'network computing' and work stations, such as Sun Microsystems and later on the dominant incumbents of HP, IBM and DEC.

Telecommunications Union) where all nations participate. The IETF is the closest equivalent to a standardization body. This voluntary organization updates standards, informs about changes and controls the use of global addresses but has no formal power.

As opposed to the standards organizations involved in developing the mobile telecommunications standards, the IETF is mainly a voluntary organization without any central management.[22] To the extent that IETF has management, it is embodied in the working group charters. These working groups are the main drivers in development of Internet standards. The work is voluntary and as such often dominated by large actors (telecommunication operators and manufacturing firms). As a consequence of the Internet's US origin, the protocol has been highly influenced by US actors via IETF. In other words, US firms have dominated the standardization process related to the Internet.

The organizations that managed the establishment of Internet technical standards were informal yet responsive. They developed open standards and rapidly adapted these to new technical and economic challenges – and this contributed powerfully to the quick diffusion of the Internet (Mowery 2001: 42).

An important institutional change that made the rapid diffusion of fixed Internet possible was the deregulation or liberalization of the telecommunications sector. Internet penetration came earlier and was more rapid in countries where liberalization took place early (UK in 1984; US in 1985; Sweden in 1993) than where it has occurred late (Italy in 1998).

Early deregulation in the UK had a significant impact on market structure. It also impacted the rate of technical change, since it opened entry to new companies and forced incumbents to engage in the development of innovations. Further, liberalization of the telecommunications sector resulted in substantially reducing the charges for telephone calls (Corrocher 2002b; and ch. 7, this publication).

As Corrocher notes in chapter 7 (this publication), Sweden has the highest Internet penetration in Europe and the most advanced Internet service sectoral system of innovation. The telecommunications market in Sweden was liberalized in 1993 and Sweden now has the most liberalized telecommunications industry in the world. This has been a major driver for the development of alternative networks to the one of the former incumbent operator (Telia). However, the unbundling of the local loop has not yet been achieved since Telia's price of interconnection is too high to allow others to compete on an equal basis (Corrocher 2002b; and ch. 7, this publication).

---

[22] Mobile standards are addressed in section 4.3.2.

In contrast to the UK, one of the major obstacles to the development of the Internet in Italy has been the slow process of deregulation of the telecommunications sector, which in turn has been caused by the lack of a clear policy for the implementation of an appropriate competition policy and of an independent regulatory authority. A telecommunications authority was established in 1997 and deregulation occurred in 1998. This delay has hindered not only the development of a competitive industry but also the diffusion of new technologies and applications (Corrocher 2002b; and ch. 7, this publication).

In the 1970s and 1980s the data transmitted via the Internet were primarily related to research activities and to communications in large firms having branches in different locations. However, in the 1990s, thanks to innovations made at CERN (European Organisation for Nuclear Research) in Switzerland, data traffic became increasingly demanded by final consumers. Tim Berners-Lee and Robert Cailliau at CERN released in 1991 a new document format called HyperText markup language (HTML) and a related document retrieval protocol called HyperText transfer protocol (HTTP). Together they turned the Internet into a vast cross-referenced collection of multimedia documents. Berners-Lee and Cailliau called their invention the 'World Wide Web' (WWW). Many start-up firms drew upon the protocols. One of them was called Netscape, which was listed on the stock exchange in 1995. Hence, although the HTML and the HTTP were not invented in the US, that is where they were first commercialized – i.e., transformed into innovations.

There were prototype networks designed, which constituted alternatives to the ARPANET, e.g., in the UK and France. 'U.S. dominance thus did not result from a first-mover advantage in the invention or even in the early development of a packet-switched network. The factor that does seem to separate ARPANET from these simultaneous projects was sizeable public funding and flexibility in its deployment' (Mowery 2001: 9). This resulted in a network of a large (continental) scale that included different kinds of organizations: DARPA, universities, consulting firms, research institutes, etc. Its size and inclusion of different kinds of organizations distinguished the ARPANET from its British and French counterparts (Mowery 2001: 9).

In the US, public intervention was crucial for the development of the Internet. Public funds were used to develop many early inventions that spawned the Internet and federal R&D spending played an important role in the creation of the entire complex of 'new' post-war information technology industries. 'The origins of the Internet can be traced back to these efforts' (Mowery 2001: 24).

However, the influence of public policy was not restricted to funding. Federal policies concerning regulation, antitrust, and intellectual property rights were also important. According to Mowery, the overall effect of these policies was to encourage rapid commercialization of Internet infrastructure, services and content by new, frequently small firms (Mowery 2001: 28). As a result, use of the Internet exploded in the US in the 1990s.

From the late 1980s onwards, US firms achieved a dominant position in the production of equipment for the Internet.[23] This occurred very much because of their 'headstart' in serving the large – and early developing – US domestic market just as US packaged computer software firms had benefited from the rapidly growing domestic personal-computer (PC) market during the 1980s. In the Internet field the firms that came to dominate were not large system vendors like IBM or DEC. Instead, a group of smaller firms, most of which were founded in the 1980s, became the most important. Examples are Cisco, Bay Networks and 3Com (Mowery 2001: 16). Cisco is still a very dominant player on this market, although it is certainly no longer a small firm.[24]

As Dalum and Villumsen point out in chapter 2 (this publication), there are currently five ways for consumers (and small business enterprises) to access the Internet:

1. 'Ordinary' modems connected directly on the telephone line.
2. ISDN-modems connected directly on the telephone line.
3. xDSL, primarily ADSL connected directly on the telephone line.
4. TV networks via 'cable modems' for cable TV or 'set-top boxes' forsatellite TV.
5. Fixed wireless access.

Dalum and Villumsen explain that the first three access technologies use a 'twisted pair' of copper wires for the last mile to the consumer, which can be installed as an integral part of an ordinary fixed-line telephone system. In practical terms this means the incumbent telecommunications operators have a clear advantage in delivering access modes. Competing companies must use the existing infrastructure on the last mile to reach the customers, i.e., they must make arrangements with incumbent operators. Dalum and Villumsen (ch. 2) argue that this has preserved the powerful position of the incumbents, which appears to be a major inhibiting factor in the diffusion of high-speed Internet access in many countries.

Because traditional subscriber lines only support analogue transmission, it is necessary to use a modem to transport data. The simple modem access (1) converts analogue to digital signals and does not require changes or enhancements to the network. Maximum speed is currently 56 Kbit/s. A first enhancement of modem technology is (2) ISDN (integrated services digital

---

[23] As we saw earlier, they also highly influenced the standard creation in the Internet field.
[24] The role of venture capital for the rapid growth of these firms is strongly stressed by Martin Kenney (Kenney 2002).

network), which runs at a higher speed (maximum 144 Kbit/s). In addition ISDN makes parallel connections of data and voice possible.

As demand for faster access increases, several digital subscriber line technologies have made higher speeds possible. Their common name is (3) xDSL, with x indicating the variant. Since demand for sending and downloading is asymmetrical for most users, a technology with higher bandwidth for downloading is required. Currently ADSL (asymmetrical digital subscriber line) is the most common technology for high-speed 'broadband' (above 2 Mbit/s) access over a 'twisted pair'.

An alternative to the telecommunications cables is access via TV networks (4). This option has been growing rapidly in some countries since many telecommunications operators (the previous state monopolies) have been slow to deliver high-speed access solutions. Dalum and Villumsen (ch. 2) note that there has been little incentive since they have been able to acquire enormous revenues due to the low speed generating high telephone bills.[25]

According to one source reporting data for 'broadband' subscriber trends without specifying what exactly broadband is,[26] there were over 40 million subscribers worldwide in 2001 divided among three shares of equal size: ADSL, digital set-top boxes and cable modems (for cable TV). The US lead in the absolute amount of broadband subscribers is, however, concentrated on cable modems and set-top boxes. The TV network-based broadband access share appeared to be around 80 per cent in the US in 2001. It has mainly been the alternatives to the incumbent telecommunications operators – i.e., the TV networks – that have been the 'carriers' of broadband access in the US.

A final access channel is (5) fixed wireless access (FWA), which uses a wireless connection on the 'last mile'. Potentially very large amounts of data can be transmitted through the air over reasonably short distances. Several European countries have recently been through contests of FWA licences, which have attracted much less attention than the recent UMTS (universal mobile telecommunications system) auctions and/or beauty contests for mobile systems.[27]

---

[25] Rate structures and levels will be discussed in more detail in section 4.3.4.

[26] *The Financial Times*, 13 December 2001.

[27] An emerging – and potentially very important – access method is via wireless local area networks (WLANs) which may become a core part of what is now considered to be 4G communications systems involving a true integration of mobile telecommunications and the fixed Internet. See further in section 4.3.2.3.

4.3.2. Mobile telecommunications

4.3.2.1. First generation (NMT)

The first standard for modern cellular telecommunications began to be speci-fied in January 1970 and was called NMT 450, i.e., the Nordic mobile teleph-ony standard based on the 450 megahertz bandwidth.[28] Important characteristics were that it was an analogue standard, that it was fully auto-matic and that it had a roaming function within the Nordic countries.[29] The development of the standard was initiated by the Nordic public telephone operators (PTOs), which were state-owned monopolies at the time. A working group, manned by the PTOs in Finland, Norway, Denmark and Sweden, de-signed the technical specifications. The Swedish PTO had a leading role in this work. In 1971 the NMT group gathered around forty national and interna-tional companies that were potential suppliers for NMT 450. They received preliminary specifications. The technical specifications were further devel-oped in discussions within the group and were finalized between 1975 and 1978 (McKelvey et al. 1998: 16, 25).

In 1977–78 the implementation of the project began and the Nordic PTT (post, telephone and telegraph) operators started to look for suppliers of the different component technologies, i.e., radio base stations and switches. The NMT group opened bidding for supplying switches to a number of compa-nies. This means that the mechanism of public technology procurement was used as an instrument to initiate the development of equipment. Bidding was international, but Sweden's Ericsson won the order to deliver switches to Sweden, Norway, Denmark and Finland. Ericsson's main competitor was Japan's NEC. However, Ericsson first offered a computer-controlled switch with electromechanical switch elements (called AXE-13). Then, Televerket (the Swedish PTO) wanted an adapted version of Ericsson's fully digital switch (AXE) and made clear to Ericsson that they would choose the digital switch from NEC if Ericsson did not offer AXE (McKelvey et al. 1998: 26).

The NMT 450 was very specific, which meant that a network operator had the possibility of buying components from different producers and putting them together. NMT 450 was implemented in Sweden in October 1980 and early 1981 in Denmark, Finland and Norway. However, the first implementa-tion occurred in Saudi Arabia in August 1980[30] (McKelvey et al. 1998: 16). In other words, it took ten years to specify the standard and get it functioning.

---

[28] NMT is not covered elsewhere in this study of the fixed Internet and mobile telecommunica-tions sectoral systems of innovation.

[29] Roaming means locating the mobile phone handset of the person called.

[30] This turned out to be an important order for equipment producer Ericsson.

The NMT 450 was much more successful than expected. It was initially forecasted to have 50 000 subscribers by 1990, whereas by 1992 it had approximately 250 000. Since more subscribers were joining than the standard could handle, the Nordic PTTs developed and added the NMT 900 (megahertz) standard in 1986. The NMT 900 system was developed as an intermediary system, between the NMT 450 and the future European digital standard (which was later agreed to be GSM) (McKelvey et al. 1998: 16).

The Nordic countries had the highest rates of penetration of mobile phones even before the advent of liberalization and before GSM – i.e., during the NMT era. It was about 7 per cent in Sweden in 1992, thanks to high-quality service provision and low tariffs. In 1990 market penetration in the UK was only 2 per cent, despite its much more extensive market liberalization for mobile (and fixed) telecommunications.[31] The rapid penetration in Sweden was largely due to the consolidation of a strong market for mobile telecommunications via concerted action by the Nordic public telephone companies in defining the first-generation NMT standard and through low prices. Sweden's fixed subscription rates were much lower than in the UK, and call charges were about half of what they were in the UK. Rapid subscriber penetration contributed to rapid market growth – which was important for the ability of equipment suppliers to benefit from economies of scale.

NMT 450 can be considered an institution in the sense of being a set of rules. This set of rules decreased the degree of uncertainty and risk for equipment suppliers. The NMT standard was conceived primarily as a regional standard, though it later verged on becoming pan-European.

The institution of NMT 450 provided the cradle for the development of pan-European mobile telecommunications. It actually spurred the development of a whole new industry – or sectoral system – of very large economic significance. Public-sector organizations dominated the development of the standard. The development was actually initiated and led by a few Nordic national public telecommunications operators.

In techno-economic development there has often been an institutional lag, i.e., institutions (rules and regulations) lag behind technical change (innovation) and constitute an obstacle to such change. This was the case with the diffusion of fixed Internet in Italy (see section 4.3.1). However, in the case of NMT 450 the opposite happened. When this institution was created it pushed – or rather pulled – the whole development, e.g., by decreasing uncertainty for equipment producers and operators. We might call this an 'institutional push' (or 'pull') instead of an 'institutional lag'.

---

[31] As mentioned earlier, liberalization was initiated in the UK in 1984 and in Sweden in 1993.

The development and implementation of NMT was actually an example of the importance of user–producer relations in innovation processes, which is stressed so strongly in the systems of innovation approach. The public organizations provided a technical framework for private equipment producers and decreased uncertainty. The Nordic equipment producers, Ericsson and Nokia greatly benefited from this, which is an important contributing factor for their leading role in mobile telecommunications equipment production today.

However, NMT was not the only standard that was developed in the proto-period of mobile telecommunications. In the 1970s cellular systems R&D gained similar momentum in a few countries (with the US, the Nordic countries and Japan as forerunners).[32] This resulted in the introduction of as many as eight cellular standards between 1979 and 1985[33] (Lindmark and Granstrand 1995: 386).

The advanced mobile phone system (AMPS) was developed by Illinois Bell Telephone, Bell Labs and Motorola. The first AMPS system was launched in 1983 (as opposed to 1981 for NMT), delayed by arguments over access to radio frequencies and a complicated licensing procedure. NMT 450 was the first standard adopted by multiple standards and by the end of 1993, 36 countries had introduced the system (Funk 2002: 41). AMPS was quite successful; it was diffused to a larger number of countries than NMT and had a larger number of subscribers worldwide (Funk 2002: 40).[34] However, NMT in the Nordic countries showed the highest penetration rates in the world, constantly outstripping forecasts (Lindmark and Granstrand 1995: 386–8). In addition, NMT was the basis for the development of GSM – which became the globally dominant standard in second-generation mobile telecommunications.

4.3.2.2. Second generation (GSM)

A. Europe Introduced in 1992, the GSM standard is also an institution. It was conceived from the start as a pan-European standard intended to cover many countries. And it came to do so. In 1992 commercial GSM services were initiated in 15 countries, but by 1996 GSM operated in 103 countries. It was possible to make phone calls between countries – even between continents – thanks to the fact that the national systems could be integrated in order to

---

[32] Bell Labs is usually credited with having invented the design concept of cellular mobile telecommunications (in 1947), the main idea being to overcome radio spectrum congestion by combining space division with radio spectrum division (Lindmark and Granstrand 1995: 386).
[33] The standards were: NAMTS, NMT, AMPS, TACS, C-450, RC-2000, RTMS and Comvik, although some experts argue that RC-2000, RTMS and Comvik were not fully functional cellular systems.
[34] This is explained not only by the size of the home market (in the US), but also by the diffusion to some large markets in the Asia-Pacific region and Canada (Lindmark and Granstrand 1995: 392).

trace where a certain terminal was located (roaming). This means that the development of the GSM standard was characterized by the involvement of a far greater number of organizations than the NMT standard(s) and a far greater complexity in the relations among them. There were other differences. Until the 1980s, public telecommunications companies in Europe often had monopolistic positions with regard to network operation and service provision. They also had the role of regulating the telecommunications sector. By the mid-1990s, they were much more oriented towards network operation. Separate regulatory organizations had been created and in turn these new organizations created new institutions.

In Sweden, the National Telecommunications Council was created in 1990, followed by the National Telecommunications Agency in 1992. This ended the double role of Televerket (the former PTO) in the area of frequency management and it meant the creation of an independent telecommunications regulator capable of ensuring competition in the non-monopoly telecommunications sector, which now included the mobile sector. As a network operator, Televerket was increasingly exposed to competition from new entrants, domestic and foreign based.

As in the case of NMT, public-sector organizations were crucial to the development of GSM (see Hommen in ch. 3, this publication). For instance, national telecommunications agencies were central in initiating and developing the new standard. However, there were now more numerous organizations of this kind than was the case with NMT's development. The development of GSM occurred within the formal organizational framework (and not in an ad hoc consortium) provided by two European standards development organizations: CEPT (Conference on European Post and Telecommunications) and ETSI (the European Telecommunications Standards Institute). CEPT was an association of European telecommunications organizations while ETSI – which gradually took over the role of standard creation – was a European Union organization.[35] In addition, equipment suppliers and public research organizations actively participated in this work. This reflected the fact that the (former) public monopolies no longer had a monopoly of knowledge and expertise in the telecommunications field (Hommen 2002a; Glimstedt 2001).

The Swedish former monopoly Televerket/Telia was very active in GSM's implementation, along with other Nordic operators and equipment production firms like Ericsson and Nokia – which formed a 'Nordic coalition'. Televerket – which later transformed from a public enterprise to a joint-stock, limited liability company and in due course partly privatized in the form of Telia – effectively led the Nordic alliance. This consortium was based on his-

---

[35] For an account of the European Commission's role in the development of GSM, see Glimstedt (2001).

torically close collaborations between Nordic PTOs and Nordic equipment producers. In competition with a Franco-German group the Nordic proposal was selected and supported by 13 of CEPT's voting members. In this way GSM may be said to have developed out of NMT – i.e., along the same trajectory (Hommen 2002a). ETSI adopted GSM without German and French support, but the two countries were still forced under EU law to use GSM as the basis for the public mobile telecom network (Glimstedt 2001).

Although Ericsson produced equipment for all three major international standards, it developed and tested the first prototype of a full GSM system in collaboration with Televerket/Telia. This consolidated Ericsson's technological leadership. However, Nokia benefited even more from the GSM decision, since it produced the standard's base stations and switches. The way GSM developed contributed significantly to increasing impressive advantages already enjoyed by Ericsson, Nokia and other Nordic firms in relation to equipment manufacturers elsewhere.

However, the Nordic proposal was based upon well-established technologies to which a number of non-Swedish firms held the IPRs; Motorola held many (50 per cent) of the important patents, and it licensed them selectively to the main Nordic equipment manufactures, Nokia and Ericsson. The second largest share (16 per cent) was claimed by AT&T. Bull and Phillips claimed 8 per cent each. Hence, at least 82 per cent of the patents for the GSM standard were of non-Nordic origin. In this light, it is quite surprising that Nordic firms attained such a dominant position as GSM equipment producers. A relevant question is why Motorola did not (successfully) push their technology in the US. Motorola sold licences to Ericsson and Nokia and thereby benefited directly by collecting licensing fees. However, Motorola was not in the position to produce equipment for GSM to any large extent. A possible explanation for Motorola's behaviour is that it felt unable to compete with European equipment producers in Europe, and perceived GSM as a European standard that would not necessarily develop into a world standard[36] (Hommen 2002a; and ch. 3, this publication).

In the first generation of mobile telecommunications, telephony and radio were combined. In the second generation, digital technology was fully implemented, creating possibilities for data transmission, in addition to voice transmission. In GSM data transmission was first introduced through SMS or short messaging service, a two-way variant of the previously existing paging system, which has become unexpectedly popular. GSM can also provide Internet access through HTML compatibility, currently developed in the form of wireless applications protocol.

---

[36] But at the time no one could foresee that GSM would evolve to become the world's dominant standard.

Finally, a remark on the role of deregulation for the diffusion of GSM. As Hommen points out (ch. 3), GSM was developed and implemented before large-scale liberalization took place in Europe, and hence the deregulation process did not play a major role. The relation was rather the reverse. GSM was actually used as a 'spearhead' of the EU strategy for telecommunications deregulation in the 1990s; it was used as a tool to change the telecommunications sector in Europe.

B. US and Japan In the US, one standardization agency, the CTIA (Cellular Telephone Industry Association), chose the digital advanced mobile phone system (D-AMPS) standard which was compatible with existing first-generation (analogue) systems. The idea was to facilitate a gradual shift between generations.[37]

Another relevant regulatory agency, the Federal Communications Commission (FCC), decided there would be no national digital standard for the US as a whole; rather operators were free to adopt any standard. On this basis another digital standard came into use, the CDMA (code division multiple access). It emerged later, but attracted more operators.[38] These two main standards were not directly compatible with each other; they were so only through the use of analogue channels. This was the so-called 'backwards compatibility' insisted upon by the FCC (Hommen 2002a; and ch. 3, this publication).

Partly because of this, both digital standards diffused relatively slowly in the US. The US had a mobile phone penetration rate of 20 per cent in 1997 – as opposed to 40–50 per cent in the Nordic countries. In addition, 60 per cent of subscriptions were to the analogue standard, while Europe was almost completely digital. The slower diffusion of digital systems in the US was due to the presence of several standards and a weaker migration from the first generation to the second because of backwards compatibility. Furthermore, the structure of tariffs on mobile services was different in Europe and roaming and caller pay issues were resolved much earlier[39] (Hommen 2002a; and ch. 3, this publication).

The two main US digital standards diffused to Latin America and Asia only to a limited degree, and never became a serious international competitor to GSM. Foreign standards were used to a very small extent in the US. But during 2000 and 2001 the most important US operators transferred to GSM,

---

[37] This is in contrast to Europe, where the standard creators did not need to worry about backward compatibility with a first-generation standard.

[38] CDMA was technically superior to D-AMPS, but CDMA had limited availability of terminal equipment and was implemented differently by each operator.

[39] The tariff structure will be discussed in section 4.3.4.

beginning with AT&T wireless in late 2001 and followed by six mobile operators. Among the reasons for switching was the fact that GSM accounted for 60 per cent of the world market even before the transfer and that economies of scale and thus lower prices could be realized. In addition, the transfer to third generation (W-CDMA) would be facilitated. GSM has thereby effectively become a world standard. The transfer has also strengthened the position of Ericsson and Nokia.

The US standard regulatory organizations seemed to have wanted to secure competition between standards as well as between operators in the US. In Europe competition only took place between operators.

In Japan the adopted digital mobile telephone standard, PDC (Pacific digital cellular), never diffused outside Japan and was incompatible with all other standards. The Japanese market remained closed to other (foreign) standards.

4.3.2.3. Third generation (UMTS/WLAN)

Unlike the NMT 900 and GSM standards, the development of the universal mobile telecommunications system standard was not driven primarily by the need to accommodate unexpectedly rapid growth in the number of subscribers. Instead, as Hommen points out in chapter 4, improved functionality seems to have been the main driving force behind UMTS.

Although UMTS is a standard supported by ETSI, i.e., it is a European standard, it also has the official sanction of the ITU, an organization 'with truly world-wide coverage and authority' (see Hommen, ch. 4, this publication). At the same time, ETSI chose NTT DoCoMo's W-CDMA (wireless code division multiple access) technology in January 1998 as the European third-generation standard[40] (Funk 2002: 78–82; 206–8). The previous development was pursued within ETSI in very general terms. When it came to an actual decision W-CDMA was chosen because ETSI believed that standard offered greater capabilities than an enhanced version of GSM and because W-CDMA included the evolution of the GSM network interface (Funk 2002: ch. 6: 6). Hence UMTS can be seen as an extension of GSM, and the two systems are intended to be compatible.

The choice of W-CDMA has been seen as a major victory for Japanese manufacturers and its two European supporters, Ericsson and Nokia. The decisions made by ETSI and ITU also made W-CDMA a global standard. The 'UMTS alliance' includes the European Union and some national operators, such as Japan's NTT DoCoMo. It also includes multinational telecommunications equipment manufacturing firms such as Ericsson and Nokia. The choice

---

[40] NTT DoCoMo is the largest mobile phone operator in Japan. It is a spin-off of NTT; the former operator monopoly. NTT is still a majority equity holder in DoCoMo.

of W-CDMA was a blow to supporters of other standards such as TDMA (time division multiple access) and CDMA2000.

UMTS will be, in important respects, a significant departure from existing mobile telecommunication systems, and will constitute a 'third-generation' system. It involves several important breaks with GSM:

- the use of broadband, as opposed to narrow-band, radio frequencies;
- full integration of voice and data communications;
- full integration of 'fixed' and 'mobile' telecommunications networks; and
- provision of 'seamless' global roaming, in addition to high functionality.

However, a certain level of wireless data transmission is already possible within GSM. For example, the further development of GSM technology (and other, second-generation counterparts) has proceeded for some time within a framework consistent with UMTS objectives. A case in point is the wireless application protocol (WAP) created in 1998. WAP constitutes an intermediate stage of development between existing GSM capabilities for wireless data transmission and the UMTS goal of making 'wireless Internet' a reality through an integration of fixed and mobile communications networks. WAP is HTML compatible since Internet material is in HTML format. WAP allows a great advance in GSM wireless data transmission by enabling Internet information to be delivered on mobile devices that already support GSM-based SMSs.[41] WAP was in operation by 2001 in many countries, but it had not become a success in terms of number of users until early 2002.

Another 'intermediate' solution – between 2G and 3G – is GPRS (general packet radio service). It brings the IP into the GSM network and thus enables data to be sent in small packets, with users to be charged for these packages as opposed to connection times, and data transmission speeds up to 115 Kbit/s. GPRS also makes multimedia services possible (Funk 2002: 211–12). Many GSM operators introduced GPRS during 2001.

The first operator to put UMTS in operation was NTT DoCoMo in Japan, who initiated the service in October 2001.[42] DoCoMo was a natural first mover since the company has operated the I-Mode mobile Internet system since February 1999. Like WAP, I-Mode is somewhere between second- and

---

[41] As mentioned before, SMS is data transmission of a 'paging' character, but in both directions. Here there is a direct link between mobile phones and fixed Internet, i.e., SMS can be sent to and from fixed computers as well as mobile phones.

[42] However, the system has suffered from a number of technical problems that have made many potential subscribers hesitate. Therefore the 3G system had fewer than 55 000 subscribers in March 2002, which was well below DoCoMo's objective.

third-generation mobile telecommunications, and had 31 million subscribers by March 2002.[43] The fact that UMTS was first introduced in Japan might provide Japanese equipment manufacturers with an advantage over other manufacturers.

Reasons for the success of I-Mode in Japan include low fixed Internet usage and DoCoMo's effective strategy. The reasons why DoCoMo has the largest number of subscribers and content sites are its early release of compatible handsets, a packet service, a clearinghouse, and its use of compact HTML. The packet service enables small packets of information to be sent inexpensively. In the clearinghouse, DoCoMo collects money for the content provider's fee-based services and takes 9 per cent as a handling charge. This organizational or managerial innovation is crucial since it makes it easy for content providers to earn money without actually being responsible for collecting the charges from the users themselves (Funk 2002: ch. 6).

In Europe, auctions for UMTS licences were held in many countries during 2000 – and operators in some cases agreed to pay enormous fees. This has created financial difficulty for some operators and will be an obstacle to the diffusion of UMTS in Europe. Some people believe that shortsighted governments thought they could finance the increasing costs of an ageing society by taxing new economy agents, such as the mobile telecommunications operators, and that this may hurt an important part of European high-tech industry. In some countries – e.g., Sweden – licences were allocated by means of 'beauty contests', i.e., a comparison of the characteristics of the proposed systems was the basis for granting licences and no fee was paid. The investments in 3G systems will be very large and are expected to be carried out during 2002 and 2003 in Europe. The US will be a laggard (also) with regard to UMTS, partly because other users, e.g., the military, tie up the relevant radio frequencies.

Whether third-generation mobile telecommunications systems (including mobile Internet access) will diffuse rapidly or slowly will depend on:

- the quality and importance of the services provided (as evaluated by those who pay);
- the structure and rate of the tariffs; and
- the cost of accessing similar services in other ways.

If operators want to enhance rapid diffusion of third-generation mobile telecommunications subscriptions they must ensure the services are good and probably offer flat subscription rates of a limited size. In addition, cultural

---

[43] I-Mode is a transitional system, based on narrow-band frequencies and a development of the Japanese PDC standard. DoCoMo established I-Mode in the Netherlands, Germany and Belgium in early 2002.

differences between countries may be important, as in the way everyday life is organized. For example, lengthy commuting via public transportation as in Tokyo may contribute to rapid diffusion of 3G.

The European success in NMT and GSM will not necessarily be repeated for the third generation of mobile telecommunications because some conditions contributing to the success of the first and second generations no longer apply. In particular, liberalization has reduced the central role of monopolistic PTOs, diminishing their close interaction with equipment producers. Consequently, producers may find that large domestic markets are initially more difficult to obtain for new products.

There are also alternatives and supplements to 3G. As Dalum and Villumsen (ch. 2, this publication) point out, 3G systems will not provide users with the full range of broadband services available to fixed Internet users. 3G systems are based on rather low-speed data communications. The absolute maximum speed for UMTS is currently 2 Mbit/s and speeds lower than 400 Kbit/s will be the norm at least for the next few years. Much higher speeds will be provided by a complement to UMTS, called WLAN. This began with the development of customer premises networks (CPNs) or wireless local area networks (WLANs) for professional users (firms). Recently WLANs also started to be installed in public areas. Public WLANs can cover only small geographical areas or 'islands', e.g., an office, an airport or an Internet café. In these islands a PC or a Palmtop can be used to access the Internet at speeds of 10 to 50 Mbit/s.

Dalum and Villumsen argue that WLAN will rapidly diffuse in the near future (ch. 2, this publication). By April 2002, there were some 300 public areas covered by WLAN in Sweden (Ny Teknik 2002). A 4G mobile telecommunications system may be considered an integration of a 3G mobile telecommunications system and WLAN access to the 'traditional' fixed Internet (and integrated with other wireless options such as GPRS, Bluetooth,[44] etc.). The customer will be automatically connected to the network with the highest capacity and the same subscription is used for all. The standard now emerging as the winner within WLAN is the American IEEE 802.11a and b. The 802.11a operates in the 5 GHz band with a potential speed of 50 Mbit/s, while 802.11b operates with 10 Mbit/s in the 2.4 GHz band. As Dalum and Villumsen state, ETSI's HiperLAN 2 standard appears the loser in this standardization game.[45]

---

[44] Bluetooth is a mode of transmitting data and voice over very short distances using radio signals instead of cables.

[45] HomeRF is yet another variant while Bluetooth-based solutions basically operate only within 10 metres of distance and act more as substitutes for cables. See, e.g., Garber (2002); Mannings and Cosier (2001); and *The Financial Times* (2002), FT Review 'CEBIT 2002 and beyond'.

The frequencies used by WLAN are unlicensed, i.e., free, and therefore encounter interference from other WLAN systems or from different applications. The 2.4 GHz band currently mainly used for WLANs is also used by – and can therefore be disturbed by – Bluetooth, microwave ovens and car-parking sensors. The 5 GHz band, which is the frequency proposed for new WLAN systems, is free from interfering competitors and allows many operators to co-exist.

Currently the US is probably most advanced in private and public WLAN installations, with Cisco strongly supporting the 802.11 standard. At the same time 3G is delayed because no radio spectrum has been allocated. For these reasons it is highly probable that WLAN will become more important than 3G in the US than in other countries (although WLAN cannot, of course, cover large areas). In Europe 3G licences have been awarded in most countries and will be installed fairly soon. However, operators who did not get 3G licences may be pushing WLAN. The country most committed to 3G is Japan, where 3G is already operating, and where there is very little discussion about WLAN (Wireless Web 2002).

Within the mobile telecommunications sector the number of categories of actors as well as the number of actors in most categories will increase. Currently the dominant categories are suppliers of equipment and access providers (operators). The vendors of systems (base stations and switches) are not likely to be threatened, since economies of scale and barriers to entry are very large. They need only wait until the current crisis is over and the operators start investing again. On the handset side we are, however, likely to see additional producers, probably with niche strategies focusing on cheap mass-market phones or very advanced ones. This increased competition will mainly influence Nokia, Motorola and Siemens.

The number of access providers will increase in many markets in the near future. In Sweden, for example, two new large mobile operators will enter when the 3G networks start to operate during 2002 and 2003. In addition, operators who own networks may start renting capacity to others, i.e., operators without networks will enter. Hence competition will increase in several ways.

A major obstacle to the breakthrough and growth of 3G is the supply of mobile Internet content. Just as in the fixed Internet sector, content providers independent of access providers will have to mitigate the obstacle of the supply of content for mobile Internet. This pertains to content such as games, music, news, information, financial services, etc., where the division of labour and the relations between access providers and independent content providers are not clear and have to be sorted out. How, for example, should the final customer pay? Via the invoice from the access provider, via a bank account or via some other intermediate actor? There is a struggle here between various interests.

An even more difficult issue to resolve is how the cake will be divided between providers of access and of content. Currently the operators appropriate most of this cake, and it is probably necessary that more be handed over to content suppliers in order to create stronger incentives for the development of content for mobile Internet. This conflict must be resolved no later than when handsets with larger displays in colour (3G phones) have emerged, i.e., in late 2002 or 2003. When discussing NTT DoCoMo's I-Mode, I stressed that organizational and managerial innovations are important in this field. 3G will not become successful without content that is so attractive the final customer is willing to pay! Such content will not be developed if its providers cannot charge for it.

4.3.3. Satellite communications

Wireless access to the Internet and to telephone lines can also be achieved via satellite communications (see Dalum, ch. 5, this publication). A communications satellite is basically a microwave repeater revolving around the earth in a specified orbit. On earth the signals can either continue in cable or mobile systems or be transferred to private houses by means of small discs. The satellites are primarily used for TV and radio transmission. For example, the European EUTELSAT system was broadcasting 750 analogue and digital TV channels and 450 radio channels by the end of 2000. In 1999, however, 20 per cent was used for a range of broadband services, including Internet backbone and access and corporate networks. EUTELSAT was initially government based but in 2001 was in the process of being privatized. At the start, members of US-dominated INTELSAT were also national governments, with privatization measures beginning during 2001 (Dalum 2002; and ch. 5, this publication).

So-called 'set-top boxes' may facilitate high-speed Internet access in remote areas. These represent an alternative solution if incumbent telecommunications operators are reluctant to make high speed available. They also make it easier for people without computer skills to reach the Internet through their TV screen. This convergence between TV broadcasting and Internet access represents an enormous potential for television networks (Dalum 2002; and ch. 5, this publication).

At the beginning of the 1990s four large consortia announced plans for mega projects of satellite-based mobile telecommunications systems. Iridium, Globalstar and ICO are the best-known examples. All became established, but in the first half of 1999 Iridium and ICO went bankrupt and Globalstar significantly adjusted its plans. Operations were geographically focused on areas where there were no terrestrial mobile communications systems available – which decreased the number of customers as well as their purchasing power.

The success and vigorous growth of cellular mobile telecommunications was significantly underestimated, bringing commercial failure to many enterprises. The 'new millennium' fostered huge ambitions for voice and data transmission among global mobile satellite-based systems that have been drastically scaled down (Dalum 2002; and ch. 5, this publication).

With widespread 3G mobile communications – or WLANs – within reach in the next five to ten years, satellite-based mobile phone systems will serve complementary roles in areas with weak coverage of terrestrial mobile communications networks. They will also play a role in maritime communications and perhaps also in systems intended to be used by the airline industry.

4.3.4. Rate structures and levels

The structure and level of rates and tariffs may also be considered to be 'rules of the game', i.e., a form of institution. In this case, it is an institution created, to a large extent, by firms, i.e., at the micro level – although firms are also influenced by other institutions, e.g., regulations. The quality and value of a telecommunications or Internet service, as perceived by the user, influence the rate of the service's diffusion. The cost of the service also influences diffusion. This implies that comparative prices of different modes of accessing certain services are important – and so are comparative prices of content provided over the networks.

In GSM there was agreement that calling charges were to be billed to the caller. However, when calls were placed to a mobile handset located in another country at the time of calling, the caller was charged the local rates, and the cost for forwarding the call outside the home country was paid by the receiver.[46]

In the US, however, the receiver has traditionally been charged. If a call is placed from a fixed telephone line to a mobile phone, only the receiver is charged (if the receiving handset is located in the vicinity). This is because there is normally no variable cost for local phone calls from fixed lines in the US, but only a fixed subscription fee. For long-distance calls there is also a variable cost. If the receiver is located outside the local area, then both the caller and the receiver pay. If a call is placed between two mobile phones, both are also paying a variable fee. This posed an obstacle to diffusion of mobile telecommunications in the US that Europe did not experience. It constituted a disincentive to subscribe to mobile services while creating an incentive for users to switch off the handsets – which led to non-availability. There was also a disincentive to give out mobile numbers because of this.

---

[46] This decision was taken since the caller would otherwise not know the cost of calling.

The importance of the level of charges (related to quality and value of ser-vice provided as well as to the cost of alternatives for access to the same or similar service), can be illustrated by the fact that mobile subscriptions dif-fused rapidly in Sweden (as compared to the UK), because of low tariffs even in the analogue era (see section 4.3.2.1).

The introduction of the prepaid card was also instrumental in increasing the diffusion in those countries where it became available. In Sweden these cards were first introduced in 1997 by Comviq – one of the three operators (now called Tele 2). The prepaid cards are, for example, used by people not able to subscribe, e.g., young people and those without credit for other reasons.

The structure and level of access costs to the fixed Internet also vary be-tween countries and continents. In the US a flat rate is all that is normally charged, which makes possible unlimited Internet access. Local dial-up is not metred.[47] In the UK and also in Italy, Internet access has been provided to a large extent free of charge, although this phenomenon might be gradually disappearing in the near future. In Sweden most consumer Internet access has been mediated by a modem and a variable cost has been paid (in addition to the subscription fee). However, the US pricing structure is currently becom-ing increasingly common in Sweden. In Japan the cost structure is similar to that in Sweden, i.e., both fixed and variable costs are charged.

The rate structure probably explains in part the high penetration of Internet access in the US – and the low ratio in Japan. However, rapid diffusion in Sweden cannot be explained by rates. Nor is the slow Internet penetration rate in Italy a consequence of pricing structure, but rather a lack of familiarity with information and communication technology (ICT) applications, the iner-tia of Italian consumers and their limited knowledge of English.

The low diffusion of fixed Internet in Japan – together with the low den-sity of home PCs – may, in turn, partly explain the rapid diffusion of the I-Mode mobile Internet operated by NTT DoCoMo. Further, this may be a reason why DoCoMo was the first operator to install a full-scale third-generation mobile telephone system in October 2001 (as discussed in section 4.3.2.3).

4.4. Boundaries Between Systems and Convergence Between Subsystems

What is the sectoral system of innovation in the telecommunications field? Is there one sectoral system or are there several systems? The telecommunica-tions sector – in a wide sense – is growing rapidly and there is convergence

---

[47] Other OECD countries with unmetred local telecommunications services are Australia, Canada and New Zealand. In these countries and the US there is also a high penetration of Internet hosts (Mowery 2001: 37).

between various parts or subsystems. It is possible to talk about convergence in several senses and respects.

First, we saw convergence between information technology (IT) and communication technology into information and communication technology, which occurred in the 1980s. There was then convergence between ICTs and the broadcasting/audiovisual technologies in the 1990s. This constituted the starting point of the so-called multimedia revolution.

The transfer to digitized mobile telecommunications systems in the 1990s implied a convergence of formerly separate technologies. The technological base had broadened to include innovations from outside the traditional tele-communications sector, mainly from computer and software firms. This meant that telecommunications equipment producers in essence became IT and software firms, although with a specialization in telecommunications. It also meant that traditional telecommunications firms had to confront new entrants whose competence had originated in other sectors. In addition, stan-dard-setting organizations became important. There has also been consider-able growth of publicly funded research in telecommunications in Europe during this past decade.

In the 1990s we have experienced convergence between traditional tele-communications and the Internet. The emergence of the Internet meant that another subsystem entered the telecommunications sector. This implied that new functions had become important, and new kinds of organizations entered the sector – new Internet access providers (such as telecommunications opera-tors and cable TV operators), Internet content providers (such as e-commerce companies) and consulting companies specializing in software and the Internet.

In the near future we are bound to see a convergence between fixed Inter-net and mobile telecommunications with the emergence of third-generation mobile telecommunications. This convergence has already started with SMS and with WAP and GPRS (and with UMTS in Japan). What WLANs will mean in terms of convergence is still unclear.

We have also seen a convergence process with regard to receiving devices or customer premises equipment. For example, third-generation cellular phones offer Internet connection and narrow-band services. Similarly, desk-top computers can be used to make telephone calls or to watch a video, and set-top boxes are also starting to become an alternative device for Internet access. Palm pilot organizers may also be used for Internet access. There are combinations of these devices. In 1994, Nokia introduced one of the first data interface products – a 'PC' card that could be inserted into a portable com-puter connected to a mobile handset by means of a cable.

All this has meant that the knowledge base for the telecommunications sectoral system has become increasingly complex. Convergence means that boundaries are changing and that sectoral systems may be moving targets, becoming larger and more complex. However, boundaries may also change in the opposite direction and sectoral systems may become more specialized, more isolated from other (sub)systems because of increasing specialization, and smaller. Therefore, both convergence and divergence might occur.

In section 3, we concluded that there is a certain degree of arbitrariness when it comes to specification of sectoral boundaries. Therefore, we can consider data communications to be one sectoral system, and mobile tele-communications to be another. However, we can also see both as belonging to one combined system (particularly if they are converging). It is partly a matter of choice and convenience. Some minimum degree of coherence is nevertheless required to make it useful to talk about a sectoral system. We would not regard paper pulp and telecommunications to be the same sectoral system of innovation.

Here, we take a very pragmatic view of whether we are talking about one sectoral system of innovation or about several within telecommunications in a wide sense. Sometimes it may be useful to regard the whole field as one system. Other times it might be more fruitful to consider the Internet or mobile telecommunications to be separate sectoral systems of innovation. It depends upon the context – e.g., on the purpose of the study to be carried out. In addition, equipment production, network operation (access provision) and content provision can be regarded as separate systems or as one common system.

However, *when* an empirical study is to be carried out it is absolutely necessary to identify the boundaries of the sectoral system to be scrutinized. The boundaries have to be specified in a sectoral as well as functional sense (and in a geographical sense, if the system is not global).

In section 3, we discussed the functional boundaries of systems of innovation and identified them with the determinants of the relevant innovation processes. If we can identify the determinants of different kinds of innovations in fixed Internet and mobile telecommunications, then we can say that these determinants constitute the functional boundaries of the relevant SSI. However, we do not know these determinants in detail, given the present state of the art. Hence, this is a clear example of the 'catch 22' problem mentioned in section 3.

REFERENCES

Abbate, J. (2000), *Inventing the Internet*, Cambridge MA: MIT Press.

Braczyk, H.-J., P. Cooke and M. Heidenreich (eds) (1998), *Regional Innovation Systems: The Role of Governance in a Globalised World*, London and Pennsylvania: UCL Press.

Breschi, S. and F. Malerba (1997), 'Sectoral Innovation Systems: Technological Regimes, Schumpeterian Dynamics, and Spatial Boundaries', in C. Edquist (ed.), *Systems of Innovation: Technologies, Institutions and Organizations*, London and Washington: Pinter/Cassell Academic.

Carlsson, B. (ed.) (1995), Technological Systems and Economic Performance: The Case of Factory Automation, Dordrecht: Kluwer.

Carlsson, Bo and Rikard Stankiewicz (1995), 'On the Nature, Function and Composition of Technological Systems', in B. Carlsson (ed.), *Technological Systems and Economic Performance: The Case of Factory Automation*, Dordrecht: Kluwer.

Cooke, P. (1998), 'Introduction: Origins of the Concept', in H.-J. Braczyk , P. Cooke and M. Heidenreich (eds), *Regional Innovation Systems: The Role of Governance in a Globalised World*, London and Pennsylvania: UCL.

Corrocher, N. (2002a), 'The Internet Services Industry: Sectoral Dynamics of Innovation and Production', report written within the study of the 'Fixed Internet and Mobile Telecommunications Sectoral System of Innovation' carried out within the EU-financed TSER project 'Sectoral Systems in Europe – Innovation, Competitiveness and Growth' (ESSY), co-ordinated by Franco Malerba, Bocconi University.

Corrocher, N. (2002b), 'The Internet Services Industry: Country-specific Trends in the UK, in Italy and in Sweden', report written within the study of the 'Fixed Internet and Mobile Telecommunications Sectoral System of Innovation' carried out within the EU-financed TSER project 'Sectoral Systems in Europe – Innovation, Competitiveness and Growth' (ESSY), co-ordinated by Franco Malerba, Bocconi University.

Dalum, B. (2002), 'Data Communication – The Satellite and TV Subsystems', report written within the study of the 'Fixed Internet and Mobile Telecommunications Sectoral System of Innovation' carried out within the EU-financed TSER project 'Sectoral Systems in Europe – Innovation, Competitiveness and Growth' (ESSY), co-ordinated by Franco Malerba, Bocconi University.

Dalum, B. and G. Villumsen, (2002), 'Fixed Data Communications – Challenges for Europe', report written within the study of the 'Fixed Internet and Mobile Telecommunications Sectoral System of Innovation' carried out within the EU-financed TSER project 'Sectoral Systems in Europe – Innovation, Competitiveness and Growth' (ESSY), co-ordinated by Franco Malerba, Bocconi University.

Edquist, C. (1997), 'Systems of Innovation Approaches – Their Emergence and Characteristics' in C. Edquist, (ed.), *Systems of Innovation: Technologies, Institutions and Organizations*, London: Pinter/Cassell. (Also published in Swedish.)

Edquist C. (2001a), 'Innovation Policy – A Systemic Approach', in D. Archibugi and B.-A. Lundvall (eds), *The Globalising Learning Economy: Major Socio-Economic Trends and European Innovation Policy*, Oxford: Oxford University Press.

Edquist, C. (2001b), 'Innovation Policy in the Systems of Innovation Approach: Some Basic Principles', in M.M. Fischer and J. Fröhlich (eds), *Knowledge Complexity and Innovation Systems*, Berlin: Springer Verlag.

Edquist, C. (2001c), 'The Systems of Innovation Approach and Innovation Policy: An Account of the State of the Art', paper presented at the DRUID Conference, Aalborg, 12–15 June.

Edquist, C., M.-L. Ericsson and H. Sjögren (2000a), 'Collaboration in Product Innovation in the East Gothia Regional System of Innovation', *Enterprise & Innovation Management Studies*, 1.

Edquist, C., and L Hommen (1999). 'Systems of Innovation: Theory and Policy from the Demand Side', *Technology in Society*, **21**: 63–79.

Edquist, C., L. Hommen and M. McKelvey (2001), *Innovation and Employment: Process versus Product Innovation*, Cheltenham: Edward Elgar.

Edquist, C., L. Hommen and L.Tsipouri (eds.) (2000b), *Public Technology Procurement: Theory, Evidence and Policy*, Boston/Dordrecht/London: Kluwer Academic Publishers.

Edquist, C. and B. Johnson (1997), 'Institutions and Organisations in Systems of Innovation', in C. Edquist (ed.), *Systems of Innovation: Technologies, Institutions and Organizations*, London and Washington: Pinter/Cassell Academic.

Edquist, C. and B.-Å. Lundvall (1993), 'Comparing the Danish and Swedish Systems of Innovation', in Richard R. Nelson (ed.), *National Innovation Systems – A Comparative Analysis*, Oxford: Oxford University Press.

Edquist, C. and M. McKelvey (eds) (2000), Systems of Innovation: Growth, Competitiveness and Employment. An Elgar Reference Collection (two volumes), Cheltenham: Edward Elgar.

Edquist, C. and C. Riddell (2000), 'The Role of Knowledge and Innovation for Economic Growth and Employment in the IT Era', in K. Rubenson and H. Schuetze (eds), *Transition to the Knowledge Society*, Vancouver: Institute for European Studies, UBC.

Edquist, C. and F. Texier (1996), 'The Growth Pattern of Swedish Industry, 1975–91', in O. Kuusi (ed.), *Innovation Systems and Competitiveness*, Helsinki: Taloustieto Oy in collaboration with ETLA (The Research Institute of the Finnish Economy) and VATT (The Government Institute for Economic Research).

Fagerberg, J. (2001), 'The Economic Challenge for Europe: Adapting to Innovation-based Growth', in D. Archibugi and B.-Å. Lundvall (eds), *The Globalising Learning Economy: Major Socio-Economic Trends and European Innovation Policy*, Oxford: Oxford University Press.

The Financial Times (2001), 'Broadband's slow start hides its potential', 13 December.

The Financial Times (2002), 'Wireless world offers true laptop mobility',13 March.

Freeman, C. (1987), Technology Policy and Economic Performance: Lessons from Japan, London: Pinter.

Funk, J.L. (2002), Global Competition Between and Within Standards. The Case of Mobile Phones, New York: Palgrave.

Garber, L. (2002), 'Will 3 G Really be the Next Big Wireless Technology?', *IEEE Computer*, **35** (1).

Glimstedt, H. (2001), 'Competitive Dynamics of Technological Standardization: The Case of Third Generation Cellular Communications', *Industry and Innovation*, **8** (1): 49–78.

Hommen, L. (2002a), 'The Global System for Mobile Telecommunications (GSM) – Second Generation', report written within the study of the 'Fixed Internet and Mobile Telecommunications Sectoral System of Innovation' carried out within the EU-financed TSER project 'Sectoral Systems in Europe – Innovation, Competitiveness and Growth' (ESSY), co-ordinated by Franco Malerba, Bocconi University.

Hommen, L. (2002b) 'Universal Mobile Telecommunications System (UMTS/MBS) – Third Generation', report written within the study of the 'Fixed Internet and Mobile Telecommunications Sectoral System of Innovation' carried out within the EU-financed TSER project 'Sectoral Systems in Europe – Innovation, Competitiveness and Growth' (ESSY), co-ordinated by Franco Malerba, Bocconi University.

Kenney, M. (2002), 'The Growth and Development of the Internet in the United States', in B. Kogut (ed.), *The Global Internet Economy*, Cambridge, MA: MIT Press.

Lindmark, S. and O. Granstrand (1995), 'Technology and Systems Competition in Mobile Communications', in D. Lamberton, (ed.), *Beyond Competition: The Future of Telecommunications*, London: Elsevier Science B.V.

Lundvall, B.-Å. (ed.) (1992), National Systems of Innovation: Towards a Theory of Innovation and Interactive Learning, London: Pinter.

Malerba, Franco (2000), 'Sectoral Systems of Innovation and Production', ESSY Working Paper No. 1, Milan.

Mannings, R. and G. Cosier (2001), 'Wireless Everything – Unwiring the World', *BT Technology Journal,* **19** (4).

McKelvey, M., F. Texier and H. Alm (1998), 'The Dynamics of High Tech Industry: Swedish Firms Developing Mobile Telecommunications Systems', Department of Technology and Social Change Working Paper No. 187, Linköping University, Sweden.

Mowery, D. (2001), 'Is the Internet a U.S. Invention? An Economic and Technological History of Computer Networking', paper presented at the DRUD Conference, Aalborg, 12–15 June.

Mowery, D. and R. Nelson (eds) (1999), *Sources of Industrial Leadership: Studies of Seven Industries*, Cambridge: Cambridge University Press.

Nelson, R. and N. Rosenberg (1993), 'Technical Innovation and National Systems', Introductory chapter in R.R. Nelson (ed.), *National Innovation Systems: A Comparative Study*, Oxford: Oxford University Press.

Nelson, R.R. (ed.) (1993), *National Innovation Systems: A Comparative Study*, Oxford: Oxford University Press.

Nelson, R. and S. Winter (1982), *An Evolutionary Theory of Economic Change*, Cambridge, MA: Harvard University Press.

North, D.C. (1990), *Institutions, Institutional Change and Economic Performance*, Cambridge: Cambridge University Press.

Ny Teknik (2002), '290 heta platser för surfing med datorn', 4 April.

Porter, M. (1989), *The Competitive Advantage of Nations*, Macmillan: London.

Wireless Web (2002), 'Battling a mindset: WLAN could threaten 3G future', http://wireless.iop.org/article/feature/3/2/5, April.

2. Fixed Data Communications: Challenges for Europe

Bent Dalum and Gert Villumsen

1. INTRODUCTION

This chapter deals with equipment for the wirelined or 'fixed' data communications networks. It is focused on the hardware perspective, although heavily influenced by software development. The analysis thus concentrates on the physical channels for fixed line communications, more precisely the technological and economic development of the data communications equipment industry. The mobile communications equipment industry is analysed in chapters 3 and 4. Recently, the emergence of 3G mobile communications systems – and its forerunner the so-called 2.5G – has created a widespread interest in the field of convergence between fixed and mobile telecommunications networks.

Due to deregulation and liberalization efforts during the 1990s telecommunications service provision and management of telecommunications networks do not necessarily coincide in one company, as they did previously. Voice calls were the basic services available by the public switched telecommunications networks (PSTNs) less than a decade ago. But now there is a wide range of services available for business applications as well as for individual consumers. Rapid diffusion of the Internet has especially fostered the emergence of specialized Internet service providers (ISPs), such as Tiscaly in Italy (see chapters 5 and 6).

Related to these developments, the ESSY project (running from 1999 to 2001) has witnessed rather dramatic changes. From 1999 until well into 2000 represented the end of a sharp increase in equity prices for telecommunications hardware companies – wirelined as well as wireless. These increases were used as vehicles for an extraordinary 'acquisition spree' into small and medium-sized firms specialized in developing Internet Protocol (IP)-based solutions for data communication systems. The 'new economy' bubble, which finally burst during the late spring of 2000, was concentrated on this kind of firm – as well as the pure 'dotcom' start-ups not to be dealt with in this context. The discussion here will focus on the broader perspectives of this 'acquisition spree', especially the relations between the fixed and mobile segments of the hardware suppliers as well as some of the international differences in strategies between EU- and US-based firms. Preliminary consequences of the burst will be discussed.

The chapter begins with a brief review of the basics of classical telephone systems in section 2 followed by a discussion in section 3 of the previous mode of interaction between telecommunications operators and the equipment industry. Sections 4 and 5 give brief summaries of some main features of the Internet Protocol versus the ATM (asynchronous transfer mode) standardization processes. Section 5 deals with the competing as well as complementary roles of IP and ATM. The structure of the fixed data communications industry is outlined in section 6, and various access technologies to the Internet are discussed in section 7. The 'acquisition spree' of the telecommunications hardware industry in the late 1990s is analysed in section 8, based on a detailed mapping for the 1998–2000 period shown in appendix 2A. Section 9 discusses the financial turmoil of this sector from 2000 and examines whether this has altered the European industry's perspective.

2. STYLIZED FEATURES OF 'CLASSICAL' TELEPHONE NETWORKS

A telephone network consists of *terminals* connected by telecommunications *cables*, made of copper wires or optical fibres. Between the terminals is a hierarchy of switches at different levels (companies, local, regional, national, international etc.) and various types of equipment for amplification of the signals. In most developed countries the switches at the regional level are currently connected by a 'backbone' of optical fibres that may be supplemented with satellite communication channels if extra capacity is needed.[1]

The capacity of the networks and the share of optical fibres vary from country to country, basically as a function of their level of economic development. In most developed countries the 'last mile' from the main lines to the individual user is still dominated by so-called 'twisted pair' copper cables. The networks are, however, common for the Internet and present-day voice telephone systems.

Although an integral part of telecommunications networks, the cable technology can also be seen as a separate field with its own technology base. The optical fibre industry integrates digital electronics, semiconductors and fibre optics and is highly research intensive. The central technology is focused on

---

[1] Data communications based on satellite transmission are discussed in chapter 5.

dense wavelength division multiplexing (DWDM) methods. The technology based on these principles has emerged from traditional so-called frequency division multiplexing (FDM) of electrical signals. But DWDM is based on transmission of optical signals – light with different wavelengths – capable of increasing the bandwidth significantly. The development of optical technology has accelerated since the mid-1990s. The technology is quite complex and has involved new types of components such as lasers, detectors and optical amplifiers (Nellist and Gilbert 1999).

But the core technology in a 'classical' telephone system is *the switch*. Although radical innovations have occurred during the history of telephone systems (starting with Graham Bell's patent on a telephone in 1876) the history of the switch can also be seen as following an evolutionary trajectory. It all began with the switch where operators manually put plugs in jacks. The electromechanical switches from the 1920s represented a major breakthrough as they took over the manual functions of the operators. The modern digital switches, introduced in the late 1970s, were prerequisites of the advent of data communications and were, as such, true radical innovations. The switch has, however, done exactly the same job during more than a century – i.e., connecting two subscribers via an open channel (a 'circuit').

Based on innovations in electrical technology during the 19th century, the telecommunications hardware industry (telegraph and telephone equipment) was well established more than a century ago. The partly evolutionary features of the industry are indicated by the composition of the major firms. Many present industry leaders, such as Lucent (the hardware and R&D arm of the original Bell empire of AT&T), Siemens and Ericsson, were already fairly large in the late 1880s. Differing national regulations and standards and/or protectionist efforts (especially in the inter-war period) gave the industry a 'multi-domestic' structure. Until the 1980s most industrialized countries had a relatively developed telecommunications hardware industry, although often foreign owned. Due to deregulation efforts and the introduction of digital telecommunications networks (characterized by very high development costs) the industry became significantly more concentrated and characterized by 'global' features from the late 1980s (Dalum et al. 1988).

Most national markets were in the early stages served by local suppliers. But from the early decades of the 20th century the core technology of telephone networks, public switches, became increasingly complex systems. Already the first generation of electromechanical, semi-automatic switches, introduced from the beginning of the 20th century, required a certain amount of R&D among system manufacturers. This introduced a growing divergence between ever larger and gradually more internationalized 'system' companies and local manufactures of 'terminal' equipment, such as telephone handsets.

The early post-war period witnessed the introduction of a new generation of automatic switches, the electromechanical Crossbar system. Ericsson was among the first to launch this technology and, thus, established itself as one of the technical leaders in the late 1940s. During the following decades these switches were improved by the adoption of new components (transistors and integrated circuits) and control equipment (computer systems).

But in contrast to computers, the replacement of components and parts in telephone networks has been more of a gradual process. The diffusion of new technology in the networks has to some extent been a function of income per capita. For the Nordic countries this has implied that their markets, though small, have been among the most advanced in the world. This has been further strengthened by the ambition of securing services in remote geographical locations on terms equal to those in more urban areas.

During the 1970s digitization of entire telecommunications networks emerged as a major technological opportunity. Ericsson was among the first to launch a digitized public switching system (AXE). During the 1980s the digitization process has transformed the switching industry from a state of 'extended maturity' (Van Duijn 1983) to one characterized by renewed growth and significantly increasing scale requirements. A wave of mergers and acquisitions in the mid-to-late 1980s followed. The OECD established the number of public switch manufacturers in its member countries at 15 (OECD 1988). At the beginning of the 21st century there are less than 10 left, of which the most noticeable are Lucent and Nortel in the US and Canada, respectively, Siemens, Ericsson and Alcatel in Europe as well as Fujitsu and NEC in Japan.

3. TRANSFORMATION OF THE 'CLASSICAL': INTERACTION BETWEEN THE EQUIPMENT INDUSTRY AND INCUMBENT OPERATORS

Equipment producers are dependent on the economic conditions of telecommunications operators. Until the massive diffusion of the Internet the decision making for the operators was – in principle – rather simple. In most cases they had a monopolistic position and it was fairly clear which technology was best. The main option was to decide when to invest in new generations of switches. The latter transported voice between two subscribers once a connection was established. Depending on the distance, voice calls went through a range of switches from local central offices to intercontinental switches.

The world also appeared rather stable from the point of view of the equipment producers. Once a contract with an operator was established a love-hate relationship emerged. The protocols and operating systems were proprietary and made it difficult for operators to turn to another switch producer. The development costs for new generations of switches were very high. New entrants faced high barriers to entry. A propensity to choose 'national champions' as equipment vendors was prevalent, such as France's Telecom-Alcatel, Germany's Telekom-Siemens and the Nordic PSTN, Ericsson.

Lock-in to previously favoured system vendors was rather obvious. One example, given by Shapiro and Varian (1999), was the Bell Atlantic case. In the 1980s Bell invested US$3 billion in digital switches to run its telephone networks. They chose Lucent (then AT&T) to deliver the switches. At that time Nortel, Siemens and Ericsson also produced digital switches. The Lucent equipment used a proprietary operating system. When Bell wanted to add new capabilities or connect the switches to other types of hardware it was dependent on Lucent to provide the necessary upgrades and to develop the required interfaces. Since it was extremely expensive to replace the equipment, Bell was locked into switches from Lucent.

However, in some countries, typically those that were not the home of a big domestic equipment producer, operators often chose two producers. This was the case in Denmark where the national (then monopoly) operator chose Ericsson's AXE switches and Siemens' equipment. But even with two producers, the operator was still heavily dependent on switch suppliers. Control over a wide range of enhancements and upgrades were in the hands of the latter.

Shapiro and Varian characterize the consequences of this lock-in as an 'extremely valuable asset for AT&T' (1999: 105f). According to Bell Atlantic, AT&T's after-market software upgrades account for 30–40 per cent of its switch-related revenues. The costs of annual upgrades of the operating system for Bell Atlantic (one of several switch buyers in the US) amounted to around US$100 million. In addition AT&T made lucrative sales of peripherals equipment to Bell Atlantic (Shapiro and Varian 1999). This case was brought to the courts in 1995 when Bell Atlantic sued AT&T for monopolization.

This pattern has changed especially during the last five to ten years. The main driving forces have been:

- Competition between operators;
- Movement towards open standards;
- Emergence and widespread diffusion of the Internet; and
- Increased demand for data relative to voice.

As the data-to-voice ratio has increased, the incumbent – previous monopoly – operators can no longer ignore data traffic as a major source of revenue; and they meet increased competition from newcomers using the Internet as a platform. They are also facing problems with digital circuit switches in handling the much higher volumes of data traffic on the 'last mile' to the consumers (see section 7). The incumbent operators are thus forced to upgrade their networks to capture a share of the increasing data communications transmission market (see chapters 3 and 4).

With the rapid diffusion of the Internet, especially after the emergence of the World Wide Web in the mid-1990s, equipment producers envisaged the emergence of new networks with smaller barriers to entry mainly due to a higher degree of openness both at network and system levels. Another major change was the emergence of public mobile communications networks, which took off especially in Europe in the 1990s and became a large business segment for telecommunications operators, whether incumbents or new competitors.

4. THE INTERNET – RADICAL CHANGES IN STANDARDIZATION PROCEDURES

While telephone networks aimed from the beginning to transmit *voice* between two subscribers, the Internet aimed to transmit *data* in terms of bits. The Internet was mainly used by universities and large public organizations until around 1990, but the development graphical interfaces radically changed this pattern (Anttalainen 1998).

The Internet grew out of experimental computer networks in the 1960s supported by the US Department of Defense. In 1968 the Department of Defense Advanced Research Projects Agency (DARPA) granted a contract to a Massachusetts-based firm. The resulting switch was called an interface message processor (IMP) and linked several computers. The result was ARPANET, the earliest forerunner to the Internet (Mowery and Simcoe 2001).

In 1973, DARPA engineers developed an improved data communications protocol that allowed separate networks to be interconnected. The idea of an open architecture that allowed network-to-network connectivity was called transmission control protocol (TCP). Later it was split into TCP/IP (transmission control protocol/Internet protocol). The TCP handles the transmission characteristics, while the IP manages the routing and network anomalies. TCP/IP is embedded in distributed customer hosts located in the network periphery, which reduces the need for centralized control. The software is located on the servers and the user hosts.

TCP/IP was rapidly adopted. It was a highly reliable open standard and arrived just as the computing research community began to standardize on the common platform of Unix. As a result TCP/IP became the dominant protocol for most networking applications from the early 1990s.

In the late 1970s the National Science Foundation and DARPA founded a set of organizations to oversee the standardization of the TCP/IP backbone.

The Internet Configuration Control Board (ICCB) was established in 1979. In 1983, when ARPANET switched over to TCP/IP, the ICCB was reorganized and renamed the Internet Activities Board (IAB). The IAB organized two main sub-groups, the Internet Engineering Task Force (IETF), which managed the architecture of the Internet as well as standard-setting processes (including editing and publishing), and the Internet Research Task Force (IRTF), which focused on long-term research (Mowery and Simcoe 2001).[2]

The IETF is not a formal standardization organization, such as the International Telecommunications Union (ITU) where all nations participate. The IETF updates standards, informs about changes and controls the use of global addresses, but it is not an organization with formal power or central management. The working groups are the main drivers. Given the voluntary character of the activities, the IETF is often dominated by large actors, i.e., US telecommunications operators and hardware manufacturers. On the other hand the ITU, although modernized in 1992, is still an organization where the decision processes may be very slow (Bekkers and Smits 1999).

A specification related to the Internet standard is published as part of the Request For Comments (RFC) document series, which is the official publication outlet. The RFC series covers a wide range of topics in addition to Internet standards, from early discussion of new research issues to status memos about the Internet. One central requirement for obtaining an Internet standard is a request for at least two independent and interoperable implementations from different code bases. Successful operational experience should also be obtained. Together with huge development costs this request may be an important factor in the growth of strategic alliances.

5. ATM AND IP – COMPETITION AND CONVERGENCE? OR CO-EVOLUTION OF TWO STANDARDS?

The two dominant protocols for transport of fixed data communications are ATM[3] and IP. ATM was originally proposed within the context of broadband integrated services digital network (B-ISDN). ATM is a typical result of the 'traditional' standardization process of the ITU. The aim of ATM was to integrate services for voice, video and data traffic in one single network.

The main actors – telecommunications operators as well as equipment producers – have strongly influenced this development (McDysan and Spohn

[2] For a historical overview, see the Internet Engineeing Task Force website (http://www.ietf.org/ especially http://www.ietf.org/tao).
[3] For extensive information of the history of ATM and the present functions of the ATM Forum, see http://www.atmforum.com/.

1998). From the beginning a major requirement of ATM was that it should combine the advantages of circuit switching (as guarantee for quick pass through) with the flexibility of packet switching. After examination of many different technologies, such as synchronous transfer mode (STM) and packet switching technologies, the ITU in 1988 agreed to base the development of B-ISDN on the principle of asynchronous transfer mode (Rahman 1998). By 1990 the decision was extended to let B-ISDN be based on ATM as well as SONET/SDH (synchronous optical network/synchronous digital hierarchy), where SONET describes the optical standards for transmission of data and SDH specifies how the data can be packaged, multiplexed and transmitted.

ATM was thus originally created as the backbone of data communications in terms of wide area networks (WANs) or 'public' networks. The actors represented the dominant 'classical' telecommunications firms, whether operators or equipment producers. However, an interest in ATM for local area networks (LANs) or 'private networks' attracted other actors as well. That led to the establishment of the ATM Forum in 1991, originally founded by Nortel, Sprint, Adaptive and Cisco, i.e., established firms as well as newcomers in the equipment market. Subsequently, all the major actors in the industry have joined. Their goal was to ensure interoperability between public and private ATM-based networks. In this respect, the ATM Forum has moved quickly to set the fundamental standards to allow the development of early ATM-based equipment for private networks. Because of its capacity to move faster than the ITU, the ATM Forum was used as a vehicle by the large US incumbent operators (such as Bellcore, AT&T and Sprint) to define and diffuse ATM-based services.

IP and ATM are often presented as two competing protocols. This is a misunderstanding of their roles. According to the ATM Forum: 'Most IP/Data carriers maintain (and have maintained for years) an ATM layer over which IP traffic rides because of the traffic-engineering and other features that are inherent to ATM and lacking in traditional connectionless IP' (ATM Forum 2002). However, it makes more sense to consider them as two protocols with their own characteristics and serving different purposes. As expressed also by the ATM Forum: 'Simply put, by combining IP and ATM, carriers enjoy the reach of IP and management, security, versatility and predictability of ATM'.

A potential problem with the IP is its connectionless nature in which each packet is transmitted independently. Some packets are queued and arrive in a sequence not necessarily identical to the pattern of departure. Furthermore, the process of identifying the destination slows the transmission rate significantly. Therefore a widely used transmission procedure is 'IP over ATM' (Hallenstål et al. 2000). The wide area backbone networks use high data rate technologies such as ATM. The reason is that ATM routing is efficient because it is based on virtual circuits and the configuration of a route is set up only at the beginning of the connection. When the virtual circuit is set up, the fixed length cells are routed by hardware (Anttalainen 1998).

Since IP is the major kind of traffic transmitted through ATM networks, combined routing is implemented to improve the overall performance of end-to-end connections. IP switching is the means to reach this end; it combines the IP and the ATM hardware. An IP switch routes IP packets through an ATM switch matrix. This speeds up the routing by a factor of ten or more compared with conventional IP routers. IP switching is efficient because most traffic is 'long term' between two parties. When a document is transmitted a large number of packets are sent from the source to the destination. This series of packets is transmitted as a single traffic flow instead of routing each packet independently. IP switching performs the routing process only once, and the rest of the packets are routed via the established virtual connection as a series of ATM cells. In an IP switch the incoming series of packets is analysed. When it is recognized that there is a long stream of packets, it dedicates an ATM virtual connection to this steam.

These are the basic reasons why equipment producers try to enhance their competences to cover IP as well as ATM. The blurred borders between the technologies are illustrated by the fact that an increasing part of voice is sent over IP networks; users may be unaware that a telephone call or a portion of a call is routed over an IP network. The transmission network is today (partly) common for Internet and voice telephone networks.

While US firms have dominated the IP standardization process, European firms have historically played a more central role within more 'traditional' telecommunications standardization. This has especially been the case in mobile communications with huge success for the European industry. However, there seems to be a shift away from de jure standards in telecommunications towards creation of de facto standards via alliances between the main actors. This trend naturally raises the question of how European companies will be able to adapt to these new institutional settings. More and more work on standardization is done in special forums, such as the ATM Forum, the 3G.IP Group, the Bluetooth Special Interest Group (SIG), 3GPP, 3GPP2, etc. The larger hardware producers and/or operators create, so to speak, 'their own' standardization organizations. The market will then decide whether these agreements will be de facto standards. The European Telecommunications Standards Institute (ETSI) has found itself marginalized from these organizations (Raja 1999).

6. STRUCTURE OF THE DATA COMMUNICATIONS HARDWARE INDUSTRY

The volume of data communications has exploded in the most recent 10 to 15 years, changing the structure of the hardware industry significantly. Table 2.1 contains some stylized features of the industry in 1999. By far the largest chunk of the market consists of equipment for telephone networks managed mainly by large incumbent operators, dubbed incumbent local exchange carriers (ILECs) in the industry's jargon. The estimated US$225 billion market represents such equipment as digital switches and ATM-based equipment as well as IP-based equipment for the backbone of the data communications networks, and is dominated by the large (and old) telecommunications hardware companies.

With the explosion of the Internet, a new industry segment with a new technology base emerged, dubbed competitive local exchange carriers (CLECs). The core technology is routing. This segment can roughly be divided into two sub-segments: routers for ISPs and routers for large and medium-sized corporations (Taylor 1999). The two types of routers can mainly be divided according to the geographical distance they support, i.e., 'local' or 'remote'. But basically the function is the same: routers route. Therefore the same firms dominate the market for LANs and for long-distance routing via ISPs.

The Internet's emergence in the US gave that country's equipment producers a leading position. As evident in table 2.1, the emerging IP equipment hardware success, Cisco, is the dominant producer in all segments for Internet devices, with a market share, according to different sources, ranging from 60 to 80 per cent. However, operators are not locked in to Cisco systems, because open standards are used. From Cisco's point of view there are two sides of the open standards coin: they make products attractive to operators, yet the company is constantly exposed to (potential) competition.

There is a clear trend towards open systems in telecommunications equipment. The IP is gaining more and more influence. New generations of equipment will increasingly be based on packet-switched solutions. This trend is especially clear in the field of convergence between the fixed and wireless telecommunications systems.

The universal mobile telecommunications system (UMTS) and other 3G systems in mobile communications will not provide users with the full range of broadband services available to fixed users. 3G systems are based on rather slow-speed data communications. Two Mbit/s is at present the absolute maximum for UMTS and a maximum speed of 384 Kbit/s will be normal for at least the next few years. The huge amounts spent by large mobile communications operators in especially the UK and Germany on the 3G spectrum auctions have created a wide gap between the costs of starting the rather slow 3G systems and the evident potential for much cheaper Internet access through wireless local area networks (WLANs). While these were designed as private networks in companies, the so-called public WLANs open the possibility for wireless access to the Internet at very high speeds if users move to 'hot spots' at airports or Internet cafés. In these 'islands' a personal computer (PC) or a personal digital assistant (PDA) can be used to access the Internet at speeds of 10 to 50 Mbit/s.

Table 2.1: Stylized features of the data transmissions equipment market, 1999

Type of user	Equipment function	Market size in US$ (billions)	Main producers & market share
Large companies	Data mgmt in large corporate networks	16.5	Cisco (40%), Cabletron, 3Com, Nortel
SMEs	Networking	13.6	Cisco (18%), 3Com Intel, Nortel, Alcatel
Internet service providers	Routers, data switches, gears	9	Cisco (33%), Lucent, 3Com, Juniper
Consumer networking	Networking gear in the home	0.25	Cisco (10%), 3Com, Nortel, Intel
Telephone networks	Switches, network boxes	225	Lucent, Nortel, Alcatel, Siemens, Fujitsu, NEC, Ericsson

Source: Levinson (1999).

Currently there are signs that public WLAN access will diffuse very rapidly in the near future. While a 4G system until recently has been reserved as a buzzword for wireless Internet access up to 100 Mbit/s, a kind of 'pre-4G' can now be envisaged as a combination of a 3G mobile telephony system and WLAN to access the 'traditional' fixed Internet. The standard now emerging as the winner is the US IEEE 802.11a and b. The 802.11a operates in the free 5 GHz band with a potential speed of 50 Mbit/s, while 802.11b operates with 10 Mbit/s in the 2.4 GHz band. The 802.11b is already working (and marketed as WiFi) and the 802.11a is very close. The European ETSI standard HiperLAN 2 appears to be a loser in this standardization game.[4]

---

[4] HomeRF is yet another variant, while Bluetooth-based solutions basically operate only within a distance of 10 metres and characteristically substitute for cables; see, e.g., Mannings and Cosier

Rather radical consequences may be envisaged and the current debate in this field is whether the IEEE 802.11x are 3G 'killers' or 3G 'helpers'. Although it may be premature to see the result of this discussion it is evident there is a major need – and a huge market potential – in solutions that are capable of creating high-speed wireless Internet access at short distances.[5]

This requires a fundamental integration of the fixed line and wireless communication technologies, based on the IP. New organizations are set up to cope with this development, such as the 4G Mobile Forum and the IPv6 Forum (Fourth Generation Mobile Forum 2002; IPv6 Forum 2002). The latter reflects the need to prepare the emerging wireless Internet access solutions (and the mobile Internet itself) for the transition from IPv4 to IPv6, which in itself is necessary for many of the potential new mobile applications. The explosive growth of Internet users has caused a lack of available IP addresses, which cannot be solved by the present IPv4 standard, but requires the 128 bits address capacity of IPv6. The convergence between fixed and wireless communication systems may thus be hastened more quickly than expected by the negative effects of the 3G spectrum auctions. At the analytical level this requires – even more than previously – a sectoral systems approach. The co-evolution of and mutual interaction between the different subsystems of the entire telecommunications innovation system has become a core feature of the dynamics of the system.

Table 2.1 indicates the various kinds of access equipment needed by final consumers in order to connect to the Internet. Although of a less challenging nature in terms of technological sophistication, this part of the entire system appears to be a very significant factor for the diffusion of the Internet to consumers. The allegory of a system never being stronger than its weakest link, applies amply in this case.

7. INTERNET ACCESS TECHNOLOGIES

In the 1970s and 1980s data communications were primarily related to research activities and internal communications inside large firms having subsidiaries at different locations. However, in the 1990s, in relation to the launch of the World Wide Web and hyperlinks developed at CERN, smooth and rapid flows of data became increasingly demanded by final consumers.

Currently there are basically five ways for consumers (and small business enterprises) to access the Internet:

(2001) and the *The Financial Times* (2002). Yet another standard in this field, IEEE 802.11g is presently emerging.
[5] See interview with Professor Arto Karila at Helsinki University of Technology: '4G boom will follow 3G gloom' in the February 2002 *wirelessweb* newsletter at http://www.wireless.iop.org.

1. 'Ordinary' modems (connected directly on the telephone line).
2. ISDN-modems (connected directly on the telephone line).
3. xDSL, primarily ADSL (connected directly on the telephone line).
4. TV networks (via 'cable modems' for cable TV or 'set-top boxes' for satellite TV).
5. Wireless access.

The first three use a twisted pair of copper wires in the last mile to the consumer. They can all be installed as an integral part of an ordinary fixed line telephone system, which means that the incumbent telecommunications operators have a rather clear advantage in delivering these access modes. Competing companies will have to use the existing infrastructure on the last mile to reach the customers, i.e., they will have to make arrangements with the incumbent operators. This has preserved the powerful position of the latter, which appears to be a major inhibiting factor in the diffusion of fast Internet access in many countries.

Since a traditional subscriber line supports only analogue transmission, it is necessary to use a modem to transform data. The (1) *simple modem access*, which converts analogue to digital signals, does not require changes or enhancements in the network. At present the maximum speed is 56 Kbit/s. A first enhancement of the modem technology is (2) *ISDN* (integrated services digital network), which runs at higher speed with a maximum 144 Kbit/s. In addition ISDN makes possible parallel connections of data and voice.

As the demand for faster access modes increases, there are several digital subscriber line technologies that make higher speeds possible. Their common name is (3) *xDSL*, where the x indicates the specific variant. Since the demand for sending and downloading for most users is asymmetrical, a technology where the bandwidth is higher for downloading is demanded. ADSL (asymmetrical digital subscriber line) is currently the most common technology for high-speed access – between 0.2 and 2 Mbit/s – over twisted pairs.

However, circuit switches in central offices can only handle digital traffic up to 144 Kbit/s (as with ISDN). Above this the digital signals need to be connected through packet switches, causing operators to upgrade the networks with the necessary equipment. Furthermore, there are some limitations concerning the distance to the central office. In practical terms this means that not all consumers have access to ADSL or similar high-speed DSLs.

An alternative to using the telecommunications cables is access via (4) *TV networks*. This alternative has been growing very rapidly in some countries since many telecommunications operators (previous government monopolies) have been slow to deliver high-speed access solutions. There has been an incentive problem since they have been able to acquire enormous revenues because the low speed simply generates high telephone bills.

According to one source[6] there were slightly more than 40 million 'broadband' subscribers worldwide in 2001, divided in three groups of equal size: ADSL, digital set-top boxes and cable modems (for cable TV). The US lead in the absolute amount of broadband subscribers is, however, concentrated in cable modems and set-top boxes. The TV-network-based broadband access share appeared to be around 80 per cent in the US in 2001, and is an alternative to incumbent telecommunications operators – i.e., TV networks, which have been the main carriers of broadband access in the US.

A final access channel is (5) *fixed wireless access (FWA)*, which uses a wireless connection on the 'last mile'. Potentially very large amounts of data can be transmitted through the air over reasonably short distances. Several European countries have recently experienced contests/auctions of FWA licences, which have attracted much less attention than the recent UMTS auctions and/or beauty contests for mobile systems. Until now FWA has not been of any major importance.

8. THE 'ACQUISITION SPREE' OF THE LATE 1990s

Theories of the firm have increasingly put more focus on the importance of capabilities. Teece and Pisano (1994) argue that the competitive advantages of firms stem from dynamic capabilities rooted in high performance routines, embedded in the decision and innovation processes of the firm and conditioned by its history. 'Because it is hard to transform organizational processes, the dynamic capabilities approach sees value to augmenting strategic change as being difficult and costly. Moreover, it can in general occur only incrementally. Because capabilities cannot easily be bought and must be built, opportunities for growth from diversification are thus likely to be limited, lying "close in" to the firm's existing lines of product' (p. 554).

This approach emphasizes the importance of building competences in 'stable' periods, when incremental innovations dominate. However, in periods of more radical technological innovations and technological convergences between previously separate fields, internal R&D seems to be insufficient for staying at the technological frontier. This appears to have been the case for the telecommunications equipment industry in the 1990s, when convergences between traditional telecommunications and the Internet brought a dramatic wave of mergers, acquisitions and strategic alliances. Many large telecommu-

---

[6] *The Financial Times* (2001b). An exact definition of 'broadband' is not given by this source. A reasonable interpretation is the interval of 0.5–2 Mb/s.

nications equipment companies obtained new competencies through acquisitions of small and medium-sized IP-based firms.

In terms of national characteristics Hayes (1985) found that American firms tend to favour 'strategic leaps' while European (and Japanese) firms tended to favour incremental, but rapid, improvements. Table 2.2 shows an account of identified acquisitions from 1995 to 2000, of which the 1998 to 2000 cases are listed in appendix 2A. The outstanding growth performance of Cisco has basically been created through a series of acquisitions.

Table 2.2: Acquisitions by large North American and European
telecommunications equipment firms, 1995–2000

	Cisco	Lucent	Nortel	Ericsson	Nokia	Alcatel	Siemens	Marconi
1995	4							
1996	7	1						
1997	6	3	1	1				
1998	9	11	3	2		3		
1999	18	14	5	8	6	3	3	5
2000	22	9	8	1	3	2	2	7
Total	66	38	17	12	9	8	5	12

Note: Acquisitions are not weighted. The 1998–2000 cases are documented in appendix 2A.
Source: Company web sites and annual reports.

Convergence between various segments of the telecommunications hardware system has obscured the boundaries of the equipment industry. The firms covered in table 2.2 are the largest North American and European producers of traditional telephone network equipment (Lucent, Nortel, Alcatel, Ericsson, Siemens and Marconi) as well as Internet equipment (Cisco, Ericsson, Lucent and Nortel). While Cisco (and 3Com) represent the newcomers, the old hardware firms Lucent and Nortel have entered the IP equipment field through an aggressive acquisitions strategy. The tremendous growth of Cisco in the 1990s – basically through a series of acquisitions of small and medium-sized innovative network equipment start-ups – caused a major shift of strategy among the dominant 'old' equipment producers.

Cisco made nearly 50 acquisitions from 1998 to 2000 (see table 2A.1), which made it the biggest supplier of hardware for IP networks. Its staff grew from 3 000 in 1995 to 44 000 in mid-2001 when the acquisition spree was temporarily stopped. The biggest acquisition was Cerent Corporation in 1999 with 285 employees at a cost of US\$6.9 billion. These acquisitions enhanced Cisco's technological competence, especially in routing technology but also within packet-switching technologies, which are an important part of optical networks.

Cisco's success depends on the quality of its products and its capability to offer a full line of equipment to new operators. Its acquisitions have been directed towards this strategy by enhancing its portfolio of LAN technology. In fact the acquisitions have helped Cisco stay ahead of competitors and get access to new proprietary technologies.

When Active Voice was acquired in 2000, the circuit-switched PBX voice mail was sold immediately after. This was a clear indication that Cisco did not give any priority to traditional circuit-switched-based products. The strategy appears to be aimed at delivering unified communications via a single end-to-end IP network combining data, voice and video where packet technologies (IP and/or ATM) are used.

Lucent defined a strategy to address the data networking business in 1998, and introduced an enhanced portfolio of intelligent switching, access and network management products as part of its plan to dramatically improve data networking performance (Lucent Technologies *Annual Report* 1998). During 1998–2000 Lucent aggressively acquired 38 data networking firms (see table 2A.2). Its biggest acquisition was Ascend Communications in 1999 at a cost of US$24 billion, which was a strategic reaction to Nortel's acquisition of Bay Networks in 1998 and the Cisco purchase of Cerent in 1999.

Lucent was relatively late to offer optical network switching. Nexabit, a firm acquired primarily to supplement Lucent's competence in this area, failed to develop its switching and routing equipment on time. Part of the severe problems Lucent faced during 2000–2001 can be traced to the fact that the company almost missed a generation of optical backbone systems (transmission at 10 Gb/s), leaving a market share of around 90 per cent to Nortel.[7]

As with Lucent, *Nortel* acquired firms to offer integrated solutions in voice, data and video, although its acquisitions numbered 'only' 16 firms from 1998 to 2000 (see table 2A.3). The Bay acquisition in 1998 was Nortel's biggest at a cost of US$9.1 billion. This purchase appears to have been a 'trigger' for Lucent to buy Ascend and for Cisco to acquire Cerent. Later Nortel bought several firms with specific competence in optical networking, e.g., Qtera, Xros and CoreTek. Nortel appears to be the market leader in optical networks.

Ericsson formulated a strategy for acquiring firms within data communications and router technology in 1995–96 (Ericsson *Annual Report* 1996). The first was an investment in Juniper Networks Inc., USA, in 1997.[8] Subsequently, except for Ericsson's acquisition of Qualcomm's activities related to W-CDMA (wireless code division multiple access), which was a result of

---

[7] *The Financial Times* (2000).
[8] In 2000 Ericsson made a divestment of part of its share in Juniper, but co-operation has continued. The divestment appears to have been cash motivated.

patent troubles for the third generation UMTS versus the CDMA2000 standard, its acquisitions all appear to seek the enhancement of capabilities within IP technology (see table 2A.4).

Ericsson's main acquisitions took place from mid-1998 to mid-1999, when the company purchased several companies in IP and ATM areas. According to an Ericsson spokesman,

> Through the acquisitions and our own activity in the area, we have essentially achieved a complete IP product portfolio. No doubt we still need to incorporate further, smaller investments into our acquisitions strategy, but our main concern now is to take care of the acquisitions we have made. (Nilsson 1999)

Since mid-1999 Ericsson has acquired only two companies, both in wireless technology. Overall, its acquisitions have been relatively minor companies with expertise in IP networks. Further, those acquired have had competences primarily in the wireless world. There are two possible interpretations. Either Ericsson is concentrating on the wireless communications it already possesses or is attempting to develop technologies for optical backbone and fixed net infrastructure. Since 70 per cent of the company's sales are generated from mobile systems and terminals (Ericsson 1999), the focus has clearly shifted away from the fixed Internet.

An example illustrating Ericsson's strategy was the acquisition of ACC, a US-based company with competencies in routing and access technology. The convergence of Internet and telecommunications equipment producers became visible at the firm level when Ericsson integrated the access router from ACC into its own AXE switch.

Nokia does not appear to be as active as Ericsson in acquisitions, having attained only a few IP hardware firms in fixed data communications (see table 2A.5). When Nokia acquired firms with specific IP competencies the purpose seems to have been to secure knowledge about (future) Internet access via mobile phones. The acquisition of Ipsilon Networks in December 1997 and Vienna Systems Corporation, Canada, in December 1998 are such examples. The Canadian firm specialized in IP telephony solutions and designs and it manufactured hardware as well as software products for distribution of data and voice over IP networks. In general it appears that Nokia is strongly oriented towards mobile communications, terminals as well as infrastructure. However, it is difficult for Nokia to offer a fully integrated solution to operators that would include, for example, optical switching. In 1999 Nokia sold its SDH/DWDM (synchronous digital hierarchy/dense wave division multiplexing) transport equipment business, including the brand name Synfonet, to Marconi for £46 million. Nokia thus abstained from being active in the optical equipment segment of the market.

In the case of *Alcatel* the pattern seems to be acquisition of fewer but larger firms (see table 2A.6). This is exemplified by its purchase of Newbridge, a world leader in ATM technology, for US$7 billion in 2000. Alcatel is the only European actor that has acquired such a large American firm possessing core knowledge within optical networks.

Siemens is one of the oldest players in telecommunications. However, it has in the past been active in several other industries, such as automation, construction, power generation and transportation systems. Today sales from the information and communication segment accounts for one-third of its total sales (Siemens *Annual Report* 2000).

Siemens is active in three areas: (1) information and communications networks (including equipment for old networks such as circuit switching and communication access equipment) as well as broadband network products; (2) information and mobile communications, with handsets and mobile networks; and (3) business services, which design, build and sometimes operate information and communications systems. These areas cover one-third of Siemens' total sales.

In 1999 Siemens withdrew from the copper cable and optical fibre industry, when in 1999 it sold its share in the jointly owned Siecor to Corning. This sale completed the Siemens exit from the communications cable business.

Historically, Siemens has been one of the large producers of equipment for traditional telecommunications networks. Its main activities have been within equipment for service providers. Siemens has until 2001 delivered packet switches (DSL-switches) to service providers but did not have the competence within the DSL modems to serve small business and private consumers. With the acquisition of Efficient Networks in February 2001 Siemens has closed this gap (Rendleman 2001; see table 2A.7).

Marconi emerged from a reorganization of the previous GEC of the UK. Marconi has tried to concentrate on optical equipment, but performed extraordinary poorly during 2000–2002 (see table 2A.8).

Very limited acquisition activities were registered for Japanese telecommunications network majors Fujitsu and NEC during 1998–2000. Activities in development of fixed Internet equipment appear mainly to have been created through in-house R&D.

9. TURMOIL IN 2001 AND CHALLENGES FOR EUROPE

The burst of the equity bubble in 2000 had significant effects on the fixed data communications industry as well as the wireless equipment producers. In September 2001 one source estimated job losses in the telecommunications hardware industry at 350 000 persons.[9] Lucent and Nortel have been espe-cially hard hit. Lucent struggled on the verge of a financial collapse, which forced the company to divest activities and/or axe staff to a level of half the employment of early 2000. In May 2001 a merger between Alcatel and Lu-cent seemed very close, but was cancelled by Lucent at the last minute. The deal was basically an Alcatel take-over of Lucent. Likewise, Nortel cut 45 000 staff by October 2001 and halved its turnover.

The consequences have also been noticeable for Ericsson, Siemens and Alcatel, and less so for Cisco and Nokia. Marconi, however, by concentrating on optical systems, appears to have been fairly hard hit.

The bubble's burst coincided with the spectrum auctions for 3G mobile communications systems, which in a European context has removed around US$100 billion from the mobile telecommunications operators, thereby se-verely delaying the introduction of 3G systems and, accordingly, slowing demand for 3G infrastructure equipment. With rapidly increasing possibilities for combining fixed and wireless Internet access these two subsystems are becoming significantly interdependent. Developments in one segment of the telecommunications innovation system will inevitably have important conse-quences for the other parts.

European hardware producers in the equipment market for fixed data com-munications appear to be in relatively weak competitive positions. This is most evident in IP-related equipment and less so in the ATM field, although it is dif-ficult to distinguish between these two areas as they are often complementary. The former strength of the remaining major European players in the wirelined field – Ericsson, Siemens and Alcatel – is evidently under pressure from North American companies, mainly Cisco, Nortel and Lucent. But the severe financial problems of Lucent and Nortel blur the pattern. This is further complicated by the future role of the wireless data communications field where European strength *vis-à-vis* North American companies is still quite clear, although Japa-nese strength in this segment may cause acute competitive pressure on Euro-pean companies in the coming years.

REFERENCES

Anttalainen, T. (1998), *Introduction to Telecommunications Network Engineering*, Boston and London: Artech House.
ATM Forum (2002), http://www.atmforum.com/ [cited 30 June 2002].
Bekkers, R. and J. Smits (1999), *Mobile Telecommunications: Standards, Regulation, and Applications,* Boston: Artech House.

---

[9] In *The Financial Times* series of articles, entitled 'The telecom crash', see especially Dan Rob-erts, 'The tangled legacy of a derailed revolution' (2001a).

Dalum, B., U. Jørgensen and J. Fagerberg (1988), 'Small Open Economies in the World Market for Electronics: The Case of the Nordic Countries', in C. Freeman and B.-Å. Lundvall (eds), *Small Countries Facing the Technological Revolution*, London: Pinter Publishers .

Ericcson (1996), *Annual Report*, Stockholm.

Ericcson (1999), *Annual Report*, Stockholm.

The Financial Times (2000), 12 December.

The Financial Times (2001a), 7 September.

The Financial Times (2001b), 13 December.

The Financial Times (2002), 13 March FT Review 'CEBIT 2002 and beyond'.

Fourth Generation Mobile Forum (2002), http://www.4gmobile.com [cited 30 June 2002].

Hallenstål, M., U. Thune and G. Öster, (2000), 'Engine Network Server', *Ericsson Review*, (3), 126–34.

Hayes, R.H. (1985), 'Strategic Planning – Forward in Reverse', *Harvard Business Review*, **63** (6), 111–19.

Internet Engineering Task Force (2002a), http://www.ietf.org/ [cited 30 June 2002].

Internet Engineering Task Force (2002b), 'The Tao of IETF: A Novice's Guide to the Internet Engineering Task Force', available: http://www.ietf.org/tao [cited 30 June 2002].

IPv6 Forum (2002), 'The New Internet: Internet for Everyone', available: http://www.ipv6forum.com [cited 30 June 2002].

Karila, A. (2002) '4G boom will follow 3G gloom', February *wirelessweb* newsletter, available: www.wireless.iop.org [cited 30 June 2002].

Levinson, A. (1999), 'Mr. Internet', *Business Week* 13 September 1999.

Lucent Technologies (1998), *Annual Report*.

Mannings, R. and G. Cosier (2001), 'Wireless Everything – Unwiring the World', *BT Technology Journal*, **19** (4).

McDysan, D.E. and D.L. Spohn (1998), *ATM Theory and Application*, New York: McGraw-Hill.

Mowery, David C. and Timothy Simcoe (2001). 'Is the Internet a US Invention? An Economic and Technological History of Computer Networking', paper presented at the DRUID conference, Aalborg, 12–15 June.

Nellist, J.G. and E.M. Gilbert (1999), *Understanding Modern Telecommunications and the Information Superhighway*, Boston and London: Artech House.

Nilsson, T. (1999), Ericsson press release, 26 August 1999.

OECD (1988), *The Telecommunications Industry: The Challenges of Structural Change*, Paris: OECD.

Rahman, M.A. (1998), *Guide to ATM Systems and Technology*, Boston and London: Artech House.

Raja, S. (1999), *Mobile Communications*, (267), 22 July 1999.

Rendleman, J. (2001), 'Siemens Makes Bid to Enter Broadband', *Information Week*, 26 February 2001.

Shapiro, C. and H.R. Varian (1999), *Information Rules – A Strategic Guide to the Network Economy*, Boston: Harvard Business School Press.

Siemens (2000), *Annual Report*.

Taylor, E. (1999), *Internetworking*, New York: McGraw-Hill.

Teece, D. and G. Pisano (1994), 'The Dynamic Capabilities of Firms: An Introduction', *Industrial and Corporate Change*, **3** (3), 537–56.

Van Duijn, J. (1983), *The Long Wave in Economic Life*, London: Allen and Unwin.

APPENDIX 2A

Information in the tables has been obtained from company annual reports, web sites and press releases. Where possible the information has been checked with *The Financial Times*.

Table 2A.1 Cisco

Acquired firm	Year	Capability	Employs	Price (US$)
ExiO Communications	2000	Wireless technologies for corporate networks based on standard, CDMA technologies	38	155 million
Radiata	2000	Chipsets for high-speed wireless networks	53	295 million
Active Voice Corporation	2000	IP-based unified messaging solutions	na	266 million
CAIS Software Solutions	2000	Software applications for service providers	65	170 million
Vovida Networks	2000	Communications software & networking protocols	65	369 million includes IP cell technologies
IPCell Technologies	2000	Software for broadband access networks combining IP & telephony services	110	na
ArrowPoint Communications	2000	Content switches that optimize web content	337	5.7 billion
Netiverse	2000	Content acceleration technology that enhances performance & functionality of networking devices	34	210 million
Qeyton Systems	2000	Developer of metropolitan dense wave division multiplexing (MDWDM)	52	800 million
PixStream	2000	Hardware & software solutions to distribute & manage digital video across all types of broadband networks	159	369 million
Seagull Semiconductor	2000	Developer of silicon technology	17	19 million

Acquired firm	Year	Capability ·	Employs	Price (US$)
IPmobile	2000	Software systems that enable service providers to build the next generation IP-based wireless infrastructure	na	na
NuSpeed Internet Systems	2000	Technology connecting storage area networks and IP Networks	56	450 million
Komodo Technology	2000	Developer of voice-over-IP (VoIP) devices allowing analogue telephones to place calls over IP-based networks	25	175 million
HyNEX	2000	Intelligent access devices for ATM networks	49	127 million
Compatible Systems	2000	Virtual private networks technology	68	na
Altiga Networks	2000	VPN technology	76	567 million (including compatible systems)
JetCell	2000	Developer of standards-based, in-building wireless telephony solutions for corporate networks	46	200 million
Atlantech Technologies	2000	Network element mgmt software designed to help configure & monitor network hardware	120	180 million
InfoGear Technology Corporation	2000	Internet appliances & software used to manage information appliances	74	301 million
Pentacom	2000	Products implementing spatial reuse protocol (SRP) which allows IP-based metropolitan networks to offer the same protection & restoration benefits as SONET-based networks while doubling bandwidth efficiency	48	118 million
Internet Engineering Group	1999	Optical software	13	25 million

Acquired firm	Year	Capability	Employs	Price (US$)
Growth Networks	2000	Internet switching fabrics, a new category of networking silicon	53	355 million
Pirelli Optical Systems (first multi-billion acquisition in Europe & first acquisition within DWDM)	1999	DWDM	701	2.1 billion
Worldwide Data Systems	1999	Consulting & engineering services for converged data & voice networks		25 million
Aironet Wireless Communications	1999	Wireless LAN	131	799 million
Tasmania Network Systems	1999	Network caching software technology	16	25 million
Cocom	1999	Access solutions over Cable TV networks	66	65.5
Cerent Corp.	1999	Telecom equipment, gears	285	6.9 billion
V-Bits	1999	Standards-based digital video processing systems for cable television service providers	30	128 million
WebLine Communications	1999	Customer interaction mgmnt software for Internet customer service & e-commerce	120	325 million
Calista Systems Inc.	1999	Voice interoperability technology	na	na
MaxComm Technologies	1999	Residential voice over DSL	na	na
Monterey Networks	1999	Optical transport networks	na	na
StratumOne Communications	1999	Semiconductor technology	na	na
TransMedia Communications	1999	Gateway technologies to combine ATM, IP & PSTN	na	na
Sentient Networks	1999	ATM gateways	na	na
Fibex Systems	1999	Products combining voice & data over ATM	na	na

Acquired firm	Year	Capability	Employs	Price (US$)
Amteva	1999	Unifying means for voice-mail, fax & e-mail messages over IP-based networks[10]	na	na
Geotel Corporations	1999	Software managing corporate phone networks & call centres	na	2 billion
Selsius Systems Inc.	1998	IP PBX	51	145 million
PipeLinks	1998	SONET/SDH routers capable of simultaneously transporting circuit-based traffic and routing IP traffic	73	126 million
American Internet Corporation	1998	Internet access over cable networks	50	56 million
Precept Software	1998	Multimedia networking software	50	84 million
NetSpeed	1998	DSL technology	140	236 million
Clarity	1998	Wireless communicationtechnology for computer networking & Internet service markets; fixed wireless access	39	157 million
CLASS Data Systems	1998	Software solutions that enable policy-based quality of service in IP networks	34	50 million
WheelGroupCorp.	1998	Network security software	75	75 million
Summa Four	1998	Programmable phone switches	210	116 million

Table 2A.2 Lucent

Acquired firm	Year	Capability	Employs	Price (US$)
Spring Tide Networks	2000	Network switching equipment	na	1.3 billions
Herrmann Technology	2000	DWDM optical networks	na	468 million

[10] The three acquisitions of Selsius, Geotel and Amteva aim to provide basic voice services and advanced voice functionality over IP networks.

Acquired firm	Year	Capability	Employs	Price (US$)
Chromatis Networks	2000	Metro optical networking systems	na	4.5 billion
Ignitus Communications LLC	2000	High-speed optical communications at the network edge	75	na
DeltaKabel Telecom , Netherlands	2000	Cable modem & IP telephony	60	na
Ortel Corporation	2000	Optoelectronic components for cable TV networks	550	2.95 billion
VTC	2000	Semiconductor components to computer hard disk drive manufacturers	230	100 million
Agere	2000	Programmable network processor technology	na	415 million
SpecTran Corporation	2000	Design & manufacture of specialty optical fibres & fibre optic products	550	64 million
Xedia Corporation	1999	Internet access routers for wide area networks	na	246 million
Soundlogic, Canada	1999	Software aiding 'knowledge workers' in handling large volumes of multi-media communications	22	na
Excel Switching	1999	Programmable switches	460	1.7 billion
CCOM Information Systems	1999	Computer telephony integration (CTI) software	10	na
International Network Services	1999	Programmable switches	na	na
Nexabit Networks	1999	IP WAN switching/ routing equipment	120	900 million
Mosaix	1999	Customer relationship management solutions	550	145 million
Ascend Communications	1999	na	na	24 billion
Batik Equipamentos, Brazil	1999	Digital switching equipment systems	400	na
Enable Semiconductor (Ethernet LAN division)	1999	Fast Ethernet & Gigabit Ethernet transceivers	na	50 million

Acquired firm	Year	Capability	Employs	Price (US$)
Zetax Tecnologia, Brazil	1999	Telecommunications infrastructure equipment to network operators	na	na
Kenan Systems	1999	Billing and customer care software		
Sybarus Technologies, Canada	1999	Integrated circuit (IC) technology for high-speed data & telecom transmission systems known as synchronous optical network (SONET) & synchronous digital hierarchy (SDH) systems	35	na
Yurie Systems	1998	ATM access technology & equipment for data, voice & video networking	na	na
Prominet Corporation	1998	Gigabit Ethernet	na	na
Pario Software	1998	Network security software for IP-based networks	na	na
WaveAccess	na	Packet radio technology for wireless Internet access & metropolitan area networks	65	na
Optimay, Germany	1998	Devpt of software products & services for global system mobile communications (GSM)	na	65 million
JNA Telecommunications Australia	1998	Supplier of data networking & telecommunications systems & services	na	na
Lannet, Israel	1998	Ethernet & ATM switching solutions for local area networks	na	na
MassMedia Communications	1998	Products that manage connections across data, voice & video networks	12	na
SDX Business Systems, UK	1998	Business communications systems	na	na

Acquired firm	Year	Capability	Employs	Price (US$)
TKM Communications, Canada	1998	Call centre integration	45	na
Quadritek Systems	1998	IP network administration software	70	50 million
Hewlett-Packard Company's LMDS (local multipoint distribution service) Wireless Business	na	Microwave radio technology	na	na

Table 2A.3 Nortel Networks

Acquired firm	Year	Capability	Employs	Price (US$)
Sonoma Systems	2000	Carrier managed services to business	na	na
Alteon WebSystems	2000	Content aware switching	na	7.8 billion
Photonic Technologies	2000	Optical components	na	35.5 million
CoreTek	2000	Optical components	na	1.43 billion
Architel Systems	2000	Software systems (IP) for service providers	na	395 million
EpiCON	2000	Software development (application delivery & mgmt software)	na	275 million
Xros	2000	Photonic switching	na	3.25 billion
Promatory Communications	2000	DSL platforms	na	778 million
Qtera Corporation	1999	Optical networking systems	na	3.25 billion
Clarify	1999	Office solutions for e-business	na	2.1 billion
Periphonics Corporation	1999	Interactive voice solutions	na	436 million
X-CEL Communications	1999	Network performance management	na	Undisclosed
Shasta Networks	1999	Gateways and subscriber policy management	na	340 million
Aptis Communications	1998	Remote access	50	290 million

Acquired firm	Year	Capability	Employs	Price (US$)
Bay Networks, US	1998	IP switching	na	9.1 billion
Cambrian Systems, Canada	1998	Technology to speed up flow of network traffic	170	300 million

Table 2A.4 Ericsson

Acquired firm	Year	Capability	Employs	Price (US$)
Microwave Power Devices	2000	Design & manufacture of radio frequency & microwave linear high power amplifier products for 3G	340	100 million
Part of LCC International (Field Measurement Systems & Network Planning Software divisions)	1999	Network-optimizing technologies	185	22 million
MATEC S.A.	1999	Enterprise solutions	475	53% share
Saraîde	1999	Wireless Internet service	150	na
OZ.Com	1999	Internet applictions	90	na
Qualcomm infrastructure division	1999	CDMA infrastructure	1300	na
Telebit	1999	IP router software	60	30 million (75% share)
Torrent Network Technologies	1999	Aggregation routers	80	50 million
TouchWave	1999	IP-based PBX IP-telephony	27	46 million
Advanced Computer Communications (ACC)	1998	Access equipment, routers & concentrators	200	300 million
Mariposa	1998	ATM service access	50	na
Juniper	1997	Backbone routers	270	na

Table 2A.5 Nokia

Acquired firm	Year	Capability	Employs	Price (USS)
Ramp Networks, US	2000	Internet security appliances designed specifically for small office applications	na	na
DiscoveryCom, US	2000	Solutions that enable communications service providers to rapidly install & maintain broadband DSL services for fast Internet access	50	220 million
Network Alchemy, US	2000	IP clustering solutions	na	335 million
Security software business from TeamWARE Group, Finland & Sweden	1999	Security solutions that maximize cost-efficiency	na	na
Telekol Group, US	1999	Solutions for ISPs	60	57 million
Rooftop Communication,US	1999	Wireless IP routers	20	57 million
Aircom International, UK	1999	Network planning tools	50	40% stake
Diamond Lane Communications, US	1999	xDSL solutions	na	125 million
InTalk Corporation, US	1999	Wireless LAN	na	na

Table 2A.6 Alcatel

Acquired firm	Year	Capability	Employs	Price (USS)
Newbridge Networks Corporation, US	2000	ATM WANs	6000	7 billion
Innovative Fibers, Canada	2000	DWDM optical filters known as Fibre Bragg Grating technology	220	175 million
Xylan	1999	Data switching equipment	na	2 billion
Assured Access	1999	Remote IP access gear	96	350 million
Genesys Telecommunications Laboratories	1999	CTI & enterprise interaction mgmt solutions	na	1.5 billion
DSC Communications	1998	Access & switching technologies	na	3 billion

Acquired firm	Year	Capability	Employs	Price (US$)
Applied IT (Fraud mgmt division)	1998	Fraud mgmt software (for telecom operators)	na	na
Packet Engines	1998	Gigabit Ethernet & routing switch technology	na	315 million

Table 2A.7 Siemens

Acquired firm	Year	Capability	Employs	Price (US$)
Efficient Networks	2001	DSL technology	na	1.5 billion
Bosch (mobile comm. development)	2000	2 and 3G (handsets)	200	172 million
Broadsoft (Via Mobisphere)	2000	Web-enabled business telephony applications	na	1.5 billion
Argon Networks	1999	na	na	240 million
Castle networks	1999	IP networks	na	300 million
Redstone Communications	1999	na	na	450 million

Table 2A.8 Marconi

Acquired firm	Year	Capability	Employs	Price (US$)
Mariposa Technology	2000	Integrated devices for voice, video & data	60	268 million
MSI	2000	Global wireless planning and operational support systems provider	na	618 million
AMTEC	2000	IP secure access systems	na	na
Albany Partnership	2000	Service provider to wireless telecom network operators & equipment suppliers	350	105 million
Scitec (Australia)	2000	Communications, network design,integration & services solutions	na	50 million
Telit Networks (Italy)	2000	Devpt of products for public network infrastructure	150	50 million
Davies Industrial Communication	na	Specialist provider of personal radio equipment	na	14 million

Acquired firm	Year	Capability	Employs	Price (US$)
SMS	na	Provider of data centres & IT outsourcing services	600	113 million
Robert Bosch Public Networks (Divisional Purchase)	1999	Supplier of public telecom network equipment to network operators & service providers	na	550 million
SDH, WLL & services Atlantic Telecom Plc (25%)	1999	Provider of cable & satellite television broadcasting & telecom services	na	na
Nokia Oy AB-SD H/DWDM (Divisional Purchase)	1999	SDH/DWDM	120	90 million
Reltec	1999	Broadband access technology	6600	2.1 billion
Fore Systems	1999	ATM & IP technology	2000	4.2 billion
RDC Communications Ltd (Israel)	1999	Wireless networking systems; wireless Internet protocol local loop system (WipLL) which provides users with VoIP, data & Internet access at speeds exceeding 3 Mbit/s	na	39 million

3.   The Global System for Mobile Telecommunications (GSM): Second Generation[1]

Leif Hommen with Esa Manninen

1. INTRODUCTION[2]

This chapter describes and analyses the development of the global system for mobile telecommunications – the GSM standard, the major European contribution to the second generation of mobile telecommunications. The aim is to illustrate the evolution of the GSM standard sectoral system of innovation. The sectoral and systemic dimensions are captured by providing a comprehensive account of the main organizational actors involved in its development, as well as the institutional frameworks governing their interaction. The chapter primarily focuses on Sweden, but also refers to broader international developments, particularly at the level of the European Union (EU). Parallel developments in other areas are discussed for comparative purposes. The case of Sweden is used for specific illustration and explanation. The chapter is structured as follows.

The second section offers a *historical overview* of how the standard was developed, its gestation and introduction to the market. The geographical coverage and organizational provenance of installed systems are also explained. The third section gives a brief description of the main *technical characteristics*. The different kinds of equipment involved and their relations within the system, as well as services offered, are discussed. The services are described mainly from an end user's perspective. In the fourth section *systems and standards* related to GSM are discussed, focusing on technologies of the same generation. Two main kinds of 'relations' are distinguished: the first is

[1] We wish to thank colleagues in the ESSY Research Network – particularly, Nicoletta Corrocher, Bent Dalum, Charles Edquist and Gert Villumsen – for reading and commenting on earlier drafts.
[2] This section is adapted from a text originally authored by Esa Manninen.

complementarity; the second, rivalry. Complementary systems and standards include a number of European innovations in digital mobile telecommunications that were introduced in connection with GSM. Rival systems and standards refer to non-European second-generation technologies for mobile telecommunications that were direct competitors to GSM.

The fifth and sixth sections discuss key actors, as well as the organizational and institutional changes that the creation of the new technical standard entailed. A detailed analysis makes it possible to study the relevant knowledge base, and how it changed over time. The fifth section discusses *public-sector actors*, and the sixth focuses on *private-sector actors* (telecommunications equipment producers and private service providers). The seventh section assesses the commercial success of the new standard, covering the equipment and services sides of the industry. Detailed statistics are provided. In the eighth and final section, *conclusions* are presented. These are stated in relation to some general questions addressed by research on sectoral systems of innovation. It should be noted that the generalizations made are of an empirical, rather than theoretical, character.

2. HISTORICAL OVERVIEW

The GSM standard was developed during the 1980s and 1990s in response to the widely perceived need for a pan-European standard in mobile telecommunications. Diverse first-generation systems had been implemented in Europe, limiting international 'roaming' and fragmenting the equipment market. There had also been remarkable market growth and it was soon evident that new systems with greater subscriber capacity and more extensive roaming would be required. However, the lack of market co-ordination provided insufficient incentive for the development of such systems. In 1982, CEPT (Conférence Européenne des Administrations des Postes et Télécommunications) moved to resolve this problem by forming 'a new standards group – Groupe Spécial Mobile – with the mandate to specify a new radio telephone system for Europe' (Garrard 1998: 126).

In 1985 and 1986, the Groupe Spécial Mobile developed and tested eight prototype systems submitted by different consortia (Lindmark 1995: 111). The test results were presented at a plenary session of Groupe Spécial Mobile held in Madeira in 1987 (Garrard 1998: 129). During the same period, the European Commission became increasingly involved with the GSM standardization process. In 1987, a Memorandum of Understanding (MoU) was drafted by the Groupe Spécial Mobile and signed by telecommunications operators and regulators from 13 countries. It committed signatories to introduce GSM in 1991 (ibid.: 131). Due to technical difficulties, the planned initiation of commercial GSM services in 15 European countries was only fully accomplished by 1992 (ibid.: 161–4).

A second phase of the GSM standard was introduced in 1995–96. By this time, the involvement of the European Commission had led to a gradual hand-over of both the Groupe Spécial Mobile and the responsibilities for the standardization of GSM (and other European telecommunications standards) from CEPT to the recently established ETSI (European Telecommunications Standards Institute) (Garrard 1998: 134–6). After its migration to ETSI, the Groupe Spécial Mobile was renamed the Special Mobile Group (SMG).

Though conceived from the outset as a pan-European standard, GSM spread rapidly to countries and regions outside Europe. By September 1996, signatories to the GSM MoU included 167 operators from 103 countries and states, 20 applicants from participating countries and 10 new applicants from previously non-participating countries (Garrard 1998: 164). The non-European regions included Africa, Asia, Australasia and the Middle East. 'To the surprise of many Europeans, GSM had even made inroads into North America where a number of newly licensed PCS [personal communications services] operators in the USA and Canada chose to use GSM technology in their allocated spectrum band at 1900 MHz' (ibid.: 164). In more recent years, such inroads have continued to grow.

The European Commission's involvement in the standardization process and the resulting hand-over of GSM from CEPT to ETSI marked an important regime-shift in European telecommunications standard setting. Historically, monopolistic national public telephone operators (PTOs) or post, telephone and telegraph operators (PTTs) had been the dominant actors in this process, al-though equipment manufacturers had become increasingly important to such activities. In the early stages of developing the GSM standard, manufacturers participated in the process only by invitation. However, it became increasingly apparent that the co-operation of manufacturers was vital to the success of so large and complex a project. Thus when ETSI was formed in 1988, CEPT members agreed to open membership to any European organization involved in telecommunications (Temple 1992: 177). This was in keeping with the princi-ple that future telecommunications standards in Europe should be developed by a forum 'that would allow, as a right, contributions from manufacturers, users, research bodies and private network operators' (Garrard 1998: 133–4).[3]

---

[3] This author does not provide a clear definition or specification of the term 'users'. However, he uses the term primarily in reference to individual end users of the services provided through telecommunications networks (Garrard 1998: 145–57, 469–70). Another source, more specifi-cally focused on issues of user involvement in the development of telecommunications standards, differentiates between individual end users and commercial 'intermediate-users' (Hawkins 1995: 23). The former type of user can usually be defined in the traditional sense of a 'subscriber' – 'an entity utilising and/or extending telephony based facilities but not primarily involved in providing

3. TECHNICAL CHARACTERISTICS

In GSM and other 'second-generation' standards for mobile telecommunications, voice transmission between terminal and base station would be digitalized. Digital systems like GSM could accommodate many more subscribers than analogue systems, and were therefore capable of overcoming the capacity problems of 'first-generation' systems like Nordic Mobile Telephony (NMT). GSM was also an 'open' standard, allowing producers to configure communications between the system's components in different ways, thus shifting responsibility for system configuration from network operators to equipment producers. An important competitive consequence for the producer firm was that it 'either ha[d] to be a system provider or have alliances with others' (McKelvey et al. 1998: section 2.3).

3.1. Equipment

For most users, digitization meant primarily that their terminal equipment had greater capabilities – for example, with respect to roaming – and more functions. For network operators, digitization required the build-up of an entirely new infrastructure, with implications for the division of labour among key actors. Digitization facilitated not only improvements in the quality of voice transmission and enhanced security functions, but also the capability to receive transmissions of data, as in so-called 'short messaging'. This made possible a wide range of new services. Some involved actors in sectors such as financial services that formerly had little or no involvement with mobile telecommunications.

Infrastructural developments also implied new relationships. In the GSM access system, radio base stations became 'smarter' at the expense of switches. Compatibility of radio base stations from different manufacturers meant that they could be easily substituted for one another. However, they also became much more complex, requiring much more software and programming. This implied a reconfiguration of the knowledge base of producing firms. Developments with respect to switching both presumed and made possible increased co-operation among network operators. Using 'home' and 'visitor' location registries, network operators could effectively track roaming subscribers and extract payment from them.

GSM *terminals* further improved voice quality and made bugging more difficult with encryption of voice signals (Meurling and Jeans 1994: 170). In

---

such facilities to other parties' (ibid.: 23). The latter type, however, is more amorphous. The 'intermediate-user' is likely to be involved in some form of 'third-party service provision' and to have 'acquired a measure of control over the addition of value to basic public network facilities' (ibid.: 23).

addition, a wider variety of terminal equipment became available with GSM and other digital standards. Of five original classes of terminals, portable handsets were by far the most popular. By 1994 there were 18 different models available from 11 manufacturers, as well as basic models and new prototypes available from original equipment manufacturers or OEMs (Garrard 1998: 150–51). Separation of the subscriber's identity and the mobile telephone greatly improved access and security. A separate electronic subscriber identity module (SIM) could be plugged into different terminals by the same subscriber. The SIM could record a wide variety of details about preferences and could also store received short text messages of up to 160 characters (ibid.: 156). Thus users could develop fairly detailed service profiles, and new services could be offered. For example, the SIM's compatibility with financial cards created new possibilities, not only for the billing and payment of mobile telephone services, but also for the delivery of other financial services via mobile telephones (ibid.: 151–3).

Later developments included the dual-band handset designed by Ericsson to operate on GSM networks using both the 900 MHz and 1800 MHz radio frequency bands (Holst 1997: 108). Short Message Service (SMS), first demonstrated by Nokia in 1994, underwent considerable development. By 1998, the original transmission rate of 9.6 Kbit/s was improved to 14.4 Kbit/s (Emmerson 1998: 40). However, serious problems still remained with the connection of SMS applications to existing information systems. 'Average' users, moreover, found the SMS interfaces 'awkward' (Pohajakallio 1998: 48).

GSM *radio base stations* were more 'intelligent' than their analogue predecessors, incorporating a more complex and important control unit. It required much more software development and computer programming, and development of the access system required a much broader competency base (McKelvey et al. 1998: section 2.3). For network operators, the use of multiple voice channels on a single radio 'carrier' made possible considerable economies of scale. Despite higher development costs, the associated infrastructural costs were lower than in analogue systems. GSM radio base stations required only one-eighth the number of transceivers needed to achieve a similar level of carrying capacity. They were also capable of doubling this capacity by adding only one more eight-channel radio module at a relatively low cost. By the mid-1990s, average GSM investment costs per individual business subscriber were initially only three-quarters, and would soon fall to nearly one-third of analogue investment costs per subscriber (Garrard 1998: 158).

In *switching*, the decision to concentrate network intelligence in the radio base stations rather than in switches ensured the inter-operability of switches and radio-subsystems and also drove down infrastructural costs. Switches produced by different suppliers were interchangeable, providing operators with competitive sources of supply. Ironically, Ericsson, a main supplier of switches for NMT, which had a similar compatibility, opposed this principle in the case of GSM – but was, however, over-ruled (Garrard 1998: 144). The most notable initial developments in switching were made to achieve extended international roaming. The register that enabled subscribers to be traced and calls routed to them was divided into two components: the Home Location Register (HLR) and the Visitor Location Register (VLR). Using these registers in combination, co-operating network operators could jointly monitor and bill their roaming subscribers (ibid.).

3.2. Technical Capabilities

Basic capabilities of the GSM system were outlined above. Here, additional details are discussed and features of the initial version of GSM are linked to more recent developments.

In GSM *terminals*, speech-coding made possible a greater *reliability* of voice quality (Garrard 1998: 147–8). SIMs also made possible the reception and display of data transmissions. Their capacity to receive and download data has been under constant improvement since 1994, when Nokia introduced one of the first data interface products (ibid.: 148–9). Dual-band handsets naturally accompanied the development of new GSM networks, which used different bands of the radio spectrum. They also facilitated extensive 'roaming' among GSM networks, in different continents as well as different countries (Johnston 1998: 53).

The GSM *access network* contrasted sharply with analogue precursors. In the latter, each frequency transmitted corresponded to only one traffic channel, while the initial GSM system had eight traffic channels and could handle both speech and data transmissions via time-division multiplexing. Later, half-rate voice-encoding doubled the number of channels for each carrier from 8 to 16 (Garrard 1998: 144–5). The original data transmission rate was 9.6 Kbit/s, but by 1998 the development of high-speed circuit-switched data (HSCSD) made possible a 14.4 Kbit/s service. The further development of HSCSD was expected to double this increase several times, eventually reaching 57.6 Kbit/s data rates (Pohajakallio 1998: 42). More recently, the development of general packet radio service (GPRS) has made possible 'data transmission at rates ranging from 14 Kbit/s to 115 Kbit/s and higher' (Clever 1999: 41).

Switching, already digitized, was not a focus for development in GSM. Instead, 'the access system [became] the focus of attention, in the hunt for new and more cost-effective technology' (Meurling and Jeans 1995: 243). Nevertheless, the interface between the radio access system and the switching system acquired increasing importance, especially with regard to data transmission.

Progression from SMS to more 'comprehensive' solutions such as HSCSD and GPRS has required specialized complements to switching and base station control systems (Clever 1999: 44). Other developments – for example, high-capacity PCNs (personal communications networks) – have greatly increased the exchange of signalling information that must be processed by the control systems. There has been an ongoing effort to increase the capacity of processors connected to the switching system. In the mid-1990s, for example, Ericsson was engaged in a project intended to achieve a tenfold increase in current processor capacity (Meurling and Jeans 1995: 253).

3.3. Functions

Thus far, the discussion has been limited mainly to outlining some key implications for manufacturers, network operators and service providers. Here, focus will be on specific facilities offered by the GSM system, considered from the end user's perspective. The main concern is with three general functions: mobile voice telephony (including issues of both quality and mobility); data transmission; and security.

Regarding *mobile voice telephony*, GSM was associated with not only improvement of voice quality but also progress in handsets. Handsets became smaller and more lightweight, and dual-band capabilities were introduced, enhancing both portability and mobility. Extensive international roaming capabilities also enhanced mobility (Garrard 1998: 155).

Mobile telephony's main competitors in *data transmission* were special mobile data networks, which continued their operation into the 1990s (Lindmark and Granstrand 1995: 381). The most successful of these was a Swedish system, 'MOBITEX, jointly developed by Ericsson and Telia' (ibid.: n. 3). However, MOBITEX had a poor growth record, even in Sweden, evidently because 'the effort required to share a limited-capacity data channel between many users is just too great' (Garrard 1998: 431). Analogue mobile telephony systems like NMT were not readily capable of transmitting data reliably (Paetsch 1993: 28). However, digital systems possessed the basic capability for data transmission. In GSM, SMS originally emerged as an equivalent to paging systems, but proved 'unlikely to provide a substitute' (Garrard 1998: 156). However, the two-way data exchange capability of SMS has great potential. It can provide Internet access through HyperText markup language (HTML) compatibility, now being developed in the form of the wireless application protocol, or WAP (Pohajakallio 1998).

Security, privacy and confidentiality were problematic in analogue systems like NMT (Paetsch 1993: 159). In GSM and other digital systems encryption militated against the bugging of ongoing calls (Meurling and Jeans, 1994:

170). Generally, user security has been one of the strongest features of GSM from its inception (Garrard 1998: 151–4).

3.4. Services

GSM could handle a much larger number of subscribers than the older ana-logue standards, making it possible to accommodate unexpectedly rapid growth in the number of subscribers (McKelvey et al. 1998: 16). In addition, extended international roaming within and beyond Europe was, from the outset, one of the key services in GSM (Meurling and Jeans, 1994: 125). The EC, in its 1994 *Green Paper on a Common Approach in the Field of Mobile and Personal Telecommunications,* took the position that 'roaming agree-ments should be promoted' (Commission of the European Communities 1994: 29). However, some analysts pointed out that GSM, as the spearhead of EC efforts to internationalize competition in telecommunications, was likely to create some unprecedented regulatory problems. One observed that 'the system allows for the import and export of services, by using cards from all over Europe' (Pisjak 1994: 299) without any regulatory framework to govern the roaming contracts. Instead, network operators were left to decide over the trade in mobile telephony services. In this respect, it was noted, 'the technical system challenges regulation' (ibid.).

The possibilities of greatly increasing GSM's capacity for data transmission through solutions such as HSCSD and GPRS have held out the promise of developing a 'mass market for mobile data' (Clever 1999). As one observer noted in the late 1990s, 'the general packet radio service ... will make multime-dia services and high-speed Internet access possible' (Shankar 1997: 44). Ear-lier, the SIM had already created new possibilities for the payment and billing of mobile telephone service, enabling network operators and service providers to reduce their administrative costs (Garrard 1998: 151–3). Moreover, there were accompanying possibilities for competition that should ultimately benefit users by ensuring that costs would be lowered, where possible. The SIM intro-duced a separation between service subscriptions and specific items of terminal equipment, making it possible for users to switch either or both service provid-ers and terminal equipment with relative ease. Moreover, the European Com-mission, from an early stage in the development of GSM, remained committed to the principle that using additional means to lock terminals to any one net-work was an 'anti-competitive' practice (ibid.: 246).

All of these aspects of GSM had significant implications for the development and provision of services. However, the most important development in relation to services was complete 'digitization'. This advance 'allowed the decoupling of the transmission and processing functions, formerly integrated, thus opening the possibility of decoupling services provision from transmission' (Pisjak 1994: 292). Digitization facilitated the entry of many new services (and new providers of both new and existing services) into the market. Ultimately, it raised 'the regulatory question of which services, if any, could or should be reserved for the operator of the telecommunications infrastructure' (ibid.).

4. RELATED SYSTEMS AND STANDARDS

In discussing systems and standards related to GSM, it is possible to distinguish two main kinds of 'relations'. The first of these is complementarity; the second, rivalry. The discussion here deals mainly with rival systems and standards – non-European second-generation technologies for mobile telecommunications that were conceived as direct competitors to GSM. First, however, it will briefly review complementary systems and standards – European innovations in digital mobile telecommunications introduced in connection with GSM.

4.1. Complementary Standards

Most complementary systems and standards introduced during the 1980s were 'new service concepts' intended to broaden the market penetration of digital mobile telephony by providing adaptations specially suited to particular market segments. These included both 'cordless' systems designed to serve very small geographical areas at very low power levels and 'cellular' systems that used low-powered terminals within networks comprised of small cells (Hawkins 1995: 31–2). Both types of system were pioneered in the UK, though variants were soon introduced in other European countries, including Sweden.

Telepoint, an early 'call only' *cordless* system developed in the UK provided the basis for ETSI's CT2 standard (FINTECH 1991), which was later followed by a technically superior 'call and receive' system standardized as CT3 (FINTECH 1990). However, the main cordless competitor to the only modestly successful CT2 in the market for wireless private branch exchanges (WPBXs) was ETSI's 'call and receive' DECT (digital European cordless telephony) standard. DECT incorporated features of both CT2 and CT3, had far greater capacity and was strongly backed by both European equipment manufacturers and the EC (Paetsch 1993: 308–13). It was regarded by ETSI as a forerunner of high-speed wireless local area networks (WLANs) (Microcell 1991: 6). Towards the end of the 1990s, diffusion of DECT was still limited mainly to the market for private automatic branch exchanges (PABXs) and it appeared 'unlikely that DECT will be adopted outside Europe' (Garrard 1998: 457). Nevertheless, DECT became 'an autonomous

Project within ETSI' and continued to be regarded as an important basis for the third-generation 'wireless local loop'; in 2001, it was hailed as 'the only IMT-2000 technology that is available today' (ETSI 2001a: 1).

The *cellular* complement to GSM was ETSI's DCC 1800 (Digital Cellular Communications) standard, originally developed in the UK as PCN (Hawkins 1995: 31; Law 1991: 14). PCN was a 'low-power, low-cost' mass-market standard (Becker 1991; Ramsdale 1991a/b), pioneering a high-density 'micro-cell' application of GSM that required operators to develop a complete network (Haddon 1991). This forced licensees to develop a common infrastructure and 'compete on the basis of services and prices' (Hawkins 1995: 32; Ramsdale 1991a/b). Technically, there were no distinctions between the services and facilities offered by GSM and DCS 1800, and special problems involved in implementing DCS 1800 dictated extremely high infrastructure costs (Garrard 1998: 180–83). Operators had to develop very large numbers of subscribers, primarily through competitive pricing (based on alternative tariff structures and interconnection fees) and aggressive marketing strategies involving new services. Such competition increased the UK mobile telephony penetration rate to 12 per cent by 1996 (ibid.: 198–217). One key lesson was that a trade-off between 'coverage' and service 'quality' was not viable. 'The only way for a new entrant to succeed in the long term is to offer a service that at least matches existing networks in *every* respect, as well as providing some additional benefit' (ibid.: 217, ital. original).

It is also possible to distinguish complementary standards for technologies that are not direct competitors to mobile telephony. Such technologies do not provide complete substitutes but can be considered to form complements (Lindmark and Granstrand 1995: 381). A clear case of this type of complementarity can be found in *paging* systems, which continued to provide a necessary complement to digital mobile telephones, due to their superior capacity for coverage (Garrard 1998: 156). The ERMES standard developed by ETSI and introduced in 1994 was a late entrant into the European market, which had earlier seen the introduction of CEPT's Eurosignal standard and the UK-based POCSAG standard (Paetsch 1993: 30–2). POCSAG out-competed both Eurosignal and ERMES on cost, though not quality, and on the world market ERMES soon lost ground to the US-based FLEX system developed by Motorola (Garrard 1998: 433–4; 444–6). The development of *public access trunked mobile radio/data systems* is another case of complementarity. Responding to problems of spectrum shortage (Hardiman 1990) and a limited but lucrative business market requiring sophisticated public mobile radio (PMR) or public access mobile radio (PAMR) systems (Paetsch 1993: 300; 319), ETSI set out, in the early 1990s, to create a pan-European standard that would be completed by 1995 (ETSI Highlights 1989: 6). The resulting

TETRA (trans-European trunked radio) standard eventually achieved both technical 'maturity' (ETSI 2001b: 3) and wide international acceptance (TETRA MoU 2001: 1). However, the total PAMR market remained small and 'dwarfed by cellular' (Garrard 1998: 423–4).

4.2. Rival Standards

This part of the discussion addresses 'rival standards' representing competing technologies of the same type as GSM – that is, second-generation (digital) systems for cellular mobile telecommunications. As distinct from 'inter-system' competition, wherein different technological systems that are only partially capable of performing the same functions contend with one another for 'market share', the type of competition considered here occurs between technological systems of the same type.[4] Such systems may have different technical specifications, but they do not differ fundamentally with respect to their main functions (Lindmark and Granstrand 1995: 380–1). The competition occurs between alternative technical standards proposed for a given type of system, and in highly regulated markets such as telecommunications, 'the adoption of a system [i.e., standard] on the market of end-users is essentially a two-stage adoption, since the system first has to be adopted by the regulatory body, handing out concessions' (ibid.: 318). Thus the acceptance of one or another standard by regulators is the first battle to be won.

There were three main rival standards for digital cellular telephony in the second generation of mobile telecommunications. In addition to the European GSM standard there were also the US-based D-AMPS (digital advanced mobile phone system) and CDMA standards and the Japanese PDC (Pacific digital cellular) standard. The discussion below will deal briefly with each of these rival systems. It will not, however, provide any detailed account of any complementary standards such as those already discussed in section 4.1.

4.2.1. D-AMPS

As in the case of European authorities and the GSM standard, the decision of the US Cellular Telephone Industry Association (CTIA) to develop a digital standard was motivated primarily by capacity problems with pre-existing

---

[4] Hence, the discussion here does not consider higher levels of system competition, such as that between 'wired' and 'wireless' telecommunications technologies. This is a topic more appropriately dealt with in relation to 'third-generation' mobile telecommunications, given that the displacement of wired by wireless telecommunications had not become a clearly defined trend prior to the advent of third-generation technologies (Lindmark and Granstrand 1995: 398–9). Similarly, the discussion here does not take up competition between first- and second-generation technologies for mobile telecommunications. It has long been established that the first generation was superceded by the second (Lindmark and Granstrand 1995: 397).

analogue systems. There was a brief initial debate about which technology the standard should be based on. The main alternatives were the FDMA (frequency division multiple access) technology backed by AT&T and Motorola and the TDMA (time division multiple access) technology supported by Ericsson and Northern Telecom, among others. The question was resolved by 1990 in favour of the TDMA technology (Lindmark and Granstrand 1995: 390). This formed the basis for the CTIA's publication that year of the IS-54 standard (ibid.). IS-54 eventually became more widely known as the D-AMPS (digital AMPS) standard.

In contrast to the European decision regarding GSM, the CTIA opted for compatibility with first-generation systems, based on 'two seamless transitions – from analog to a six time-slot digital system followed by a shift to a twelve time-slot system' (Paetsch 1993: 390). This decision made possible an incremental shift from first- to second-generation technologies, based on the gradual conversion by carriers of the radio frequencies previously allocated to AMPSs. 'This approach, however, necessitate[d] not only a dual cellular infrastructure but also a dual-mode cellular phone for the time of transition' (ibid.). This terminal equipment, in addition to being bulkier and heavier than either the analogue equipment that it replaced or the all-digital handsets that would eventually come to replace it in turn, was also more costly (ibid.). Moreover, the system as a whole required considerable time for development, and did not become commercially viable until 1993, even after which adoption rates remained slow (Lindmark 1995: 390). In these respects, D-AMPS was a laggard compared to GSM.

Even before the CTIA decided on the IS-54 standard in 1990, regulatory decisions and the development of competing standards had created the basis for ongoing uncertainty about the emergence of any single 'second-generation' standard in the US. The FCC (Federal Communications Commission), as the relevant regulatory authority in the US had already ruled, in 1988, that there would be no national digital standard defined for the US. It only insisted that existing requirements for national compatibility would continue to apply to any of the new cellular systems that carriers were free to adopt (Garrard 1998: 315). This requirement provided the underlying rationale for the CTIA's decision to opt for a 'backwards-compatible' standard in the form of IS-54, despite the drawbacks it incurred in expense and delay. In addition to these hindrances, D-AMPS also had to face competition from other domestic standards, another outcome of the FCC ruling.

As discussed below, CDMA, the main domestic competitor to D-AMPS in the US, emerged several years later than D-AMPS. Nevertheless, many of the network operators that had originally opted for the D-AMPS standard subsequently changed their allegiance to CDMA. In 1996, therefore, there were only three major network operators that continued to use D-AMPS, whereas eight operators had chosen to use the CDMA standard instead (Garrard 1998: 324). Despite this split, D-AMPS still retained a large share of the US market, due to the size of the operators (including AT&T network systems) that continued to use it. Thus, 'TDMA could potentially serve areas with a population of 204 million; major operators choosing CDMA served 256 million' (ibid.).

This partition of the market meant, in effect, that there would be only limited competition between the two standards. In some areas of the US, operators offering both standards were in competition. But in other areas, many end users would never have a real choice between the two digital standards because only one of the options would be made available to them.

There were additional problems of a more technical character that also ensued from the manner in which the two standards had evolved. Neither one was directly compatible with the other, although both were 'backwards compatible' with pre-existing analogue standards in the US. In 1998, therefore, it appeared that 'roaming between one network with CDMA and another with TDMA will only be possible using analog channels' (Garrard 1998: 325). It also appeared that 'since the FCC requirement for nation-wide compatibility still remains in force, a complete migration to digital services seems impossible from a regulatory point of view, even if operators decided that they wanted to pursue that option' (ibid.: 325–6).

The capabilities of specific systems that were developed were not only compromised with respect to 'roaming'. There were other flaws as well. In the case of D-AMPS, the 'backwards compatibility' of the standard with the pre-existing analogue standard, AMPS, meant that D-AMPS was not an entirely new system and therefore did not require extensive infrastructural development in the form of 'installed base' (Funk 1998: 434). Essentially a digital extension of its analogue predecessor, AMPS, D-AMPS was only installed in large cities whose existing AMPS networks required increases in capacity. These circumstances greatly limited the technological development potential of D-AMPS. 'This meant that although D-AMPS would be cheaper for US carriers to implement than a completely new system, it would not be as technologically sophisticated as a completely new digital system such as GSM' (ibid.).

For a number of reasons, then, neither D-AMPS nor any other US-based standard for second-generation mobile telecommunications succeeded in dominating the domestic market in the US. This outcome was, moreover, linked to technical shortcomings that had repercussions for the performance of the US standards internationally. Compared to the rapid and extensive international diffusion of the GSM standard (see section 3.3), the US standards did not fare well. In the case of D-AMPS, the main market development outside the US occurred in Latin America and some parts of Asia:

All the Latin American countries adopted AMPS/D-AMPS as their national standard, often insisting that new operators introduced digital technology from the start of service instead of waiting until they needed additional capacity. A number of Asian countries licensed D-AMPS services alongside GSM, following their policy of allowing technologies to compete, as well as competitors. (Garrard 1998: 327)

4.2.2. CDMA

The emergence of domestic standards for 'second-generation' mobile telephony that would compete with D-AMPS was partly linked to the FCC's 1988 decision. However, it was also due to the character of the Telecommunications Industry Association (TIA), the organization finally responsible for the development of telecommunications standards. As already noted, the CTIA – an organization which represented not only manufacturers of mobile telecommunications equipment but also 'carriers' or network operators and other users – played an important role in defining mobile telecommunications standards in the US. Its proposals, however, also had to be ratified by the TIA (Paetsch 1993: 143).

The TIA was essentially 'a manufacturer's trade association' that possessed a higher degree of authority than the CTIA, due to the fact that it had accreditation from the American National Standards Institute (Garrard 1998: 315). In composition, the TIA was quite unlike its European counterpart ETSI, which was dominated primarily by 'carriers' (i.e., the PTOs and PTTs). TIA was much less influenced by carriers' demands, which it only needed to take into consideration when developing what were essentially 'voluntary' standards (Paetsch 1993: 143). This difference in organizational structure resulted in a much more pluralistic approach to standards development in the US case, based on the need to accommodate competing interests among manufacturers.

In 1990, at the same time that the CTIA decided on IS-54, Motorola proposed a narrow-band analogue technology called N-AMPS that was capable of overcoming the capacity problems of first-generation cellular telephony (Garrard 1998: 318). The N-AMPS proposal failed, but another, more serious contender had already emerged.

In 1989, even before N-AMPS was announced, the US telecommunications equipment manufacturer, Qualcomm, presented the CTIA with an alternative to the TDMA technology that was the basis for IS-54. This alternative was CDMA, a 'wideband' technology which Qualcomm continued to develop as a proprietary standard, even after the CTIA had decided in favour of TDMA as the 'industry standard'. Qualcomm was joined in this effort by a number of major organizations such as Motorola, AT&T, Nynex, Ameritech, and PacTel (ibid.: 317–18). Among the major equipment manufacturers, the only firm not to join the coalition was Ericsson, 'which continued to state publicly that it did not believe that CDMA offered any advantages over GSM and that it did not intend to manufacture any new products for the new technology' (ibid.: 319).

Apart from this exception, Qualcomm had been able to mobilize strong support for its CDMA proposal, especially among equipment manufacturers. Hence the CTIA and the TIA were faced with a serious quandary, which the CTIA eventually resolved by affirming its original decision in favour of IS-54 but also resolving to continue work on a 'wideband standard'. This compromise led, eventually to CTIA's adoption in 1994 of CDMA as standard IS-95, which was 'to become the second industry cellular standard in the USA' (ibid.: 319).

CDMA thus emerged considerably later than D-AMPS as an 'industry standard', and was therefore not initially a direct competitor to D-AMPS. In the longer term, it did become a competitor, and the more lengthy period of time required for its development enabled CDMA to gain the backing of an extensive consortium of telecom carriers or operators and equipment manufacturers. In addition to this, CDMA possessed a number of features that made it technically superior to D-AMPS. For example, CDMA was capable of capacity gains on the order of 'a twenty-fold increase over the AMPS system' (Paetsch 1993: 179). These aspects of CDMA's development provide some explanation of why so many major network operators switched rather quickly to the new US digital standard when it finally emerged (see section 4.2.1, above).

In spite of the advantages gained from its delayed launch, CDMA still suffered from problems of technological 'immaturity' and the 'limited availability' of terminal equipment when it was finally introduced by those operators who had chosen to back this standard (Garrard 1998: 325). Like D-AMPS, CDMA achieved 'less growth in installed base ... than if such a standard were installed throughout the US' (Funk 1998: 435). CDMA was also implemented differently by each operator. Thus, like D-AMPS, its potential impact on the US market as a whole was seriously limited by an initial partitioning of the market based on operators' choice of one or the other standard. This, in turn, limited the standard's technological development. Consequently, CDMA, like D-AMPS, met with only limited international success.

Outside of the US, the most notable adoptions of CDMA occurred in Asia. The world's first CDMA system was launched in Hong Kong, in 1995, and had gained some 10 000 subscribers by the end of that year (Garrard 1998: 325). Even earlier, South Korea had, for reasons of industrial policy, adopted CDMA as its national standard in 1993. This decision eventually led to the launch of two CDMA services in 1996, and several more thereafter, as well as the licensing of CDMA technology to a number of Korean manufacturers of telecommunications equipment (ibid.). As of 1998, CDMA also had a number of other good prospects in the Asia-Pacific region, but these would involve serious competition with other standards – most notably GSM, which had already been implemented in these countries. Thus, while it seemed 'very likely that a number of countries ... may license additional operators for CDMA', it also had to be noted that 'many have already licensed almost every other technology that became available' (ibid.: 328).

4.2.3. PDC

The Japanese contribution to digital cellular telephony in the second generation of mobile telecommunications was the PDC standard, which never diffused widely out of its home country. This insularity has been variously attributed to the standard's lack of 'openness' (Funk 1998: 434) and Japanese telecommunications equipment manufacturers' 'lack of a track record in international markets' (Garrard 1998: 326). In any case, PDC remained essentially a domestic standard.

PDC began with a 1989 decision by Japan's Ministry of Posts and Telecommunications (MPT) to create a high-capacity digital standard for cellular telephony (Garrard 1998: 326). Technical requirements were initially defined by an internal ministry working group, the Japanese Digital Cellular Radio System Committee, and the standard was developed by subcommittees of the Standards Committee of the Japanese Research and Development Centre for Radio Systems (RCR) (ibid.: 361). The standard eventually developed by 1990 had many basic features that were highly similar to D-AMPS. The main differences were due to spectrum allocation policy (ibid.). As a result of these differences, PDC would be incompatible with any other system. 'Although Japan's MPT did require ... the same TDMA technology that GSM and D-AMPS are based on, the frequencies that it allocated for digital cellular systems were not compatible with these systems' (Funk 1998: 435).

The PDC system was first launched in Tokyo in 1993 by NTT DoCoMo, which was once the mobile subsidiary of NTT, the national telecommunications operator, but had since become a separate company (Garrard 1998: 326). This launch was soon followed in 1994, the same year that Japan's market for terminal equipment was liberalized, by the introduction in other densely populated areas of two further large digital cellular networks. Each of these networks was a joint venture of one of two newly formed consortia – Tu Ka and Digital Phone – whose composition included Japanese subsidiaries of international telecommunications equipment manufacturers (e.g., Motorola) and operators (e.g., Cable and Wireless) in addition to their domestic counterparts (ibid.: 362). These new networks were soon joined by others, with the result that NTT's network quickly found itself facing a number of competitors.

The fact that PDC was launched under competitive market conditions contributed to slower growth than expected for NTT, but a fairly rapid adoption of PDC networks within Japan. In 1995, competition had become intense and the growth of the market for mobile telecommunications had become rapid. In that year, the price of terminals for the new PDC standard had fallen below US$500, and in the last quarter all operators cut their monthly fees and registration charges. As a consequence, 'by the end of the year there were nearly nine million subscribers, with 60 per cent of them connected to digital networks' (Garrard 1998: 363).

As mentioned earlier, PDC never flourished outside Japan. In addition to the technology's lack of 'openness' and Japan's weak presence on international markets for telecommunications equipment, the lack of success abroad was at least partly due to NTT DoCoMo's continuing domination of the standardization process that created PDC. One observer noted that 'since NTT DoCoMo was not allowed to operate services overseas, it had little interest in creating a world-wide standard' (Funk 1998: 435). Consequently, NTT Do-CoMo 'used its control of the standard-setting process to create a relatively closed, unique standard that is still only used in Japan' (ibid.).

4.3. Summary

This section has dealt with both complementary and rival standards related to GSM. Both kinds of standards have been competitors to GSM, but only to a limited extent.

Section 4.1, on complementary systems and standards, discussed other types of technological systems that might originally have constituted 'competitors' to systems like GSM. They could have provided partial substitutes for GSM and other second-generation (digital) systems for cellular mobile telecommunications, in areas such as data transmission, telephony or voice transmission, and short messaging (or paging). In most of these cases, the only partial potential for substitution was eventually translated into the development of complementarities between systems. In several such cases within Europe, ETSI was able to direct these systemic complementarities towards the evolution of standards compatible with GSM.

ETSI thus created a whole 'family' of compatible technological standards. DECT, DCS 1800, and TETRA were not only complementary to, but also compatible with, GSM. Accordingly, they both benefited from and helped to advance and consolidate GSM's rapid domination of the European market. ETSI's most notable failure, ERMES, was a complementary system, but could gain no special advantage from GSM compatibility. Moreover, it fared poorly in relation to other systems of the same type that had superior technical or market features. None of these paging systems, however, was a viable

substitute for mobile telephony. Therefore, none detracted from the technological and market development of systems such as GSM.

Section 4.2 dealt with rival standards for systems of the same type as
GSM. It showed that there was never full competition among these standards,
since the initial decisions made by regulatory authorities effectively partitioned the international market. Japan was perhaps the most extreme case.
There, close relations between the standard-setting authority and the national
telecommunications operator in charge of developing the new technology led
to the latter's effective domination of the standardization process and the
creation of a closed national standard. Conversely, the market remained
closed to other standards.

Even in the case of the US, which had a competitive policy regarding standards, the entry of foreign standards was minimal, and the domestic market
was effectively partitioned only between two rival domestic standards. This
outcome ensued not only from regulatory decisions but also from the decentralized and 'voluntary' nature of standard setting and standards development
in the US context. D-AMPS – and, for that matter, any other second-
generation standard – never managed to dominate the US market completely.
Similarly, and partly as a consequence of this domestic rivalry, neither D-
AMPS nor CDMA ever emerged as a dominant force in international competition. This pattern is clearly illustrated in table 3.1, which describes the distribution of market shares for the major second-generation standards in
mobile telecommunications at the end of the 1990s.

As table 3.1 reveals, the D-AMPS standard captured a large share of international markets only in Latin America, and the CDMA standard made
somewhat more limited headway in Asia, where D-AMPS had little success
but GSM had far more. Table 3.1 also indicates the 'regional' character of the
market for mobile telecommunications. What is perhaps most notable about
the limited successes of US standards abroad is that in both cases the US-
based standards fared better internationally than domestically. This was due
not only to a 'divided market' but also to the weaker migration in North
America than elsewhere from 'first-generation' to 'second-generation' standards. By contrast, the GSM standard, based in Europe, the region of most
extensive migration, dominated not only the domestic market but also the
African market. In addition, GSM captured 35 per cent of the Asian market
and even made some inroads on the North American market.

Table 3.1: International competition among major 'second generation' and other mobile telecommunications standards: regions and market shares

	Europe	North America	Latin America	Asia	Africa
GSM	89%	4%	1%	35%	88%
D-AMPS		27%	39%	3%	
CDMA		9%	9%	14%	
Analogue	11%	60%	51%	48%*	12%

Note: *48% includes PDC & PHS – Japanese digital cellular standards.
Source: ITU World Communications Database.

5. PUBLIC-SECTOR ACTORS

Compared to the development and implementation of the NMT standard(s), the emergence of the GSM standard was marked by the involvement of a far greater number of actors and a much greater complexity in the relations among them. The playing field was no longer one region within Europe but, instead, Europe as a region of the world. For public-sector actors – in particular, the PTOs or PTTs – the 1980s and 1990s were years of transition. Until the 1980s, the PTOs and PTTs exercised extensive monopoly powers, often combining the roles of regulation, network operation and service provision. By the mid-1990s, their roles had become much more specialized. Increasingly, the functions of PTOs and PTTs were confined to network operation, and even in this area their monopolies were progressively eroded. New organizations, such as separate regulatory authorities, had been created to take over many of their former functions, and they faced domestic competition from new service providers.

Similarly, private-sector organizations were increasingly exposed to higher levels of international competition. In addition, the convergence of formerly separate technologies in the 'digitization' of mobile telecommunications meant that incumbent firms in the telecommunications sector now had to confront new entrants whose competence had originated in other sectors. Strategic alliances (among both public- and private-sector actors) became prevalent. Moreover, firms also began to rely increasingly on public-sector research. Rather than collaborating exclusively with PTOs or PTTs, telecommunications equipment manufacturing firms began joint R&D with universities and research institutes. All of these developments had far-reaching implications for the institutional framework and knowledge base of second-generation mobile telephony (Hawkins 1995: 29–30).

5.1. European National PTOs or PTTs: Televerket

As with the first-generation standard, NMT, public-sector actors were very important to the development of the second-generation standard, GSM. One of the main continuities was the leading role played by national PTOs or PTTs in initiating and defining a new standard. But there were also disconti-nuities in the part played by these organizations. For one thing, there were many more PTOs and PTTs involved in the development of GSM than in the case of NMT. For another, they did not co-operate solely on an *ad hoc* con-sortium basis, but rather within a formal organizational framework provided by two European standards development organizations (SDOs).

The first of the SDOs associated with GSM was CEPT, which initiated the standard. The second was ETSI, which saw the standard through to its com-pletion. The transfer of responsibility for GSM and other standards from CEPT to ETSI was also marked by a shift from a 'closed' to a more 'open' approach to standards development. The more inclusive approach of ETSI, which welcomed equipment suppliers and public research organizations, among others, as members, reflected a growing realization that PTOs and PTTs could no longer claim or exercise a monopoly of knowledge and exper-tise in telecommunications.

Numerous PTOs and PTTs were involved in developing GSM, since this was an initiative of CEPT, an organization that represented some 25 European PTOs or PTTs. The majority of CEPT's members were state-owned monopolies that combined several roles (Hawkins 1995: 29). Most were both network operators and service providers. In addition, many also combined these roles with that of regulating the telecommunications markets in their respective countries. They exercised a very high degree of 'market power', justified by the understanding that telecommunications formed a 'natural monopoly' (Muller 1992). As mo-nopolists in 'closed' national markets, the PTOs or PTTs also had special respon-sibilities for the development of new technology and the improvement of market conditions in the telecommunication sector. The first part of this mandate, espe-cially, often involved 'strong cooperation between the incumbent operators and the national telecommunications industry; in some cases this was almost tanta-mount to a kind of vertical integration' (Pisjak 1994: 289).

In the European Union, the publication in 1987 of the *EC Green Paper on Telecommunications* (Commission of the European Communities 1987) had profound implications for these organizations. Among other things, it spelled the end of a policy regime in which domestic telecommunications standards were 'defined internally by monopoly PTOs, sometimes in collaboration with preferred suppliers' (Hawkins 1995: 29). The EU's creation in 1988 of ETSI, which took over standard-setting from CEPT, marked a decisive shift from a closed to an open approach to developing standards. The EC *Green Paper* also initiated extensive liberalization of telecommunications markets in the EU, paralleling similar developments across the OECD world. The reforms that followed included the opening of formerly closed national markets to international competition and the end of monopoly privileges for the PTOs or PTTs. New service providers were also permitted to emerge. Other reforms included the creation of separate bodies to take over market regulation. Liberalization was a complicated and therefore gradual process, beginning earlier in some countries and later in others. Nevertheless, by the end of the 1990s it was at an advanced stage in Europe, even if not yet fully completed (OECD 1999: 11–12).

A prime example of the old regime was the Swedish PTO, Televerket (later, Telia), and its close collaboration with the Swedish telecommunications equipment manufacturer L.M. Ericsson (later, Ericsson). Televerket was mandated to develop new telecommunications technology, and to support national equipment suppliers in doing so (Karlsson 1998: 30–2, ch. 3). L.M. Ericsson's success in developing major innovations in telecommunications equipment depended strongly on its relations with Televerket. In addition to constituting a vital 'test market', the Swedish PTO had 'provided crucial resources for the innovation activities through technical and financial risk-sharing and technical collaboration activities' (Fridlund 1998: section 6). Close collaborative relationships between Televerket and Ericsson continued in the initial development of GSM (McKelvey et al. 1998: section 9.1).

The GSM consortium as a whole comprised national PTOs or PTTs and the equipment manufacturers with whom they chose to collaborate. Beneath the broader 'umbrella' of the consortium, a number of different alliances or coalitions were formed between these two types of actors. Thus, five such alliances submitted eight prototype technologies to CEPT's initial 'technology competition' for GSM, which was conducted in order to establish a technical basis for further development of the first set of recommendations for the standard (Garrard 1998: 129). The five coalitions were: (1) Televerket, the Finnish, Danish and Norwegian PTTs, Ericsson; Nokia, and Elab (a Norwegian firm); (2) ART, SAT, SEL, AEG, Italtel; (3) Philips and TRT; (4) LCT; and (5) ANT, Bosch and Telettra (Lindmark 1995: 111).

PTOs or PTTs were heavily involved in the development of the 'Nordic' alternative. However, their counterparts in other countries also played an important role. Although there were five alliances in all, these could be further grouped into two main camps: 'a Franco-German group and a narrow-band camp championed by actors in the Nordic region' (Glimstedt 2000: 9). The Franco-German group, which had developed a series of wideband or broadband solutions based on large investments in wideband TDMA, during the 1980s, included France Telecom and its German counterpart, DPT. It also had the backing of Alcatel and Siemens, the major telecommunications equipment manufacturers in France and Germany, respectively (Ruotto 1998: 257–8). National industrial interests were, moreover, overtly promoted via the French–German wideband proposals (Cattaneo 1994).

Sweden's Televerket played an important lead role in the opposing camp. The Nordic coalition, of which both Televerket and Ericsson were members, submitted four separate proposals for a narrow-band GSM prototype technology. (All other proposals were for wideband solutions.) Within this alliance, 'Televerket was the only PTT offering an alternative; all the rest were firms' (McKelvey et al. 1998: section 9.1). Televerket's alternative, moreover, was the one selected. This conferred an early lead to Ericsson, Nokia and other Nordic equipment manufacturers in the commercial development of GSM technology. Conversely, '[i]f a broadband solution would have been chosen as the new European digital standard, the Nordic actors would have been left way behind in the technological development' (ibid.).

One might infer that Televerket was not only a prominent sponsor but also a main author of the technology that became the prototype for GSM. As indicated by Glimstedt (2000: 8), however, Televerket acted less as a 'spearhead' and more as a 'figurehead' for allied private firms that had already begun to take the lead. The achievements of engineers at Televerket and Ericsson were based on technologies of which a number of non-Swedish firms held the intellectual property rights (Bekkers et al. 2000). US-based Motorola held many of the most important of these patents, which it licensed selectively to Nokia and Ericsson. With Ericsson, Motorola made cross-licensing agreements in return for access to Ericsson's previously developed expertise in digital switching (ibid.). Motorola's strategy of using licensing agreements as a means of promoting its interests and generating revenue streams based on its R&D investments is well-documented (Iversen 2000).

There is thus evidence that questions the technological leadership that might be attributed to Televerket. Of course, Televerket also played an important role as a 'user' – i.e., as an operator of GSM networks. However, this role coincided with the privatization of Televerket into the public corporation, Telia. This second aspect of Televerket/Telia's involvement with GSM is therefore dealt with in a later section (6) on 'private-sector actors'.

5.2. European Standards Development Organizations (CEPT and ETSI)

Two European SDOs – CEPT and ETSI – played prominent roles in the development of the GSM standard. The MoU group, originally formed within CEPT to administer the Memorandum of Understanding on GSM and later based in ETSI is also discussed below.

5.2.1. CEPT (Conférence Européenne des Administrations des Postes et Télécommunications)

CEPT experienced a certain degree of conflict and tension with respect to its mandate when in 1975 the European Commission requested CEPT to ensure principles such as 'market co-ordination' in its work on standards (Drake 1994; Hawkins 1992). CEPT had no power to enforce the standards that it set (Wallenstein 1990). Also, and perhaps more importantly, 'the CEPT members were reluctant to meet these requests because such harmonization attempts conflicted with their national sovereign powers' (Bekkers and Liotard 1999: 111). The European Community's new approach to technical harmonization and standards, implemented during the 1980s, could have ameliorated these problems (Schreiber 1991: 99). Nevertheless, the members of CEPT continued to agree upon standards and measures for technical and administrative harmonization through 'consensus'. In this manner, some members persuaded CEPT to establish the Groupe Spécial Mobile in 1982 for the purpose of defining a new, pan-European mobile telephone standard (Garrard 1998: 126).

The Groupe Spécial Mobile carried out most of the initial work involved in defining the GSM standard under the auspices of CEPT. These activities began with the drafting of recommendations, included the testing of prototypes to develop a more complete specification, and in addition, involved the administration of the standard. Under the direction of the European Commission, the GSM formulated in 1987 an MoU, initially signed by the PTOs or PTTs of some 13 European countries. The MoU committed the signatories to regulatory conventions and a schedule for implementation (Garrard 1998: 129–31). The Groupe Spécial Mobile sought to include manufacturers in its activities at a very early stage, although only by invitation (Lindmark 1995: 111). This marked a significant departure from the past practice of CEPT, whose membership structure 'precluded direct participation by non-PTO interests' (Hawkins 1995: 29). It also prefigured the open approach to standards development. Nevertheless, CEPT remained dominated by PTOs or PTTs, in significant contrast to the TIA, its US counterpart.

It is remarkable that the European Commission, 'lacking voice within CEPT' (Glimstedt 2000: 4), was able to intervene effectively in its development of GSM. Yet the EC managed to wrest authority over standards development from CEPT and transfer it to the newly created ETSI in 1988. Even earlier, in 1987, it had been able to direct CEPT's formulation of the GSM MoU. Apparently, the EC was also able to influence CEPT's choice of the technological basis for the GSM standard. Thus, the wideband coalition, including some of the most powerful members of CEPT, found itself very isolated. Thirteen of CEPT's 15 members voted instead for the Nordic narrowband alternative (Ruotto 1998). The main leverage of the EC was regulatory – its determination to liberalize European telecommunications after the US model (Sandholtz 1993). The *EC Green Paper on Telecommunications* (Commission of the European Communities 1987) made this explicit. It also heralded an end to using standards development in telecommunications as a vehicle for purely national industrial policy interests. These principles were already in force in the EC's single market policy requiring European standards in telecommunications (Bach 2000). Given the powerful mechanisms that could be brought to bear, CEPT had little choice but to yield to the EC. Moreover, CEPT had little interest in making any decision regarding GSM that would obviously privilege its most powerful members and their 'national champions'.

5.2.2. ETSI (European Telecommunications Standards Institute)

The EU's creation of ETSI was motivated by concern about Europe's competitiveness in telecommunications and the threat posed by US multinationals (Dang-Nguyen et al. 1993). The EC, in its 1987 *Green Paper on Telecommunications*, had called for strong and concerted effort in the development of telecommunications standards for the internal market (Commission of the European Communities 1987). GSM was a notable exception. The *Green Paper* 'set mobile telecommunications to one side for future consideration' (Commission of the European Communities 1994: section 1). By 1988, when ETSI came into being, the recommendations for phase 1 of the GSM standard were nearly complete. The transfer of work on GSM was therefore carefully staged to minimize disruption. And, when the Groupe Spécial Mobile transferred from CEPT to ETSI in 1989, it preserved the same organizational structure and agenda. Despite all this, the transfer of GSM to ETSI translated into a considerable delay in the introduction of GSM due to procedural requirements (Garrard 1998: 134).

ETSI assumed the mandate and responsibility for developing further EU telecommunication standards (Drake 1994) with CEPT agreeing to the transfer of this role only under 'intense pressure' (Garrard 1998: 134). Subsequently, ETSI ushered in a new, more open and inclusive approach to standards development. ETSI and its counterparts in the US (the TI Committee, founded in 1984) and Japan (the Telecommunications Technology Committee or TTC, founded in 1985) were 'regional in scope and oriented towards the voluntary/consensus method of standards making' (Hawkins 1995: 29).[5] Thus, ETSI, like its counterparts, has been 'virtually required to

---

[5] Earlier the US and Japanese counterparts of ETSI were identified as the TIA and the RCR, respectively. The references made here to TI and RCR may therefore be somewhat confusing. This problem arises due to the fact that a multi-purpose organization such as ETSI can have more than one functional equivalent in other settings. As Hawkins et al. explain, TI – an abbreviation for ANSI TI – is a committee of the American National Standards Institute (ANSI). It is respon-

include users from the start' (ibid.).[6] The ETSI membership consisted not only of the PTOs and PTTs and manufacturers, but also public research organizations and new entrants into service provision. The sheer number of members, well over 300, suggested 'that ETSI is reaching well down to small and medium sized enterprises' (Temple 1992: 177). ETSI also emphasized extensive public inquiry and instituted rules and procedures aimed at the effective and reasonable resolution of disputes (ibid.: 179). Rather than requiring unanimity, ETSI took decisions on the basis of '71 per cent weighted majority votes' (Bekkers and Liotard 1999: 113).[7]

To summarize, several innovations in procedure and organizational membership marked the birth of ETSI. These, together with the regulatory powers that the European Commission remained capable of exercising, ensured that standards developed within ETSI would serve the entire EU, as opposed to any particular national industrial policy interests within it. Hence, the MoU under ETSI placed manufacturers under essentially the same constraints as the PTTs and PTOs: they would be required to serve the entire GSM community on equitable terms and without discrimination (Bekkers et al. 2000).

5.2.3. The MoU Group

The original signatories to the GSM MoU were the PTOs or PTTs of some 13 European countries. By 1996, the list of signatories had grown to include 167 operators from 103 countries and continued to expand rapidly. By joining the

---

sible for the approval of voluntary standards developed by ANSI-accredited organizations such as the TIA (Hawkins 2000: 265). ETSI, however, combines approval and development, which remain separate in the US standards development regime.

[6] In this context, 'users' does not refer exclusively or even primarily to end users. The author, whose work deals with the development of technical standards in telecommunications, also excludes PTOs or PTTs from the user category. He considers that '[m]ost users can be accurately described as subscribers to a level of service as defined by a monopoly public network operator (PTO)' (Hawkins 1995: 23). Of these, he is mainly concerned with 'intermediate-users', rather than end users. Intermediate users are defined as follows:

> The "intermediate-user" extends the functionality of the basic public network facilities. This may involve something as relatively simple as the provision of customised features by means of customer-owned equipment – such as advanced private automatic branch exchanges and specialised data communication technologies. It could also involve something as complex as the interconnection of an entire private network to the public network. These service 'enhancements' may be confined to the user's own internal requirements, but they may also be extended, in that they can be sold on to other parties. In practice, this can make a user resemble a supplier and vice versa. (Hawkins 1995: 24)

[7] The voting procedures are actually more complicated than this, since there are two voting structures with different formulae for 'weighting'. Decisions on standards are·made by national delegations, according to the formula described above. Other decisions are based on weighted voting by all full members. A more complete account of voting structures and weighting formulae is given in Bekkers and Liotard (1999: 113).

MoU Group, telecom operators accepted both a timetable and a set of regulatory conventions concerning implementation. The MoU articulated a 'coordinated and phased approach to procurement of network infrastructure' (Garrard 1998: 131). It also ensured that common policies would be formulated concerning a number of issues. Many of these were commercial service issues. In addition, the MoU was also concerned with the further technical development of GSM, and its administration therefore sought to develop policies regarding intellectual property rights (IPRs) (ibid.). Here, especially, the MoU Group demonstrated a great deal of continuity with its origins in CEPT by proposing policies that clearly advantaged users over producers (Bekkers and Liotard 1999: 120).

The commercial issues that the MoU Group had to contend with were settled largely by practices and conventions established for analogue networks. Beyond agreement that there should be basic registration fees, as well as subscription and calling charges (billed to the caller), there was no attempt to standardize tariffs among the various operators (Garrard 1998: 138). Roaming, however, proved to be a more controversial matter. It was eventually decided to charge roaming callers at local rates, and then transmit the call details and charges to their home networks, which could then charge additional fees for handling when presenting the bill. Calls made to a mobile user who was roaming internationally were even more difficult. It was finally decided that, in spite of the calling-party-pays principle, callers should pay only the regular charge for a call to a mobile on its home network and the recipients should pay the additional charges. This was discouraging for mobile users – who were, however, able 'to limit use of their mobiles to outgoing calls while they were roaming' (ibid.: 139).

Infrastructure procurement and the further technical development of the GSM standard turned out to be highly problematic (Bekkers and Liotard 1999: 120–22). The initial policy on IPRs encountered opposition from manufacturers – especially Motorola. The MoU Group proposed to give manufacturers system licences only if they would agree to secure operators against any possible patent infringements. Manufacturers should also allow free use of any patents essential to the implementation of GSM (Wilkinson 1991). All manufacturers accepted the first condition, but while European manufacturers 'grudgingly accepted' the second, the US-based manufacturer, Motorola, bitterly opposed it (Garrard 1998: 140). Motorola's main hope of generating revenue from its heavy R&D investment in GSM resided in 'selective licensing' of its patents, many of which were crucial to GSM (Bekkers 2000). Firms based in the EU could rely on other forms of participation in the further development of GSM. But even among European manufacturers there was 'quiet outrage' regarding the IPR policy (Bekkers and Liotard 1999: 120).

'IPR owners could … be forced to give away the results of their research efforts without compensation simply because their technology was selected for a CEPT standard' (ibid.). Motorola's resistance therefore sparked a conflict that took much time and effort to resolve (Cattaneo 1994: 64).

ETSI sought to develop a 'balanced' approach to the relationship between standards and IPRs (Prins and Seissel 1993). In the end, the European Commission's position, that IPRs would have to be respected and compensated, prevailed. In 1993 ETSI's new IPR policy and general undertaking recognized the right of IPR holders to claim revenues from their patents, but retained the principle of non-exclusive compulsory licensing to other ETSI members with a formula characterized as 'licensing by default' (Bekkers and Liotard 1999: 121). Thus, ETSI and the MoU Group retained effective control over the GSM standard, while manufacturers retained limited claims to their IPRs. The original ETSI policy did not allow, for example, cross-licensing. However, this condition was soon annulled, in response to a more extensive complaint filed with the EC Competition Authorities (Tuckett 1993). Subsequently, manufacturers were permitted to enter into bilateral cross-licensing agreements (Bekkers and Liotard 1999: 122–3). This suited large firms like Motorola, but raised steep entry barriers to firms that had no valuable patents to bargain with (Garrard 1998: 140). Prospects for granting cheap licences for low-cost manufacture of GSM technology outside Europe were greatly reduced, if not eliminated altogether (ibid.).

5.3. Other Public-sector Actors: Research in Sweden and the EU

Other public-sector organizations were also important to the development of GSM – particularly, public research organizations like universities and research institutes. In contrast, such organizations had made few contributions to first-generation mobile telephony.

According to McKelvey et al. (1998: section 9.2), the 'Swedish competence build-up' associated with the development of GSM depended at least partly on publicly funded research involving collaboration between academic and industrial partners. Such work formed part of the state-funded 'IT4' research programme administered principally by NUTEK. IT4 supported a number of specific projects from 1987 to 1990, and '[o]ver time, universities were increasingly drawn into these projects' (ibid.: 50). University programmes in electronics and communications technologies in Sweden were also subject to growing influence, not only from Televerket, but also from Swedish private-sector actors in GSM, including both Ericsson and some smaller private-sector actors. Both Televerket and Ericsson had participated in university faculty boards and financed specific professors. Also, 'SRA (later ERA) helped universities build test equipment' (ibid.: 50). Such co-operation continued into the 1990s, with support from NUTEK for further university–industry collaboration (NUTEK 1997). Televerket, Ericsson and other actors benefited in at least two ways. An expansion of extramural research capabilities had been necessary to master the transition from analogue to digital mobile telephony. Also, building up the competencies of the universities 'seems to [have been] particularly important for the recruitment of engineers' (ibid.: 51).

There had been no concerted effort at the EU level to involve public research organizations in the development of first-generation mobile telephony. With the second generation, however, came the first efforts to bring about closer university-industry collaboration – especially after the publication of the 1987 EC *Green Paper on Telecommunications* (Commission of the European Communities 1987). The majority of the EU-funded research programmes initiated at that time were oriented more towards third-generation technologies (DaSilva and Fernandes 1995). However, certain collaborative research initiatives dealt with problems whose resolution could contribute to the evolution of GSM. One such initiative has been COST (Co-opération européenne dans le domaine de la recherche Scientifique et Technique), which was closely associated with mobile-related projects during the 1980s. COST has an independent basis as a European intergovernmental agreement for promoting research collaboration, providing a multilateral framework for co-operation aimed at improving the quality of European research in a variety of fields (Nissinen and Niskanen 1999: 15). Its various programmes or 'actions' consist of basic or precompetitive research on problems of Europe-wide interest and are directed primarily towards public research organizations. These actions often include business enterprises and other private-sector organizations as participants, and one of the general objectives of COST has been to forge collaborative links between industry and academia (European Commission 1996: 1). Telecommunications has been one of the most heavily subscribed domains of COST collaboration (ibid.: 4) and one of the most successful actions was directly linked with GSM (Nissinen and Niskanen 1999: 28). Other actions also supported the further evolution of GSM and mobile telephony (DaSilva and Fernandes 1995: 16). As a consequence of ETSI's strong reliance on co-ordinated public-sector research initiatives such as the COST actions, ongoing standardization projects like GSM and DECT have been characterized as 'RTD&D projects in all but name' (Hawkins et al. 2000: 255).

6. PRIVATE-SECTOR ACTORS

Some of the key private-sector actors in the development of GSM were national telecommunications equipment manufacturers that co-operated with the European PTOs or PTTs. In particular, Ericsson and Nokia subsequently became major producers of GSM equipment, gaining significantly increased shares of the world market for telecommunications equipment. Other private-sector actors also played important parts. Service providers emerged in national and international markets, presenting opportunities for further innovation. Moreover, some PTOs and PTTs underwent privatization, thus participating in further development of GSM as private-sector actors.

6.1. Equipment Suppliers: Ericsson

The initial development of GSM technology involved extensive collaboration between national European telecommunications equipment manufacturers and national PTTs/PTOs. Subsequent interaction was also important, especially for major Nordic equipment producers such as Ericsson and Nokia. Their collaborative activities took place within the framework of a loosely-knit alliance among Nordic firms and the PTTs/PTOs of Finland and Sweden. Ties between firms – not all of them Nordic – were also important. The Nordic alliance, which prevailed in the selection of the prototype technology for GSM, was led by the Swedish PTO, Televerket, later privatized to become Telia.[8] Subsequently, Ericsson, together with Televerket, developed and tested the first prototype of a full GSM system, thus consolidating their early technological lead. Nokia also benefited, as did other firms in the alliance.

Ericsson's collaboration with Televerket during the late 1980s proceeded from initial tests of the NMT 900 system, through construction of a trial GSM system, to development of key components for GSM (McKelvey et al. 1998: section 9.2). Ericsson and Televerket eventually demonstrated the capacity to simulate and test an entire GSM system, with the result that their system proposals became accepted as the basis of GSM in Europe (Lilliesköld 1989: 35). This accomplishment, however, also depended strongly on co-operation and the strategic exchange of technology between Ericsson and other firms. Televerket and Ericsson could not claim exclusive authorship of the prototype technology for the GSM standard. As noted earlier, the dispute over IPRs under the GSM MoU was settled by permitting firms to cross-license their

---

[8] Telia has not actually been privatized – at least not fully. Rather, what has transpired could be described as a first step towards privatization. Telia remains under state ownership, but has been transformed from a public enterprise (*Affärsverk*) to a joint-stock, limited liability company (*Aktiebolag*, abbreviated *AB*) (Karlsson 1998: ch. 3).

patents. Subsequent publication of information on essential GSM patents by ETSI has shown that of 132 essential patents in all, the largest share (50 per cent) was claimed by Motorola. The second largest share (16 per cent) was claimed by AT&T, and Bull and Phillips both claimed the third largest shares (8 per cent each) (Bekkers and Liotard 1999: 123). This record indicates that at least 82 per cent of the essential patents for the GSM standard were non-Nordic. Hence, major Nordic equipment producers such as Ericsson had to engage in extensive cross-licensing in order to acquire a full system capacity with respect to GSM. During the early 1990s, Motorola, the holder of fully half the essential patents for the GSM standard, entered into cross-licensing agreements with four other firms: Ericsson, Nokia, Siemens and Alcatel (Funkschau 1993). Since none of these firms claimed any large share of the essential patents for GSM, Motorola 'imposed a market structure by conditioning exclusive cross-licensing agreements' (Bekkers et al. 2000). Motorola thus gained significant revenue from the growth of a market from which it might otherwise have been excluded. The European cross-licensees were also beneficiaries of this arrangement. As revealed in table 3.2, all of them quickly became major suppliers for GSM.

Table 3.2 demonstrates that the licensing of essential patents conferred an important competitive advantage. The value of cross-licensing was clearly apparent at an early point to Ericsson, as well as to other firms. Ericsson, in particular, used access to its AXE switching technology as a basis for acquiring key GSM patents (Bekkers et al. 2000; Glimstedt 2000: 8). The AXE switch had already proven to be a vital component in the systems developed by US-based producers such as Motorola (Meurling and Jeans 1994: 77), making Ericsson an important supplier of mobile telecommunications infrastructure in the US (Meurling and Jeans 1995: 179). Further adaptation of the AXE switch also required considerable R&D investment. Hence, Ericsson objected to inter-operability of switches and radio-subsystems as an essential design feature of GSM – a decision originally made to ensure interchangeability of switches and their competitive sources of supply. Ericsson later used its commanding position in switching to acquire other technologies that would give the firm an advantageous position in relation to GSM. However, Ericsson did not concentrate exclusively on GSM, but pursued all major international standards (McKelvey, Texier and Alm 1998: section 9.3) – again, via extensive reliance on collaborative strategies such as cross-licensing. At the same time, Ericsson sought to build up a specialized but comprehensive 'systems' capability in mobile telecommunications – by, for example, acquiring competing domestic firms to exploit their complementary strengths in infrastructural components such as radio base stations (ibid.: section 9.1).

Table 3.2: Estimated suppliers' market share of the 33 largest GSM networks in Europe, December 1996, plus worldwide market share of GSM terminals in 1996

Supplier	Score switching	Market share switching	Score base stations	Market share base stations	Market share mobile terminals (worldwide)
Ericsson	10 297	48%	7 978	37%	25%
Siemens	4 426	21%	325	2%	9%
Nokia	3 086	14%	4 617	22%	24%
Alcatel	2 228	10%	2 084	10%	6%

Source: Bekkers and Liotard (1999), Table 3.

During the 1990s, Ericsson responded to the rapid growth of GSM and mobile telecommunications by broadening its competency base in three ways: (1) increasing R&D expenditures; (2) keeping only core activities within the firm; and (3) entering into collaborative relations with other equipment suppliers, network operators and service providers in strategic national markets (McKelvey et al. 1998: section 9.3). According to one account (Granstrand et al. 1997), Ericsson's R&D spending approached 20 per cent of sales in the 1990s. Even earlier, during the 1980s, the total number of engineers employed by the firm had risen by 82 per cent (ibid.). However, Ericsson's R&D expenditures did not simply reflect an increased concentration on a restricted set of core competencies. Rather, '[a]dditional engineering categories were added (e.g., computer science), and no broad category of engineering competence was scrapped' (ibid.: 13).

Ericsson's collaborative efforts yielded commercial success while at the same time demonstrating the superiority of Ericsson's switches and radio base stations. In Germany, Mannesman Mobilfunk relied heavily on Ericsson during the early 1990s to construct 'by far the largest GSM network that anyone had built' (Garrard 1998: 258). Ericsson 'rapidly became recognized, along with Nokia, as the surest way to achieve trouble-free roll-out' (ibid.). International collaborations also enabled Ericsson to enter new markets and build market share in strategic areas. Collaborative capability building thus complemented the strategy of focusing more closely on mobile telephony as a core business activity. Thus, Ericsson continued to rely on foreign subsidiaries and joint ventures as a means of establishing a presence in overseas markets (Fridlund 1998), but attempted to increase profitability by restricting the wide range of telecommunications equipment manufactured by 'branch factories' (Wells and Cooke 1991: 96–7). Recent acquisitions in cables and computers were shed to build up core competencies in telecommunications

(Dixon 1988). Ericsson also introduced a new, modular approach to system design, in which core systems were locally adapted by regional 'competence centres' (Meurling and Jeans 1995). Joint ventures were used to enter inaccessible key markets – as, for example in its partnership with the UK firm, Thorn-EMI in the equity joint venture Thorn-Ericsson, which Ericsson took over in 1988 (Dodsworth 1988). With increasing liberalization of national markets, joint ventures and strategic alliances also became more important for gaining shares of specific product markets. Ericsson had used alliances with Orbitel in the UK and Matra in France to build up a 40 per cent share of the world market in radio base stations. In the late 1980s, the firm still remained weak, with only 14 per cent of the world market for terminal equipment and 3 per cent of the US market (Wells and Cooke 1991: 99). A strategic alliance was therefore formed with US-based General Electric in order to increase sales and capture economies of scale in terminal equipment such as handsets (Taylor and Dixon 1989).

Ericsson, together with Nokia, eventually enjoyed considerable success with terminal equipment sales. 'By the end of 1995, just three manufacturers – Motorola, Nokia and Ericsson – still shared about 75 per cent of the GSM terminal market, with only a couple of per centage points between them' (Garrard 1998: 140). This outcome was partly due to bilateral agreements for the cross-licensing of patents, made in response to the procurement policy of the MoU Group, which, in addition to imposing stiff barriers to market entry, sought an extensive relaxation of normal patent rights from manufacturers. These demands were only grudgingly accepted by European manufacturers, and steadfastly resisted by US-based Motorola.[9] Eventually, cross-licensing agreements were accepted as a compromise solution.[10] However, this favoured concentration and oligopoly: 'Th[e] arrangement was satisfactory for the larger players, which had their own IPR to use in negotiations, but less acceptable for the smaller companies, which were less likely to have such an advantage' (Garrard 1998: 140).

Ericsson was also successful in redefining and broadening its competency-base, becoming a leading example of corporate 'technological diversity' (Granstrand et al. 1997). Even before the 1990s, Ericsson had progressed from an initially narrow focus on telecommunications equipment and related

---

[9] In this context, Motorola, despite being based in the US, was considered by the MoU Group to be a corporate citizen of the European Union. This recognition of Motorola as an 'honorary European' was 'by virtue of its extensive R&D activities in several European countries' (Garrard 1998: 140).

[10] This compromise was not reached easily, nor did it establish a precedent by which future conflicts between standards and IPRs in telecommunications could be minimized. For a detailed account of the issues and how they were resolved in the case of GSM, see Bekkers and Liotard (1999).

technologies to master computerization and digital switching technologies, later combining them with radio transmission technologies in order to develop the NMT system (Fridlund 1998). Later diversification and expansion of Ericsson's competency base, greater acquisition of new technologies from external sources, and increasing R&D are shown in table 3.3, which compares the period when GSM was first implemented with the NMT 450 and NMT 900 periods. Competency development related to two successive new cable transmission systems is also described. Clearly, Ericsson had acquired 'system competency' – i.e., the capacity to design, build, market and support entire systems for the operation of mobile telecommunications networks. Originally, Ericsson was only a supplier of certain components for PTOs or PTTs that had effectively acted as system integrators and architects. Later, Ericsson could develop comprehensive solutions addressing all three main technology areas in mobile telecommunications – i.e., radio base stations, switches and terminal equipment (McKelvey et al. 1998: section 9.4).

Table 3.3: Technology accumulation in Ericsson's product generations

Product/ Product Generation	Number of technologies				R&D costs (base = 100)	Per cent of technologies externally acquired	Main tech fields[d]	Number of patent classes[e]
	Old[a]	New[b]	Total	Obsolete[c]				
Mobile phones								
1. NMT-450	n/a	n/a	5	n/a	100	12	E	17
2. NMT-900	5	5	10	0	200	28	EPM	25
3. GSM	9	5	14	1	500	29	EPMC	29
Telecom cables								
1. Coaxial	n/a	n/a	5	n/a	100	30	EPM	14
2. Optical	4	6	10	1	500	47	EPMC	17

Notes:
(a) No. of technologies from the previous generation.
(b) No. of new technologies, compared to previous generation.
(c) No. of technologies obsolete from previous generation.
(d) 'Main' = >15% of total engineering stock. Categories are: E = electrical; P = physics; M = mechanical; C = computers.
(e) No. of international patents (IPC) at four-digit level.
n/a = not applicable.

Source: Granstrand et al. *(1992).*

6.2. Service Providers and Network Operators

With market liberalization, new network operators and service providers were also important private-sector actors in the diffusion of GSM. Their main contribution was to create and expand markets. However, this activity also involved 'incremental' technological innovation.

6.2.1. A new policy regime in the European Union and Sweden

GSM was introduced more or less simultaneously with the advent of a new EU telecommunications policy regime, whose main goal was to deregulate the sector and create a competitive common market in telecommunications equipment and services (Commission of the European Communities 1987). GSM was therefore 'taken over' by the EC and moved to ETSI, making GSM 'the spearhead for European policy to liberalise telecommunications' (Garrard 1998: 247). Mobile telephony later became the subject of a 1994 *Green Paper on a Common Approach to the Field of Mobile and Personal Telecommunications in the European Union* (Commission of the European Communities 1994). The paper contained five main proposals that subsequently engendered much controversy and were greatly revised. Their purpose was to complete the liberalization of European telecommunications markets and, thereby, to 'remove the barriers to further development' of mobile telecommunications (ibid.: 37). One proposal concerning the use of separate service providers (along with direct service provision) by network operators was later dropped. Another, concerning the right to self-provision by operators of fixed links for network connection was considerably weakened, and the debate on other proposals continued without reaching consensus. Eventually, the European Commission took unilateral action and, in January 1996, issued a directive based on its two most crucial proposals. The directive required that: (1) mobile services must be competitive, with multiple GSM licences in each member state, and (2) mobile operators should be able to construct their own infrastructures for transmission (Garrard 1998: 243–4). Subsequent implementation facilitated the entry of new network operators and service providers.

Arguably, both the 'old regime' represented by CEPT and the liberalization policies that followed GSM's migration to ETSI contributed to the market success of GSM – in different, though complementary ways. CEPT was able to achieve agreement on a common technical standard for digital mobile telephony in Europe, consolidating a huge initial market for GSM. However, new network operators and service providers allowed into the telecommunications sector under 'liberalization' aided the wide diffusion of GSM within this potential market. Hence, EU policies contributing to the success of GSM followed a 'parallel path', maintaining an almost ideal – and, perhaps, non-replicable – balance of co-ordination with competition. 'There is a high level of interaction – and interdependence – between these two approaches; harmonisation can be considered a necessary condition to achieve true liberalisation and the breakdown of (technical) trade barriers' (Bekkers and Liotard 1999: 111).

Sweden, during the first period of GSM's diffusion on the market, was not a member of the European Union. However, by the time Sweden finally joined the EU in 1995, it had already implemented many of these policies and became one of the leading countries that 'went beyond the initial competition policies pioneered in the 1980s' by the US, New Zealand and Japan (OECD 1999a: 11). The early liberalization of both the fixed and mobile telecommunications networks in Sweden was due to several related reasons. First of all, Televerket had never held a legal monopoly over telecommunications – even though it had established a de facto monopoly during the post-war period and also exercised certain regulatory powers (Karlsson 1998: ch. 5, 304). Second, the Swedish government had begun to discuss liberalization at a very early point, and was also increasingly concerned about harmonization with the policies of the European Union (Andersen and Eliassen 1993; Petersson and Söderlind 1992: 63ff, 214f.). A government bill to limit the monopoly powers of Televerket was introduced in 1980 (Karlsson 1998: 171). Open competition in mobile telecommunication infrastructure was established practice by 1988 and sanctioned by government policy that was well on its way to becoming law (ibid.: ch. 5, 284–5). Third, policies initiated at the beginning of the 1990s included separation of regulatory decision making from the regular business operations of Televerket and creation of Telestyrelsen, an independent regulator capable of ensuring fair competition (ibid.: ch. 5, 285–8). Fourth, Swedish legislation enacted EC policies regarding telecommunications, even before Sweden joined the EU. Sweden's new telecommunications law, completed in 1993, introduced measures aimed at strengthening competition in telecommunication, including implementation of the EC policy directive on Open Network Provision (ONP) (Braugenhardt and Kaaman 1991). Based on the 1987 *Green Paper*, ONP aimed at creating an open, competitive and non-restrictive Europe-wide market for telecommunications network operators (Braugenhardt and Kaaman 1991). Sweden's new telecommunications law was also accompanied by a modified Radio Transmission Law, under which frequency management and the licensing and regulation of mobile networks passed from Televerket to Telestyrelsen (Karlsson 1998: ch. 5, 296, 298–301).

Thus, Sweden's mobile telecommunications market was completely open to competition from new entrants by the early 1990s. Shortly after the GSM system was introduced, the oldest Swedish mobile telephone operator, Televerket's radio department, was reorganized as a competitive business within the specialized subsidiary, Telia Mobitel (Holst 1994: 189). It also met some competition from two new operators. The first one was Comviq GSM AB, which entered the market in September 1992 (Lernevall and Åkesson 1997: 571). At the same time Europolitan (owned by NordicTel AB) also started to offer a GSM service.

6.2.2. Telia Mobitel

Earlier, Televerket had been able to position itself as the only operator of NMT networks in Sweden. The only competitor, Comvik, had introduced a different type of system. In addition, Televerket, in its regulatory capacity, had greatly restricted the radio frequency allocations available to Comvik[11] (Karlsson 1998: 242–4). Comvik's share of the market remained low (Lernevall and Åkesson 1997: 565, 575), while Telia Mobitel could expect continued growth in demand for both analogue and digital mobile telecommunications (Karlsson 1998: 250). Even before the introduction of GSM by Televerket/Telia Mobitel in 1992, Sweden's mobile telephone market had the highest penetration rate in Europe – about 7 per cent. Sweden's market was very dynamic, compared to the UK market, which some observers thought to be saturated at a penetration rate of just over 2 per cent in 1990. Sweden's fixed subscription rates were much lower than the UK's, and charges were about half what they were in the UK (Garrard 1998: 188). In Sweden, there was no concern similar to that in the UK of developing a mass market for GSM. Consequently, the DCS 1800 standard was not introduced at a particularly early point, and it did not lead development of the GSM market (Mölleryd 1997: 45). In 1994 the NMT 900 network remained a viable consumer alternative that was capable of considerable expansion (Garrard 1998: 265–6). Competition in the open GSM market from the new entrants eventually forced Telia Mobitel to take a more profound interest in marketing GSM to consumers. By 1995 most of Telia's growth in mobile telephony was based on GSM, and the proportion of non-business subscribers had steadily increased. Telia Mobitel had intensified marketing and commission sales strategies, and also introduced several different kinds of subscriptions (Mölleryd 1997: 45).

In 1996 Telia and other Swedish GSM operators acquired licences for high-capacity DCS 1800 networks (Holst 1997: 110). However, the others were granted dual-band licences that permitted them to open DCS 1800 networks only after their existing GSM networks had reached full capacity. In contrast, Telia Mobitel and a new fixed network operator, Tele 8, were granted permission for an immediate start-up of DCS 1800 networks (Garrard 1998: 268). In Sweden, therefore, it was primarily Telia Mobitel, that pioneered the mass-market variant of GSM, rather than new entrants. At the same time, Telia Mobitel also sought to expand its 'business' and 'private' markets by offering DECT as an added service to mobile users. The technological innovation that made this competitive strategy feasible was the dual-band handset developed by Ericsson (Holst 1997: 108). Relying on both im-

---

[11] In one instance that later became notorious, Comvik's application for frequencies in the 900 MHz band was refused because Televerket planned to launch its NMT 900 system in this band.

proved marketing and technical innovation, Telia Mobitel was able to improve its share of the GSM market at the expense of its competitors during the mid-1990s. By 1997 it had re-emerged as the dominant Swedish GSM operator, controlling 54 per cent of this market (Holst 1999: 114).[12]

6.2.3. Comviq

Telia Mobitel's main competitor, the 'new entrant' Comviq, was initially more aggressive about marketing GSM to consumers. Comviq (introduced as Comvik above) had only obtained a minimal share of the market for analogue mobile telephony in Sweden. Comviq therefore made GSM the main focus of its competitive strategy during the 1990s (Karlsson 1998: 250). After obtaining a GSM licence in 1990, Comviq purchased equipment from US and German suppliers to establish its GSM network (ibid.: 273–9). Its aim was to capture about 50 per cent of the GSM market. Comviq therefore turned to the consumer market, reducing costs by relying on its own microwave link and introducing consumer-oriented tariff structures after 1994 (Garrard 1998: 268). It also offered a variety of specialized extra services (Holst 1997: 336). In addition, Comvik utilized alternative distribution channels and sales strategies (Mölleryd 1997: 45–6). By the end of 1995, Comviq had captured over 40 per cent of the Swedish market, with two thirds of its subscriber base consisting of consumers (Garrard 1998: 268). It was only in 1996, when the rate of market penetration reached 29 per cent, that Comviq, along with other operators, was subsequently permitted to implement a high-capacity DCS 1800 network (ibid.: 268). It is possible that Telia Mobitel's lead in implementing a DCS 1800 network contributed to at least a temporary loss of competitive advantage for Comvik. By 1997 Comviq's share of the Swedish GSM market had declined from the 40 per cent high-point reached in 1995 to merely 23 per cent (Holst 1999: 114).[13] At the same time, however, Sweden's market for mobile telephony had at least doubled in size compared to 1994, and Comviq had experienced steady growth in its subscriber base (ibid.: 112–13).

6.2.4. Europolitan

Europolitan, a completely new entrant, benefited from the pioneering efforts of Comviq. Europolitan was established in 1989 as NordicTel, with financing obtained from several large Swedish corporations. Subsequently, the ownership structure changed, with a 51 per cent share of the company purchased by US-based Air Touch in 1993, when the British mobile operator, Vodafone, also

---

[12] The measure of market share here is based on the revenue of operators, rather than the number of subscriptions.
[13] The measure of market share here is based on the revenue of operators, rather than the number of subscriptions.

purchased a 20 per cent share of the company (Holst 1999: 380). The year 1994 witnessed a public share offering and the sale of remaining shares by several original Swedish owners (Mölleryd 1997: 47). In 1992, the company, re-named Europolitan, established its GSM network after a difficult campaign. Nordic-Tel/Europolitan had to argue against unfavourable initial rulings on its applications for frequency allocation (Karlsson 1998: 275–7). Europolitan initially targeted the business market. However, it quickly followed the lead of Comviq in marketing aimed at consumers. Varied tariff structures and retail distribution channels, as well as agreements with wholesalers, were used to expand market share. In 1994 Europolitan also launched its own chain of retail outlets to expand sales (Mölleryd 1997: 47–8). In 1996 it obtained, along with Comviq, a dual-band GSM licence. Europolitan also continued its 'high-quality' marketing strategy, and was the first GSM operator to obtain ISO-9001 certification for its mobile networks (Holst 1997: 340). Such measures contributed to a steady growth of sales. By 1997 Europolitan held a 23 per cent share of the Swedish GSM market, rivalling Comvik (Holst 1999: 114, 380).[14]

6.3. Other Private-sector Actors: Distributors

New marketing strategies and distribution channels became increasingly important during the 1990s. These were means by which the competing network operators sought to expand both the GSM market and their respective shares of it. Businesses that specialized in these areas, particularly distributors, were thus instrumental in 'growing' the market. Two that have received special mention in Sweden are GEAB and Talkline (Mölleryd 1997: 51–2).

During the mid-1980s, *GEAB* was established as a retail shop that sold mobile telephones and mobile telephone subscriptions. The first store, opened in Stockholm in 1985, soon became one of the primary sales outlets in Sweden, selling more than 1 000 new subscriptions every year (Mölleryd 1997: 38). During the early 1990s, the business expanded into a chain of stores whose business was sought after by competing Swedish GSM network operators and equipment suppliers. GEAB became a major distributor for Comvik, as well as continuing with sales for Telia Mobitel, but could not reach any agreement with Europolitan. In 1994, GEAB was purchased as a vehicle for marketing mobile telephone services across Europe by Unisource Mobile, a subsidiary of Telia's international branch (ibid.: 51).

Talkline, a British mobile telephone company with retail outlets, established a Swedish store in 1990. Initially, the business floundered, but it later prospered under the management of a new Swedish proprietor. After the

---

[14] The measure of market share here is based on the revenue of operators, rather than the number of subscriptions.

change of ownership in 1991, Talkline focused primarily on the business market, for which it devised productivity-enhancing 'mobile solutions' that included, among other things, paging services. The business expanded rapidly, acquiring contracts with a number of large businesses. It sold subscriptions for all of the major GSM network operators in Sweden, and telephones for the major suppliers, later enlarging its business to include computers. Talkline experienced rapid expansion after 1993–94 and merged with another, more consumer-oriented, business in 1995 to form one of the leading retailers of mobile phones and personal computers in Sweden (Mölleryd 1997: 52).

7. MAIN OUTCOMES

The following discussion of economic outcomes focuses on market growth in Sweden. However, the European and broader international context is also taken into consideration.

7.1. Consequences: European Competitive Advantage; Nordic Dominance

By the mid-1990s, it was already evident that GSM had become a 'global' success. In 1996, five years after its launch in 1991, GSM had more than 21 million subscribers in 133 networks operating in more than 105 countries, with 50 000 subscribers signing on each day (America's Network 1996). This constituted a substantial share of the total world market for mobile telephony. Including all known standards, this market was estimated to amount, at the end of 1995, to some 85 million subscriptions to mobile telephone services (Holst 1997: 38). The standard was already well established in Asia and Europe, which together accounted for 45 million of the total 85 million subscriptions. These regions also had the fastest growth in subscribers. In 1995, Asian subscriptions had more than doubled to 22 million subscribers. In Europe, growth was less dramatic, but an increase of nine million subscribers in 1995 raised total subscriptions to 23 million (ibid.). By the mid-1990s, GSM was also recognized as having a wider potential market than any other existing standard, despite the fact that it still had little purchase in the US market. In early 1995, GSM was already potentially available to 4.34 billion persons in 94 countries (ibid.). The only comparable coverage by any other standard was that of the US-based 'first-generation' AMPS. In early 1995, AMPS was available to 3.01 billion people in 73 countries worldwide (ibid.). GSM clearly dominated the 'second-generation' market. In 1997 its only true technological rival, the US-based IS-95 or CDMA standard, had between 5.5

and 5.6 million users worldwide. In contrast, the GSM MoU could claim between 4.5 million and 50 million subscribers (Shankar 1997: 42).

The success of the GSM standard provided the EU with a singular and much-needed success. As one recent study of Europe and the information and communication technology (ICT) 'revolution' observes, '[t]he ETSI/GSM project has been of obvious importance for the European presence in the equipment industry for mobile telecommunications' (Dalum et al. 1999: section 4.3). This was all the more remarkable and significant against the background of a general pattern of US and Japanese dominance in the ICT sectors (ibid.). Hence, the GSM success story was also a notable exception from which strategic lessons had to be drawn for the development of future competitive advantage in ICTs. GSM also had positive economic impacts of a more immediate character. Telecommunications markets in the EU increased in size by one-third and in value by 38 billion ECU between 1995 and 1998 (European Commission 2001: 4). The increase in demand for mobile telecommunications was identified as one of the main factors contributing to this spectacular growth rate. It was further projected that by 2001, the EU market for mobile telecommunications would grow to 160 million subscribers and account for the creation of 400 000 jobs (ibid.). It was also stated in this connection that 'the GSM market could more than double to above 170 million customers, if the rest of the EU caught up to Finland's current mobile phone density of 50%', and that this increase in the number of subscriptions 'would mean at least 150 000 new jobs' (ibid.). Despite such optimistic forecasts, there remained large disparities in subscriber penetration rates and other aspects of the diffusion of GSM (and mobile telecommunications more generally) within the EU. Finland was clearly an exception in Europe and the only countries that even began to approach its remarkable subscriber penetration rate of 45.6 mobile subscribers per 100 inhabitants were the other Nordic countries and Italy (OECD 1999: 76). Sweden had a subscriber penetration rate of 35.8, Norway had a rate of 38.4, Denmark one of 27.5, and Iceland one of 24. All other EU countries, except Italy at 20.1, had subscriber penetration rates of less than 20, and some of the largest EU economies, e.g., France and Germany, were well below the OECD average rate of 15 (ibid.). Thus it was rather questionable whether the EU as a whole would ever catch up with Finland.

The existence of a large and rapidly growing market for GSM services in the Nordic countries was matched by the strong performance of Nordic producers of telecommunications equipment, who became the leading suppliers of equipment for the GSM standard. They also became world leaders in mobile telecommunications equipment more generally. Two of the three dominant firms in mobile telecommunications equipment during the 1990s have been Nordic – Ericsson (Sweden) and Nokia (Finland) (Dalum et al. 1999). The closest competitor for market share has been Motorola (US), closely followed by Siemens (Germany). Japanese multinationals have formed the third rank of competitors (ibid.). 'Nordic dominance' in mobile telecommunications is thus related to the success of the GSM standard with whose development Ericsson and Nokia were closely involved. Specific reasons include GSM's relatively rapid and thorough consolidation of a large European 'home' market as a consequence of concerted action on standard setting within CEPT and ETSI, complemented by the market-expanding liberalization policies of the EC. Additional reasons included close collaboration between the Nordic producers of telecommunications equipment and the Nordic PTOs or PTTs, as well as growing reliance on the output of public research organizations. Firm strategy was also crucially important, not only in refocusing corporate activity and building internal competence, but also in external collaboration, which was essential to acquiring key knowledge assets. Cross-licensing agreements between Nordic producers and US-based Motorola were crucial to selecting the Nordic prototype technology for GSM. The 'virtuous circle' in mobile telecommunications in Sweden and other Nordic countries was completed by rapid growth of a large domestic market. 'When a large enough initial market is created, learning effects on the production side may well provide producers with a great advantage and enable them to develop strong technological and market competencies which are a solid base for exporting' (Dalum et.al. 1999: section 5). In Sweden this depended on the liberalization policies of the EC and corresponding Swedish policies. Thereby, new private-sector actors could help to 'grow' the market, not only through competition among network operators and service providers but also through marketing services and equipment.

7.2. Changes to Charging Systems

Before presenting statistics on the growth of mobile telecommunications equipment and services in Sweden, it will be useful to review further factors contributing to the growth of the market. Here, further insight can be developed by focusing attention more closely on how liberalization and competition were manifested in changes to charging systems.

The main reasons for the relatively poor international performance of US-based standards for 'second-generation' mobile telecommunications included not only a 'divided market' but also a weaker migration in North America than elsewhere from first- to second-generation standards. Both were due to regulatory decisions that stressed the necessity of achieving 'backwards compatibility' with the pre-existing analogue standard, AMPS, rather than unified or inter-compatible digital standards. Decisions regarding charging were another factor contributing to relatively slow growth and low subscriber penetration rates in the US. The US market for mobile telecommunications had a subscriber penetration rate in 1997 of just over 20 per cent (OECD 1999: 76). This is far below the rates cited above for the Nordic countries. Moreover, there had been relatively slow market growth up to that point, characterized by 'steady progression' and a continuing dominance of the analogue AMPS standard, such that 'the introduction of digital services was ... a gradual transition that had an almost imperceptible effect' (Garrard 1998: 348). The absence of rapid growth accompanying the introduction of digital standards in the US may be explained by the existence of an adequate infrastructure based on the successful analogue standard, AMPS. But explanations for the more generally sluggish growth of mobile telecommunications in the US must be sought elsewhere – in, for example, charging, or tariffs, on mobile services.

There were clear disincentives to subscribe to mobile services in the US, since, in addition to paying fixed subscription rates, (varying) call charges and fees for extra services, such as roaming, 'cellular users in the US were also required to pay for incoming calls' (Garrard 1998: 44). Users were understandably anxious to avoid 'junk calls' and reluctant to give their mobile numbers. The problem persisted well into the 1990s, when the Clinton administration introduced a new telecommunications act. The new legislation enabled cellular operators 'to offer long-distance services to their customers along with their cellular packages, instead of handing local calls over to one of the long-distance (Inter-Exchange) carriers' without having to provide equal access to them (ibid.: 354). These changes made it possible to simplify the structure of charges for interconnection, thereby lifting the main barrier that had previously prevented the introduction of 'caller-pays' charging. In contrast, similar measures were introduced at a relatively early point in Europe, with positive effects on the increase of subscriptions, at least so far as the market development of GSM was concerned. The GSM MoU required the speedy resolution of such 'commercial issues' by the signatories. 'Roaming' and interconnection fees had proved, as in the US, to be a difficult issue. However, it was resolved much earlier and more decisively in favour of implementing a 'caller-pays' system, with additional costs for international roaming assigned to the recipients.

In the introduction of PCNs (PCN) in the UK and its subsequent adoption by ETSI in the form of DCS 1800, consumer-oriented standards based on high-density urban networks were essential to rapid market growth. The success of these mass-market adaptations of GSM in the UK depended critically upon competitive tariff structures. There were essentially no major technical differences between GSM and PCN/DCS 1800, but terminal equipment for the latter had to be sold at lower prices, and the services provided for it required much higher infrastructure costs. PCN/DCS 1800 network operators and service providers had to resort to purely 'commercial' means of achieving rapid and extensive market growth to cover their large initial investments in infrastructure and equipment. In addition to aggressive marketing and new distribution channels, such means included the use of alternative tariff structures and the renegotiation of interconnection fees with fixed networks (public switched telephone networks: PSTNs) to lower prices and fees. Network operators in the UK eventually achieved a subscriber penetration rate of 12 per cent by 1996. Sweden exhibited a different pattern from the UK. There were several factors contributing to the markedly more rapid and extensive market growth in Sweden. First, the initial rate of market penetration already achieved by mobile telecommunications during the first generation of analogue standards was much higher in Sweden. This higher density was largely due to the beneficial effects of a common analogue standard, NMT. Second, Sweden's basic subscription rate had been kept to about half that of the UK, even with a relative lack of competition. The lower rates in Sweden helped expand the market quickly to a size where it could 'naturally' sustain lower pricing. Third, increased competition on the Swedish market did not reduce already low prices for subscriptions. It only helped reorient strategies for marketing services towards consumers and non-business users. Thus, the introduction of DCS 1800 services in Sweden did not mark the advent of a mass-market pioneered by new entrants. This development had already begun in connection with the NMT standard during the first generation of analogue mobile telecommunications. Moreover, the DCS 1800 market was pioneered by the incumbent, Telia. The main innovations of the new entrants were in marketing strategies, such as the introduction of prepaid card subscriptions.

The far-sighted pricing policies of Nordic operators and service providers in the early 1990s, thanks to their positive effects on market growth, appear to have been fully vindicated by the late 1990s. At that time it became possible to introduce new strategies for further expansion of the market that were entirely different from varied tariff structures aimed at capturing niche markets. In this regard, the 1999 issue of the OECD's *Communications Outlook* observed 'the move by Telia to reduce the number of mobile pricing options from ten subscription plans to two is noteworthy'. It further commented that 'it would be a welcome development if the same impact was to occur for calls between fixed and mobile networks in terms of international roaming' (OECD 1999: 76).

7.3. Growth Statistics[15]

Against the background sketched above, it is now possible to present statistics concerning the growth of markets for telecommunications equipment and services in Sweden during the first and second generations. The preceding discussion should be referred to for explanation and interpretation of the information presented below.

7.3.1. Growth figures (equipment)

Figure 3.1 shows the number of terminals sold in Sweden during the period 1982 to 1999. Clearly, each generation of terminals was sold in ever increasing quantities. The sales of NMT 450 terminals peaked at about 41 000 in 1988. In 1994 sales of NMT 900 terminals reached a maximum of 274 000.

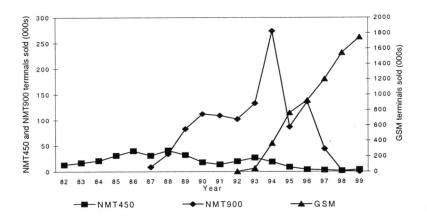

Figure 3.1: Number of terminals sold in Sweden, 1982-99

Note: The number of GSM terminals sold follows the scaling on the right-hand Y-axis.

Source: MobilTeleBranschen 1999 and 2001.

GSM terminals were introduced in 1992, and sales are still growing. The numbers of GSM terminals sold in Sweden each year are given in table 3.4. The growth in number of GSM terminals sold has been quite dramatic in Sweden since the market introduction in 1992. In 1994, the same year sales of NMT 900 terminals reached their peak, about 367 000 units of GSM termi-

---

[15] The primary author of this section is Esa Manninen, who contributed not only the lion's share of the text but also all of the statistical data presented in the form of figures and tables.

nals were sold. It took the NMT 900 terminals eight years on the market to reach that maximum, while GSM terminals passed the NMT 900 maximum during the third year after market introduction.

Table 3.4: Number of GSM terminals sold in Sweden each year, 1992–99

Year	1992	1993	1994	1995	1996	1997	1998	1999
Terminals sold (in 000s)	3	44	367	764	925	1203	1546	1746

Source: MobilTeleBranschen, 1999 and 2001.

7.3.2. Growth figures (services)

During 1994 the growth in GSM subscribers for the first time exceeded the growth in NMT 900 subscribers in Sweden (Lernevall and Åkesson, 1997: 571). In mid-1995 the distribution of GSM subscribers between the three actors in Sweden were: 355 000 for Televerket, 307 000 for Comviq, and 93 000 for Europolitan (ibid.: 571). One important reason for this rapidly increasing number of subscribers was the operators' heavy subsidization of subscriptions (ibid.: 571). For the consumer it meant that a new cellular terminal could be bought for a symbolic price. Table 3.5 gives a more detailed picture of the change in subscription numbers for the Swedish GSM system. Note that the figures for Comviq are reported under the heading Tele2. At the end of 1997 Comviq GSM AB and Tele2 AB merged, and they are now owned by NetCom Systems AB (Post och Telestyrelsen 1998: 2, n. 1; PwC and Öhrlings-Price Waterhouse Coopers 1999: 32).

*Table 3.5: Total number of GSM subscriptions and shares for each mobile
operator in Sweden, 1994–98*

Year	1994	1995	1996	1997	1998
Total subscriptions (in 000s)	422	1 033	1 571	2 414	3 605
Telia	51%	45%	52%	49%	47%
Tele2	32%	41%	30%	34%	36%
Europolitan	17%	14%	18%	18%	17%

Note: Apparent differences between *the figures presented in this table and information on the market shares of the major Swedish operators presented earlier in sections 6.2.2–6.2.4, can be* explained by the fact that this table refers to subscriptions, whereas the previously quoted figures refer to revenues.

Source: PwC, and Öhrlings-Price Waterhouse Coopers (1999): Appendix B, table 5.

The most striking feature of table 3.5 is the rapid increase in the total number of subscriptions during the period – from below 0.5 million to 3.6 million in four years. The highest growth rate was for the period 1994–95, when the number of subscriptions increased by 145 per cent. For the remaining years the yearly growth rate was about 50 per cent. During this period of high total market growth, the largest Swedish operator Telia managed to keep about half of the market in terms of number of subscriptions. Prepaid card mobile telephony was first introduced by Tele2 in the spring of 1997. Later in the same year Europolitan introduced its card, and was followed by Telia in July 1998 (PwC, 1999: 42). Table 3.5 shows the number of GSM subscriptions *including* prepaid cards. In table 3.6 prepaid card subscriptions are separated from other subscriptions.

Table 3.6: Prepaid card subscriptions in Sweden (in thousands) 1996–98

Year	1996	1997	1998
Number of prepaid card subscriptions (000s)	–	235	1 023
Other forms of subscriptions (000s)	1 571	2 179	2 582
Total number of subscriptions (000s)	1 571	2 414	3 605

Source: Derived from figures in PwC, and Öhrlings-Price Waterhouse Coopers (1999): Appendix B, table 5.

It can be seen that between 1997 and 1998 the growth rate for prepaid cards has been much higher, at 335 per cent, than that for other forms of subscriptions, which increased 18 per cent. Growth in mobile telephony services production can also be described in terms of operator revenues. In table 3.7 the total value (in terms of revenues) of the Swedish mobile services market is separated into the NMT and GSM segments. The source for table 3.7 does not indicate whether these are nominal prices. However, there was very little inflation during the period. We can see total revenues almost doubled between 1994 and 1997, and in 1998 total revenues exceeded 11 billion SEK. However, operators' revenues from interconnection fees are excluded.[16] The table also reveals that revenues from the GSM system first exceeded the revenues from NMT in 1996.

Table 3.7: Revenues of Swedish mobile services in MSEK, 1994–98

Year	1994	1995	1996	1997	1998
Total revenues	4 340	6 050	7 420	8 420	11 349
GSM revenues	1 070	2 310	4 460	6 190	9 883
NMT revenues	3 270	3 740	2 960	2 230	1 466

Source: PwC, and Öhrlings-Price Waterhouse Coopers (1999): Appendix B, table 6.

---

[16] Interconnection fees are paid by operators to get access to other operators' (fixed and/or mobile) telecommunications networks. For 1998 it was estimated that interconnection fees were between 20 and 30 per cent of the operators' total revenues. Including interconnection fees, estimated total revenues in 1998 were 15.1 billion SEK (PwC, and Öhrlings-Price Waterhouse Coopers 1999: 30; Appendix A).

8. CONCLUSIONS

The following conclusions respond to a series of 'key questions' elaborated within the research network on European Sectoral Systems of Innovation (ESSY). Those questions form the main headings for this concluding discussion.

8.1. Knowledge Base and Learning Processes

In the development of GSM, the knowledge base of mobile telephony became increasingly more complex and diffuse. This transformation was reflected in the changing division of labour between the public- and private-sector actors in mobile telephony. Previously, the private-sector actors had possessed specialized expertise in various subsystems. In contrast, the main public-sector actors – i.e., the PTOs or PTTs – possessed 'system competence' and acted as 'system integrators'. In the second-generation of mobile telephony, the same division of labour was at first maintained, but then began to erode. In Europe, regulatory reforms by the EU increasingly confined the role of the PTOs or PTTs to that of network operation. Separate regulatory authorities were established, and the PTOs or PTTs lost their monopolies over service provision. Standard setting was opened up to a much broader range of actors. The convergence between mobile telephony and information technology necessitated the entry and involvement of other actors in the formerly closed field of telecommunications. Moreover, heightened international competition led to greatly increased expenditures on R&D. National equipment suppliers and national PTOs or PTTs could no longer simply rely on one another's complementary assets to acquire and develop the knowledge they required. Hence, key actors in mobile telephony found it increasingly necessary to form strategic alliances with a wide range of other actors, often across national boundaries. Increased interaction with public research organizations also became necessary. All these considerations influenced the shift from 'closed' to 'open' standards development. In this instance, at least, institutional change followed and formalized organizational changes caused primarily by technologies and markets, rather than actually initiating such change.

PTOs or PTTs relinquished a large part of their former role as systems integrators. Even in the early phases of GSM's development, the system competence formerly associated with this role appeared to have already been transferred to major equipment producers. Televerket's largely symbolic role and Ericsson's de facto leadership in the technical development of the 'Nordic' prototype technology for the GSM standard demonstrates this point. Moreover, SDOs such as ETSI assumed increased importance, not least because of their capacity to involve many other actors in developing and defining standards. Public research organizations also became increasingly important. Among private-sector actors, the major telecommunications equipment firms remained most important. The build-up of competence through a variety of means was critical to their success. Ericsson, in order to focus its activity on mobile telecommunications resorted to corporate restructuring, mergers and acquisitions, joint ventures and various other kinds of collaboration, in addition to greatly increased expenditures on R&D and the hiring of skilled personnel. Thus the firm's narrowed focus on mobile telecommunications was accompanied by the development of a much broader and more internally diversified profile of competence. Generally, telecommunications equipment producers developed their own capabilities as system integrators. On the other hand, they entered into a greater number and wider variety of strategic alliances with other actors. Ericsson, which exemplified both trends, used cross-licensing agreements with Motorola to develop system competence with respect to GSM.

8.2. Firms, Non-firm Organizations and Networks

Organizational developments included the transition from closed to open standards making, and the emergence of a qualitatively different type of SDO (e.g., the hand-over from CEPT to ETSI). There was an accompanying shift among 'key actors' from multi-purpose and monopolistic organizations (the PTOs/PTTs and major equipment producers) to a new division of labour in which key roles were more widely distributed. Apart from the SDOs, there are no longer any true monopolists in the global telecommunications sector, including mobile telephony. Even the largest discrete organizations (the PTOs/PTTs and major equipment producers) are increasingly performing specialized roles, although they retain and seek to develop certain capacities for system integration. Thus, the evolution of mobile telephony involved greater functional differentiation and complexity in the division of labour.

The shedding of system competencies by the PTOs and PTTs was accompanied by a shedding of roles and responsibilities, many of which were assumed by other public-sector organizations. The increased diversity of non-firm organizations in the public sector created a need for new mechanisms of coordination that was only partly met by new SDOs such as ETSI. Governments – in Europe, the EC, in particular – became increasingly involved in utilizing telecommunications standards as vehicles for industrial and trade policy. With respect to specific organizational forms, such as firms and networks, second-generation standards in mobile telephony involved the formalization and consolidation of networks that were previously more informal in character. Formalization took the form of establishing consortia or strategic alliances, based on agreements such as the GSM MoU. Consolidation, at least amongst firms, often took the form of mergers and acquisitions, such as Ericsson's absorption of the telecommunications equipment sector in Sweden. As a formal institution, the GSM MoU facilitated overseas expansion of a market originally defined on a regional basis. Expansion, in turn, entailed the formation of new network relationships. Thus, the development of new kinds of governing bodies within the public sector was accompanied by the proliferation among private-sector actors of partly overlapping and partly opposing consortia, coalitions, alliances, etc. An expanded taxonomy of organizational forms and modes of governance (Hollingsworth et al. 1994: 8) might be necessary to develop an adequate organizational and institutional map of mobile telephony.

8.3. Geographical Boundaries

Standard setting in second-generation mobile telephony involved a higher level of internationalization than in the first generation. Most second-generation standards were developed as regional standards with the potential to become de facto world standards through international adoption. GSM more than fulfilled the expectation of wide international diffusion. Initially conceived as a pan-European standard, it gathered sufficient momentum to become the leading 'world' of its generation. Nevertheless, open competition with foreign standards never occurred in the regional home markets. In these key markets, co-operation between standards development organizations, standard-setting agencies and regulatory authorities resulted in decisions that effectively partitioned the international market. GSM also developed within a sheltered regional market, but one in which, unlike the US, the standard setting and regulatory regime did not require backwards compatibility with a well-established first-generation standard. Within this market, in which no first-generation standard had truly dominated, a particularly rapid migration from first- to second-generation standards occurred, providing GSM with sufficient momentum to capture external markets.

The sustained development of a strong and constantly expanding home market for mobile telecommunications clearly contributed to the competitive advantage of equipment-producing firms that had been involved with the development of standard(s) defining the market. Thus, the dynamism of the EC market for GSM helped European firms such as Ericsson and Nokia to become leading producers of terminal equipment and infrastructure for mobile telecommunications worldwide. These developments are often attributed to the market-expanding effects of the liberalization policies ushered in by the EC during the 1990s. However, the Nordic countries had achieved some of the world's highest rates of subscriber penetration for mobile telecommunications even before liberalization. This was largely due to the consolidation of a strong market for mobile telecommunications via concerted action by the Nordic PTOs and PTTs in defining the first-generation NMT standard. In Sweden, Televerket/Telia kept prices for subscriptions to second-generation GSM services very low throughout the 1990s to achieve rapid and extensive market growth. Moreover, it was Televerket/Telia, rather than the new entrants, that pioneered DCS 1800, the 'mass-market' variant of GSM. Enlightened standardization and pricing policies on the part of powerful incumbents contributed at least as much as liberalization to development of the home market. Alluding to this experience, Dalum and Villumsen (2001) now argue that 'one of the most relevant policy instruments at hand appears to be to create massive incentives for increasing the penetration ratios of broadband access among consumers in Europe' (ibid.: 16).

However, 'learning' from a dynamic home market was not the only source of the technological and market leadership in mobile telecommunications that Ericsson and Nokia acquired via their involvement with the GSM standard. There were additional influences and mechanisms at work and not all of them involved close geographical proximity, although geographical boundaries shaped their interaction. Especially important in this connection were collaborative relationships and strategic alliances between firms based in different regional markets. Both before and after GSM, Ericsson employed these means to expand into international markets, internationalizing its R&D and producing for multiple standards.

GSM was from the very outset the project of a regional consortium, eventually consolidated by ETSI under the tutelage of the EC. However, this consortium was internally divided by both national coalitions and strategic alliances. The national coalitions were generated by the near vertical integration between major equipment-producing firms and PTOs or PTTs. Contention between these coalitions was a marked feature of the process by which CEPT selected a prototype technology for the GSM standard. In that context, a Nordic coalition confronted a Franco-German one. US-based Motorola provided Nordic producers with access to technology that was crucial to their success in the selection of a prototype technology. Subsequently, Ericsson and Nokia became leading producers of equipment for the GSM standard. Motorola, although it had only very limited possibilities to participate directly in the growth of the GSM market, could still benefit from the revenues generated through strategic licensing of essential patents. However, MoU policy on IPRs gave rise to conflicts whose resolution shaped both the GSM market and positions within it. This policy was strongly resisted by the equipment producers, led by Motorola. Eventually, ETSI resolved this dispute in accordance with the EC's recognition that if European Community markets were to attract and benefit from private investments in R&D, IPRs would have to be respected and compensated. ETSI's compromise solution allowed for cross-licensing among equipment-producing firms. Large firms, which had considerable assets in the form of IPRs were satisfied with this arrangement, but it disadvantaged smaller firms without comparable resources. In effect, the solution was one that favoured market concentration and oligopoly. Firms such as Ericsson and Nokia were able to consolidate commanding positions within the market for GSM equipment and the possibilities for European-based network operators to award manufacturing contracts to low-cost producers outside of the EC were greatly reduced.

8.4. Long-term Dynamics of the Sector and Co-evolutionary Processes

Many aspects of GSM's development – for example, the increase in functional differentiation and the trend towards greater and more extensive formalization – suggest that mobile telecommunications closely followed the well-known 'industry life cycle'. However, there are also obvious departures from this pattern. Rather than simply becoming more concentrated and oligopolistic, the equipment industry continued to witness the emergence of 'new entrants' from other sectors. Similar developments have occurred in network operation and service provision, where the clear trend was away from monopoly and towards greater variety and more competition. These developments were indicative of technological renewal. In some respects, this was a matter of increase in 'degree', rather than 'kind'. For example, there was an increasing use of computer software in GSM. Consequently, firms such as Ericsson began to pose much greater demands on national education and training systems for an adequate supply of computer science graduates. However, the generational shift in mobile telecommunications also marked important changes in the quality or character of the competence requirements of firms. These were based on the convergence of formerly separate technologies. In the first generation, telephony and radio were combined. In the second, digital technology was fully implemented, creating possibilities for data transmission, in addition to voice transmission. This opened up a broad range of evolutionary possibilities for market and institutional forces to respond to. Producer firms such as Ericsson needed to develop a much broader and more internally diversified profiles of competence in order to develop second-generation systems, and the strategies to which they resorted placed new strains on existing institutional set-ups. The 'quasi-vertical integration' between PTOs/PTTs and equipment-producing firms that CEPT attempted to perpetuate in the initial procurement policies of the GSM MoU administration failed to withstand these strains. Important institutional changes in relations between these two categories of actors were eventually brought about under the aegis of ETSI and the EC.

The past record of rapid growth in mobile telecommunications has, of course, been the outcome of both supply and demand forces at work. One important reason for introducing the GSM standard was to increase the subscriber capacity. In this respect, technological development on the supply side clearly responded to a well-defined aspect of existing demand. However, the GSM standard also offered enhanced services like pan-European roaming, and improved voice quality and capabilities for data-transmission. Thus technological development on the supply side helped to create new forms of market demand. With the creation of ETSI and a new regime of open standards development, these relationships were institutionalized as an essential part of the process of standard development. There was, nevertheless, often considerable lag between technological and institutional developments. For example, 'digitization' was recognized as the technological basis for separating network operation from service provision. But this was not fully implemented with GSM. Incumbents and regulators resisted such attempts to maximize competition. On the whole, the technological evolution of GSM was a remarkably 'managed' process. Technological discontinuities in mobile telecommunications that were potentially competence destroying for incumbents were introduced in a manner that was competence enhancing. Institutions and rule-making authorities – in particular, the SDOs – played a leading part in managing the incorporation of new technologies and new sources of competition. There was a negotiated regulation of co-evolution among markets, technologies and institutions, which cannot be captured with simple terms such as 'institutional lag'.

8.5. Public Policy and European International Performance

The conventional wisdom concerning policies for innovation in telecommunications has favoured the liberalization of markets, complemented by supply-side initiatives aimed at increasing industrial R&D efforts, often through increased interaction with public research organizations. However, the success of GSM was based on very different measures. In Europe and Sweden, the first two generations of mobile telephony were conceived and introduced primarily by PTOs or PTTs which were essentially public-sector monopolists that also exercised regulatory powers in closed national markets. Deregulation of the telecommunications sector and strong supply-side R&D programmes were introduced by the EC only after the GSM standard had been defined and implemented. One lesson drawn from GSM is the strategic importance of standards as a means of creating 'organized markets' and co-ordinating supply and demand. Indeed, recent EU policies regarding telecommunications standards have been explicitly motivated by considerations of European competitive advantage. In creating ETSI and introducing an open approach to standards development, the EC made a clear effort to provide effective co-ordination mechanisms at higher levels of integration than those previously addressed in national and regional policy initiatives.

The conventional wisdom concerning Europe's international performance in mobile telephony is that Europe has emerged as a clear leader due to its success in defining standards. A 1998 feature in *Business Week* compared the US experience to Europe's under the heading 'The Cowboys versus the Committee' (Brull 1998). The article relates that while Europe was able to settle quickly on one standard, thereby securing a large initial market, and was able to keep licensing fees low in order to entice manufacturers, the US allowed four competing digital standards to flourish, none of which could match the huge subscriber base of GSM. These developments are considered to account for the subsequent loss of market share by US equipment manufacturers to European rivals. The conventional wisdom could be correct. Even so, there is no guarantee that Europe's past successes will be replicated in the third generation of mobile telephony. If standards were indeed the key to European leadership, it must be recognized that many of the conditions associated with the development of successful first- and second-generation standards no longer apply. In the wake of the institutional changes that accompanied the introduction of GSM, it may prove far more difficult to ensure 'virtuous' interaction between the supply and demand sides of the market for the third-generation standard, UMTS. As Corrocher (2001) argues for mobile Internet, 'the most important and sensitive issue is going to be the design of appropriate pricing schemes for consumers and business users: in this respect, the role of public policy is going to be crucial' (ibid.: 57). Moreover, the standard-setting regime that emerged in Europe after GSM now resembles its counterpart in the US much more closely. Nevertheless, there are some early indications that the European standard, UMTS has acquired a promising early lead over its rivals (Dalum 2001: 14).

REFERENCES

America's Network (1996), 'Wonders of the World Phone: L.M. Ericsson's Planned Development of the World Phone', *America's Network*, 46–7.

Andersen, S.S., and K.A. Eliassen (1993), 'The EC as a New Political System', in S.S. Andersen and K.A. Eliassen (eds), *Making Policy in Europe – The Europeification of National Policy-Making*, London: Sage Publications.

Bach, D. (2000), 'International Co-operation and the Logic of Networks: Europe and the Global System for Mobile Communications (GSM)', BRIE Working Paper no. 19, Berkeley: University of California at Berkeley.

Becker, F. (1991), 'PCN: The Key to Mobility', *Siemens Review* Telecommunications Special: 15–16.

Bekkers, R., G. Duysters and B. Verspagen (2000), 'Intellectual Property Rights, Strategic Technology Agreements and Market Structure: The Case of GSM', paper presented at Swedish International Symposium on Economics, Law and Intellectual Property Rights, Stockholm, Sweden, June.

Bekkers, R. and I. Liotard (1999), 'European Standards for Mobile Communications: The Tense Relationship Between Standards and Intellectual Property Rights', *European Intellectual Property Rights* 3: 110–26.

Braugenhardt, S. and J. Kaaman (1991), 'Open Network Provision – EGs koncept för öppna telenät', *Tele* (Swedish ed.) 3: 36–40.

Brull, S.V., N. Gross and C. Yang (1998), 'Cell Phones: Europe Made the Right Call', *Business Week*, 7 September, 107.

Cattaneo, G. (1994), 'The Making of Pan-European Networks as a Path-Dependency Process: The Case of GSM versus Integrated Broadband Communication', in G. Pogorel (ed.), *Global Telecommunications Strategies and Technological Changes,* Amsterdam: Elsevier Science.

Clever, M. (1999), 'Mass Market Solutions for Mobile Data', *Telecommunications* 33 (6), 40–49.

Commission of the European Communities (1987), *Green Paper on the Development of the Common Market for Telecommunications Services and Equipment*, CEC Communication – COM (87) 290 final, 30.6 1987, Brussels-Luxembourg: CEC.

Commission of the European Communities (1994), Towards the Personal Communications Environment: Green Paper on a Common Approach to the Field of Mobile and Personal Telecommunications in the European Union, CEC Communication – COM (94) 145, 27.4.1994, Brussels-Luxembourg: CEC.

Corrocher, N. (2001), 'The Internet Services Industry: Sectoral Dynamics of Innovation and Production and Country-specific Trends in Italy and the UK', ESSY project report on telecommunications, Milan: CESPRI, Bocconi University, Italy.

Dalum, B. (2001), 'Data Communications – The Satellite and TV Subsystems', ESSY project report, telecommunications paper no. 4, Aalborg: Department of Business Studies, Aalborg University, Denmark.

Dalum, B., C. Freeman, R. Simonetti, N. Von Tunzelmann and B. Verspagen (1999), 'Europe and the Information and Communication Technologies Revolution', in J. Fagerberg, P. Guerrieri and B. Verspagen (eds), *The Economic Challenge for Europe: Adapting to Innovation-based Growth*, Cheltenham, UK: Edward Elgar.

Dalum, B. and G. Villumsen (2001), 'Fixed Data Communications – Challenges for Europe', ESSY project report, telecommunications papers no. 5–6, Aalborg: Department of Business Studies, Aalborg University, Denmark.

Dang-Nguyen, G., V. Schneider and R. Werle (1993), 'Corporate Actor Networks in European Policy-Making: Harmonizing telecommunications policy', Köln: Max Planck Institut für Gesellschaftsforschung.

DaSilva, J.S. and B.E. Fernandes (1995), 'The European Research Program for Advanced Mobile Systems: Addressing the Needs of the European Community', *IEEE Personal Communications* 2 (1), 14–19.

Dixon, H. (1988), 'Ericsson Switches its Global Strategy', *The Financial Times*, 25 November.

Dodsworth, T. (1988), 'Telecom's Partners Grow Apart', *The Financial Times*, 10 June.

Drake, W. (1994), 'The Transformation of International Telecommunications Standardisation: European and Global Dimensions', in C. Steinfeld and Associates (eds), *Telecommunications in Transition: Policies, Services and Technologies in the European Community*, n.p.

Emmerson, B. (1998), 'On the Move', *Communications International* 25 (4), 40–4.

ETSI (2001a), *Key ETSI standards – DECT*, available: http://www.etsi.org/ 2001 [cited 16 January 2001].

ETSI (2001b), *Key ETSI Standards – TETRA*, available: http://www.etsi.org/ 2001 [cited 16 January 2001].

ETSI Highlights (1989), 'News of ETSI's Technical Committees', *ETSI Highlights*, 6 November.

European Commission (1996), *Introduction to COST Co-operation*, Luxembourg: Office for Official Publications of the European Communities.

European Commission (2001), *Job Opportunities in the Information Society: Exploiting the Potential of the Information Revolution*, COM (1998) 590 final – EN, http://www.europa.eu.int/comm/dg05/soc-dial/info/jobopps/joboppen.pdf [cited 1 March 2001].

FINTECH (1990), Untitled, *Mobile Communications* (March).

FINTECH (1991), Untitled, *Mobile Communications* (March).

Fridlund, M. (1998), 'Switching Relations: The Government Development Procurement of a Swedish Computerized Electronic Telephone Switching Technology', in C. Edquist and F. Texier (eds), *ISE: Innovation Systems and European Integration* [CD-ROM], Linköping: Systems of Innovation Research Programme, Department of Technology and Social Change, Linköping University, Sweden.

Funk, J.L. (1998), 'Competition Between Regional Standards and the Success and Failure of Firms in the World-Wide Mobile Communication Market', *Telecommunications Policy* 22 (4/5), 419–41.

Funkschau (1993), 'Motorola/Nokia: Austach von GSM-patenten', *Funkschau*, 50.

Garrard, G.A. (1998), Cellular Communications: Worldwide Market Development, Boston: Artech House.

Glimstedt, H. (2000), 'The Competitive Dynamics of Technological Standards: The Case of the Third Generation in Cellular Communications', paper presented at Seminar for the Systems of Innovation Research Programme, Department of Technology and Social Change, Linköping University, Sweden, December.

Granstrand, O., E. Bohlin, C. Oskarsson and N. Sjorberg (1992), 'External Technology Acquisition in Large, Multi-Technology Corporations', *R&D Management* 22, 111–33.

Granstrand, O., P. Patel and K. Pavitt (1997), 'Multi-technology Corporations: Why They have "Distributed" rather than "Distinctive Core" Competencies', *California Management Review* 39 (4), 8–25.

Haddon, A. (1991), 'DCS1800: The Standard for Personal Communication Networks', *Telecommunications* (June): 61–3.

Hardiman, E. (1990), 'The Role of Private Mobile Radio', paper presented at World Mobile Telecommunications Conference, London, 24–5 September.

Hawkins, R. (1992), 'The Doctrine of Regionalism: A New Dimension for International Standardisation in Telecommunications', *Telecommunications Policy* (May/June), 339–53.

Hawkins, R., R. Mansell and W.E. Steinmueller (2000), 'Liberalization and the Process and Implications of Standardization', in R. Mansell and W.E. Steinmueller (eds), *Mobilizing the Information Society: Strategies for Growth and Opportunity*, Oxford/New York: Oxford University Press.

Hawkins, R.W. (1995), 'Enhancing the User Role in the Development of Technical Standards for Telecommunications', *Technology Analysis and Strategic Management* 7 (1), 21–40.

Hollingsworth, J.R., P.C. Schmitter and W. Streeck (1994), 'Capitalism, Sectors, Institutions, and Performance', in J.R. Hollingsworth, P.C. Schmitter and W. Streeck (eds), *Governing Capitalist Economies*, New York: Oxford University Press.

Holst, G.-M. (ed.) (1994), *The Teldok Yearbook – 1994*, Teldok report 86E, Stockholm: Hj. Brolins Offset AB.

Holst, G.-M. (ed.) (1997), *The Teldok Yearbook – 1997*, Teldok report 116, Stockholm: Hj. Brolins Offset AB.

Holst, G.-M. (ed.) (1999), *Teldoks Årsbok – 2000*, Teldok report 130, Stockholm: Hj. Brolins Offset AB.

Iversen, E.J. (2000), 'Standardisation and Intellectual Property Rights: Conflicts Between Innovation and Diffusion in New Telecommunications Systems', in K. Jacobs (ed.), *Information Technology Standards and Standardisation: A Global Perspective*, Hershey, USA/London, UK: IDEA Group Publishing.

Johnston, W. (1998), 'Europe's Future Mobile Telephone System', *IEEE Spectrum* 35 (10), 49–53.

Karlsson, M. (1998), 'The Liberalisation of Telecommunications in Sweden – Technology and Regime Change from the 1960s to 1993', Ph.D. Dissertation, Department of Technology and Social Change, Linköping University, Sweden.

Law, C.E. (1991), 'Personal Communications Networks: What Do They Mean?' *Mobile and Satellite Single Market Review* 1.

Lernevall, S. and B. Åkesson (1997), 'Från myndighet till bolag 1966–1993' *Svenska Televerket* Del VII, Stockholm: Telia.

Lilliesköld, G. (1989), 'NMT, GSM och "sladdlös" PABX', *Modern Elektronik* (3), 35.

Lindmark, S. (1995), 'The History of the Future: An Investigation of the Evolution of Mobile Telephony', Licentiate Thesis, Department of Industrial Management and Economics, Chalmers University, Gothenburg, Sweden.

Lindmark, S., and O. Granstrand (1995), 'Technology and Systems Competition in Mobile Telecommunications', in D.M. Lamberton (ed.), *Beyond Competition: The Future of Telecommunications*, Amsterdam: Elsevier Science.

McKelvey, M., F. Texier and H. Alm (1998), 'The Dynamics of High-Tech Industry: Swedish Firms Developing Mobile Telecommunications Systems', in C. Edquist and F. Texier (eds), *ISE: Innovation Systems and European Integration* [CD-ROM], Linköping: Systems of Innovation Research Programme, Department of Technology and Social Change, Linköping University, Sweden.

Meurling, J. and R. Jeans (1994), *Mobiltelefon – En idé som skapade en världindustri*, Stockholm: Informationsförlaget.

Meurling, J. and R. Jeans (1995), *A Switch in Time: AXE – Creating a Foundation for the Information Age*, London: Communications Week International on behalf of Ericsson Telecom.

Microcell (1991), 'ETSI Eyes New PMR Specs, Runs into DECT LAN Flap', *Microcell*, October, 6.

Muller, J. (1992), 'Competition and Regulation in Telecommunications', *Telecommunications Policy* **19** (2), 161–4.

Mölleryd, B. (1997), Så byggdes en värdsindustri – Entrepreörskaps betydelse för svensk mobiltelefoni, Stockholm: Teledok 28.

Nissinen, M. and P. Niskanen (1999), *COST – Scientific Co-operation on Researchers' Terms: A Study of Finnish Participation*, Espoo, Finland: VTT (Technical Research Centre of Finland).

NUTEK (1997), Telecommunication: Evaluation of the Research Programme, 1993–96, Stockholm: NUTEK.

OECD (1999), Communications Outlook – 1999, Paris: OECD.

Paetsch, M. (1993), Mobile Communications in the US and Europe: Regulation, Technology and Markets, Boston/London: Artech House.

Petersson, O. and D. Söderlind (1992), *Förvaltningspolitik,* Stockholm: Publica.

Pisjak, P. (1994), 'Interdependence Between Regulation and Technological Innovation in the Telecommunications Sector', *Technology Analysis and Strategic Management* **6** (3), 289–303.

Pohajakallio, P. (1998), 'Casting the Cellular Net', *Telecommunications* **32** (4), 47–50.

Post och Telestyrelsen (1998), 'Konkurrenssituationen på olika delmarknader inom telekommunikationsområdet, 1997' [report on-line, cited 17 August 1999], Stockholm: National Post and Telecom Agency [Available from http://www.pts.se].

Prins, C. and M. Seissel (1993), 'The New European Telecommunications Standards Institute Policy: Conflicts Between Standardisation and Intellectual Property Rights', *European Intellectual Property Rights*, n.p.

PwC and Öhrlings-Price Waterhouse Coopers (1999), 'Den svenska marknaden för telekommunikation, 1998' [report on-line, cited 17 August 1999]. Stockholm: National Post and Telecom Agency [Available from http://www.pts.se].

Ramsdale, P. (1991a), 'PCN Implementation in the UK', *IEE Review* (February): 76–7.

Ramsdale, P. (1991b), 'PCN Infrastructure: Looking at the Options', *Communications International* (November): 53–6.

Ruotto, A. (1998), 'Governance within the European Television and Mobile Communications Industries: PALplus and GSM – A Case-Study of Nokia', PhD Dissertation, University of Sussex, UK.

Sandholtz, W. (1993), 'Institutions and Collective Action: The New Telecommunications in Europe', *World Politics* **45** (2).

Schreiber, K. (1991), 'The New Approach to Technical Harmonisation and Standards', in L. Hurwitz and L. Lequesne (eds), *The State of the European Community: Policies, Institutions and Decisions in the Transition Years*, n.p.

Shankar, B. (1997), 'Airing the Standards Debate', *Telecommunications* **31** (10), 41–4.

Taylor, R. and T. Dixon (1989), 'Ericsson and GE in Mobile Phone Venture', *The Financial Times*, 25August, 24.

Temple, S.R. (1992), 'The European Telecommunications Standards Institute – Four Years On', *Electronics and Communication Engineering Journal* **4** (4), 177–81.

TETRA MoU (2001), *TETRA – Facts*, http://www.tetramou.com/facts/index.htm 2001 [cited 16 January 2001].

Tuckett, R. (1993), 'ETSI's IPR policy: The Implications for Companies Using European Telecom Standards', *Patent World* 23 (September).

Wallenstein, G. (1990), Setting Global Telecommunications Standards, n.p.

Wells, P.E., and P. Cooke (1991), 'The Geography of International Strategic Alliances in the Telecommunications Industry: The Cases of Cable and Wireless, Ericsson, and Fujitsu', *Environment and Planning A* **23**: 87–108.

Wilkinson, S.L. (1991), 'They're Stealing Our Diamonds: The Standards Assault on Patents', *Canadian Intellectual Property Review* **8** (2): 193–7.

4. The Universal Mobile Telecommunications System (UMTS): Third Generation[1]

Leif Hommen

1. INTRODUCTION

This chapter deals with the development of the universal mobile telecommunications system (UMTS) standard, the European–Japanese member of the 'family' of third-generation standards in mobile telecommunications. The chapter seeks to describe and analyse the development of this standard in a way that captures the evolution of a sectoral system of innovation. In content and organization it parallels Chapter 3. The sectoral and systemic orientation leads to a concentration on key organizational actors, their technological and competitive assets and strategies, and the institutional frameworks within which they interact. As in the previous chapter, there is a focus on Sweden and Swedish actors, but less so. Greater reference is made to the international context, partly because of its greater importance for the development of a 'global' standard. More comparisons are made at the regional level – for example, between Europe and Japan. However, the Swedish case is still referred to for specific illustration and explanation. The chapter's structure follows that of Chapter 3.

Following the introduction, section 2's 'historical overview' introduces the rationale for developing UMTS and the complexities involved in implementing a standard intended to be profoundly global in character and coverage. These issues are addressed further in section 3 which outlines the standard's technical characteristics. Section 4 briefly introduces complementary systems

[1] The author wishes to thank colleagues in the ESSY Research Network – particularly, Nicoletta Corrocher, Bent Dalum, Charles Edquist, and Gert Villumsen – for reading and commenting on earlier drafts.

and standards, then focuses in greater detail on those rivalling UMTS. Major public-sector actors involved in UMTS are discussed in section 5, while main actors from the private sector are examined in section 6. In section 7 a preliminary evaluation of the economic effects of UMTS is provided. The conclusions drawn in section 8 reflect key issues related to the standard's role in the mobile telecommunications sectoral system of innovation in Europe.

2. HISTORICAL OVERVIEW

UMTS is the standard approved in 1998 by ETSI (the European Telecommunications Standards Institute) for third-generation mobile telecommunications. Unlike standards for previous generations of mobile telephony, the UMTS standard was not driven primarily by the need to accommodate unexpectedly rapid growth in the number of mobile telephone subscriptions. Rather, the impetus for its development came from the convergence of information and communication technologies (ICTs) and the market opportunities that this created for developing a broader range of applications for mobile telecommunications.

UMTS was first conceived in the late 1980s, on the basis of earlier deliberations within the International Telecommunications Union (ITU), beginning in 1985, concerning future public land mobile telecommunications systems. By the early 1990s, GSM and other second-generation systems had only begun to be implemented. The 'second-generation' market was still far from saturated, and second-generation systems had yet to realize their full potential for growth. During the early 1990s, therefore, 'progress on UMTS continued slowly and somewhat theoretically and was largely ignored by most of the cellular operators, who were more concerned with growing their subscriber bases profitably' (Garrard 1998: 478). In 1996, however, a special task force of the European Commission not only put forward a set of technical objectives and dates for the introduction of UMTS but also outlined a regulatory framework and organizational basis for carrying out this process (ibid.: 479). UMTS subsequently gained momentum, particularly after ETSI's 1998 approval of Euro-Japanese W-CDMA (wireless code division multiple access) technology as the basis for the standard, and its accompanying decision to introduce UMTS on a commercial basis in 2002 (Funk 2002: 206–8). However, the planned 'roll-out' of UMTS in Europe at the beginning of the new millennium has coincided with a broad and deep downturn in the telecommunications sector. As of 2002, therefore, it remains difficult to comment very extensively on the actual market performance of UMTS.

There are, however, some early indications that UMTS has good prospects for becoming one of the main third-generation standards and could even become the dominant standard. With both Japanese and European authorities having taken early and decisive action to establish a single (although 'open') third-generation standard and their US counterpart having opted instead for market selection, UMTS is assured of a much larger initial market than any of its US-based rivals (Funk 2002: 80–4). Moreover, Nokia and Ericsson, as the chief European firms collaborating with Japan's NTT DoCoMo in the development of W-CDMA, have both contributed to, and are well positioned to benefit from, these developments. In contrast, 'US firms have had relatively little negotiating power throughout the entire third-generation standard setting process' (ibid.: 81).

The UMTS story reveals new complications in the process of standard setting and its relation to market competition. Significantly, standard setting in third-generation mobile telecommunications has now assumed a much wider scope. UMTS has been conceived as a truly 'global' system of mobile telecommunications. Eventually, the standard is supposed to operate across all existing digital telecommunications networks. And, although UMTS is a European standard, approved by ETSI, it is also officially recognized by the ITU, a standards development organization with truly worldwide coverage and authority, as one of the 'IMT-2000 family' of harmonized third-generation standards (Nilsson 1999: 113; Samukic 1998: 1103–4).

3. TECHNICAL CHARACTERISTICS

Within ETSI, there was an early agreement that there should be an 'evolutionary approach' to UMTS – that is, a gradual transition from a global system for mobile telecommunications (GSM) to UMTS, based on progressive upgrading of existing technologies (Samukic 1998: 1100–101). As a consequence, much of the relevant literature has tended to present UMTS as a further extension of GSM, or to associate new developments in GSM technology with a 'migration' to UMTS. The identification of UMTS with GSM is based on the former's 'backwards compatibility' with the latter (Johnston 1998: 49). Nevertheless, UMTS departs significantly from earlier mobile telecommunications technology. It combines several important technical advances: (1) using 'broadband' rather than 'narrowband' frequencies, (2) fully integrating 'voice' and 'data' communications, (3) fully integrating 'fixed' and 'mobile' networks, and (4) providing 'seamless' global roaming, in addition to high functionality. UMTS is also not directed primarily towards solving the 'capacity' problems created by a rapidly growing market for mobile telephony, as was its predecessor, GSM. Instead, it has been oriented towards broadening the market via the development of new applications and novel services in mobile telecommunications (Rapeli 1995: 20). This orientation has required equipment producers to develop stronger capabilities as system providers, and at the same time enhanced, at least potentially, the innovative roles of network operators and service providers.

3.1. Equipment

UMTS is above all a 'broadband' standard. The frequency bandwidth chosen for UMTS is broad enough to support the transmission of so-called 'high bit-rate services' – something which is not possible with GSM and other 'narrow-band' systems (Rapeli 1995: Figure 3). The 'broadband' frequencies chosen for UMTS are capable of supporting transmissions of data at rates of over 2 Mbits per second (Öhrlings-Coopers & Lybrand 1998: Appendix II). This makes possible the wireless transmission of non-voice data (e.g., text and images) on a scale that previously could only be achieved through fixed systems (Rapeli 1995: Table 1). There is consequently a much greater potential for integration of fixed and wireless telecommunications networks, including incorporation of the Internet. In addition to facilitating the development of new services, the full exploitation of broadband capacity also places high demands on the capabilities of terminal equipment (Johnston 1998: 50).

In 1995, projections about *terminal equipment* for UMTS were still remarkably vague (DaSilva and Fernandes 1995: 18). By 1998, however, some clearer indications could be given. UMTS terminal equipment would build upon certain features associated with GSM, such as dual-mode handsets and subscriber identity modules (SIMs). With UMTS, for example, 'the capability of the SIM [would] expand so programmes can be downloaded by the air-interface' (Johnston 1998: 53). By 2001, equipment producers such as Ericsson had begun to unveil further solutions. For instance, one of the main difficulties of Internet access from mobile terminals is that such terminals have limited memory, processing power, display size and audio capabilities, compared to stationary computers – and, moreover, 'usually cannot dynamically download and upgrade software components, such as new media codecs' (Ekudden et al. 2001: 172). Mobile terminals cannot yet cope with the full range of available data, and data must therefore be adapted to the specific capabilities of the mobile terminal and network. Ericsson's solution has been to develop flexible products capable of further adaptation to specialized demands – i.e., 'mobile platforms' containing protocol and media decoder solutions enabling vendors of terminals to 'develop applications and graphical user interfaces' that would 'differentiate their products' (ibid.: 175).

Because UMTS integrates fixed and mobile telecommunications networks, its *access network* cannot be described exclusively in terms of a system of radio base stations (Rapeli 1995: 21). The radio access system (RAS) for UMTS is composed of base stations and other equipment making possible the interaction (i.e., interoperability) of mobile units and the fixed network (Buitenwerf et al. 1995: 34). As originally envisioned, the RAS would contain both the 'air interface' (the basic UMTS interface) and two fixed network interfaces (Urie 1995: 28) One fixed network interface would be with the 'core network' (broadband integrated services digital network, or B-ISDN). The other would be with the so-called 'intelligent network' or IN, providing the mobile functions needed to 'add on' a mobile network to a fixed B-ISDN. Within the RAS there would be a 'layered' approach to coverage, with different radio access bandwidths made available within different types of cells, arranged within a hierarchical cell structure (Andermo and Ewerbring 1995: 49). Thus, the 'picocell and microcell [would] be covered by a larger macrocell covering even lower bandwidth services (144 Kbit/s) over a large area such as a city', while a global system of satellites would cover remote areas (Johnston 1998: 51–2).

The basic design has remained, but there has been considerable evolution in terms of interfaces. The 'IMT-2000' decision by the ITU to create a 'harmonized family' of CDMA (code division multiple access)-based third-generation systems, requires UMTS to be interoperable within a framework consisting of 'three modes of CDMA-based radio interfaces' and 'two kinds of core network'. Moreover, 'all radio-access networks must be able to connect to either type of core network' (Nilsson 1999: 113). The IMT-2000 decision sought to include a broad range of spectrum allocations and 'migration scenarios', making it a priority to 'minimize the number of air-interface techniques' and resolve 'incompatible requirements for radio access standards' (ibid: 114).

In earlier accounts of UMTS, *switching and transmission* functions were to be handled by the 'core network', based on B-ISDN. There would also be an 'Intelligent Network' (IN), providing service and control logic for mobile systems not included in the core network because unnecessary for fixed systems. The core network would consist of asynchronous transfer mode (ATM)-based B-ISDN local and transit-level switches and interconnecting transmission systems. To cope with the added complexity of mobile switches, 'control in UMTS should have been moved off of the switches and either out into the access network or into the intelligent network' (Buitenwerf et al. 1995: 33). Then only 'functions directly involved in Call and Bearer set-up and reconfiguration [should be] kept associated with the switches' (ibid.).

Inclusion in the IN of most mobile control functions in UMTS meant both that the IN would be responsible for much of the processing of mobile terminated or originated calls and that some of the IN's control functions would be incorporated into the radio access network. 'Furthermore, the mobile terminal must be able to interact directly with the IN system (either in the RAS or deeper in the network)' (ibid.: 34). Accordingly, even in the late 1990s, 'most of the work [on UMTS] ha[d] concentrated on the wireless [access] part' (Johnston 1998: 50). The 'separation between connectivity and communication or control services' meant that within core networks conventional switching technology – for example, Ericsson's AXE exchanges – 'will continue to serve as MSCs (Mobile Service Centres)' (Enderin et al. 2001: 11). The main demands on switching are 'increased processing capacity, greater switching capacity, and conversion to packet switched technology' (ibid.). General Packet Radio Service (GPRS) has already been introduced as 'the first step towards supporting IP (Internet Protocol) based applications within the mobile core network' (Hameleers and Johansson 2002: 27). A much more extensive development programme is also under way (ibid.). In the longer run, a shift to optical switching that will obviate electronic signal processing has been forecast. One expert states that 'the direction towards time and wave-length multiplexing is obvious ... contrary to [earlier] expectations of ATM to dominate in the core network' (Rapeli 2001: 164).

3.2. Technical Capabilities

According to the specifications adopted by ETSI in 1998, *terminal equipment* in UMTS would include both mobile units and SIMs with data and application downloading capacities. The terminals would be adaptive to different user preferences specified by SIMs, based on their incorporation of multimedia capabilities (i.e., the capacity for voice, textual and graphic data, and possibly some video transmission). Terminals would also have dual-band capabilities, enabling them to operate with both GSM and UMTS bandwidths (Samukic 1998: Table 1). Second-generation short message service (SMS) evolved into enhanced messaging service (EMS) and multimedia messaging service (MMS). EMS 'offer[ed] a combination of text and simple pixel-like images and melodies', while MMS 'also allow[ed] formatted text, photos, drawings, graphics, animations, Power-point-style presentations, audio samples and video clips to be woven into the message' (Novak and Svensson 2001: 202). Ericsson introduced its first handset with these capabilities, the T68 GPRS phone, at the end of 2001 (ibid.: 108). Security capabilities were also enhanced, through the HyperText markup language (HTML)-compatible wireless application protocol (WAP) (Emmerson 1998: 41), and evolution of the SIM into the WIM (WAP identity module), enabled 'data-centric transaction-based services' (Friis-Hansen and Stavenow 2001: 162).

The main bottleneck in the development of terminal equipment has remained the limited capabilities of wireless handsets to handle the full range of multimedia content, particularly in 'streaming' (Ekudden et al., 2001: 172). Firms like Ericsson have met this challenge by developing 'capability exchange mechanisms' that allow servers to send multimedia that has been adapted to the capabilities of the mobile user's terminal equipment and mobile network. This solution permits terminal vendors to develop specialized applications of an 'integrated platform' by collaborating with suppliers of multimedia-enabled handsets (ibid.).

ETSI's specifications for the UMTS *access network* required significant advances in the capabilities of the radio access system. Implementing them would require new base station systems (BSSs) and the development of bearer flexibility. Transmission capacities would be up to 2 Mbit/s. Because of its inclusion of IN components, the 'air interface' would be capable of 'self-adaptation'. The access network would not only have a high subscriber capacity, but would also support variable bit rates and different types of traffic, including both multimedia and low bit rate speech (Samukic 1998: Table 1). The IMT-2000 subsequently elaborated by the ITU Radio Communications Section (ITU-R) imposed additional requirements for flexibility and self-adaptation, demanding interoperability within the 'harmonized family' of four optional modes (Nilsson 1999: 113–5). To accomplish this within W-CDMA, the basic radio access technology for UMTS/IMT-2000, 'several interfaces and functional splits must be standardised', including both the air interface and fixed network interfaces (ibid.). To handle mixed services, base transceiver stations require a flexible architecture, structured according to function rather than channels, and enhanced control functions housed in Radio Network Controllers (RNCs) (Eldståhl and Näsman 1999: 60). Increased network size and complexity, requiring optimal usage of the RAS, have led to the development of decentralized systems that distribute automated monitoring and control functions throughout the radio access network (Gustås et al. 2002).

According to ETSI's basic specifications, the *switching and transmission* system in UMTS would incorporate a number of new features. Many of these would be based on evolution of GSM switching and development of INs. There would also be wholly new features, such as new charging and accounting mechanisms based on the use of SIMs. SIMs would also make possible the transfer of specifically configured services, or virtual home environments (VHEs) from one network to another. Convergence with the fixed network would support, for example, packet data transmissions using Internet protocols (Samukic 1998: Table 1). Current switching technologies, capable of shifting control functions between the RNC and the MSC, and able to handle voice as well as circuit-switched and packet-switched data communication within the same node, could have met these specifications by 1999 (Eldståhl and Näsman 1999: 60). However, conflicting imperatives to standardize switching systems and cope with highly variable and heterogeneous patterns of traffic have led firms such as Ericsson to 'over-dimension' their hardware and develop software that 'limits the call capacity and functionality of the node by means of software keys', thereby facilitating rapid reconfiguration (Enderin et al. 2001: 15). Operators can now download software upgrades from the equipment supplier. These features of switching systems are consistent with more flexible relations with operators, who can now also contract with the supplier for additional services, in areas such as operation and maintenance (Carlgren 1999: 97).

3.3. Functions

The regulatory framework of UMTS clearly separates roles and identities between subscribers and users, as well as between network operators and service providers, making necessary new security provisions related to users. At the same time, the expanded technical capabilities of UMTS have introduced new user-oriented functions concerning operation and maintenance.

UMTS as a 'system concept' has explicitly separated the roles of service provider, network operator and subscriber (Rapeli 1995: Figure 5). This separation, and the possibility that 'a multitude of new services can enter the market', ultimately raises the issue for regulators of whether any services should be controlled by network operators – and, if so, which (Pisjak 1994: 292). The network operators are free to concentrate on developing the service capabilities of their networks, while service providers can compete on the cost and quality of different offerings, which users can combine in a flexible way. Although operators can choose to retain certain roles in the provision of multimedia services, balancing share of revenue against risk, the hitherto high failure rate of new services encourages them to specialize (Ekudden et al. 2001: 170). Naturally, security mechanisms are required to assure the integrity of both networks and services. The WAP and the evolution of SIMs into WIMs have emerged as a solution to this problem for both operators and the providers of 'transaction-based services'. But differences between operators and commercial service providers (e.g., banks) over control of the 'security infrastructure' for specific services (e.g., financial services), have spelled continuing market fragmentation (Friis-Hansen and Stavenow 2001: 163).

For end users, there have been fewer conflicts. The separation between users and subscribers has made it possible to safeguard subscriptions and provide security guarantees for users (Rapeli 1995: 23). Therefore, UMTS 'phase 1' specifications indicated a number of security functions, in addition to the already-mentioned user-oriented functions of automatic 'global roaming' and multi-vendor networks. These include the protection of network use, safeguards against the misuse or abuse of networks, and the provision of specialized security services to individual users (Samukic 1998: Table 1). The overarching concept is that of the VHE, describing 'the provision and delivery of personalised services across network and terminal boundaries with the same look and feel', so that 'users are consistently presented with the same personalised features, user interface customisation and services, in whatever network, whatever terminal (within the capabilities of the terminal) and wherever the user may be located' (Farjami et al. 2000: 754). The VHE thus interposes itself between the user and the concrete network, negotiating differences in system capabilities between user and provider. 'During the registration procedure, the VHE will enable a visited network to obtain information about the user's service provider, as well as other information, such as the user's service profile and the identification of service capabilities needed for the execution of... specific services' (Hagen et al. 1999: 2066).

3.4. Services

UMTS makes possible many new services, such as video-conferencing (Johnston 1998: 51). Best effort packet-switched data transmission rates of up to 470 Kbit/s provide access to the Internet and corporate intranets. High-speed connections, at least as fast as landline modems operating at 56 Kbit/s can link professional users with corporate local area networks (LANs), providing access to file servers, databases and groupware. Other business applications, such as wireless postcards and electronic business cards, as well as specialized applications for sectors as diverse as health care and traffic control, also depend on the higher data transmission rates that are possible with third-generation W-CDMA systems such as UMTS (Eldståhl and Näsman 1999: 58–9). Diverse multimedia services are available to users, with variable quality and quantity of transmissions. SIMs and Internet protocol make possible new levels of specificity in addressing and charging. Users can not only specify 'personalized' configurations of services but also measure and adjust them to control service charges. Dual-band and global roaming capabilities, combined with the VHE, also make preconfigured service 'packages' highly portable across networks (Samukic 1998: Table 1). Customization of services is thus a distinguishing feature of UMTS.

While pre-UMTS systems such as GSM have 'largely standardised the complete set of teleservices, applications and supplementary services', this has posed difficulties for operators seeking to differentiate their networks via new services. This has led to a new approach, whereby a defined technical platform supports a variety of specialized applications (Farjami et al. 2000: 754). In brief, 'UMTS will standardise service capabilities and not the services themselves' (ibid.). This facilitates both development of new services by operators and entry of new service providers, although developing specialized applications and content enhancements may require an operator to develop 'agreements with service providers' to deliver 'operator-powered services to its subscriber base' (Ekudden et al. 2001: 171).

4. RELATED SYSTEMS AND STANDARDS

The following discussion briefly addresses systems and standards complementary to UMTS, before dealing at greater length with rival ones. The term 'rival' denotes non-European standards for mobile telecommunications that were conceived as direct competitors to UMTS. However, many of these rivals are now officially recognized as 'complements' to UMTS, as a result of the compatibility requirements imposed by ITU's international mobile telephone standard – or IMT-2000 – a decision taken in 1998 to create a 'harmonized family' of major third-generation standards (Nilsson 1999: 113–5).

4.1. Complementary Standards

Standards complementary to UMTS can be classified according to its 'layered' approach to coverage, which involves a hierarchical cell structure. (Andermo and Ewerbring 1995: 49). RAS standards such as UMTS refer to the 'macrocell' level, but there are also 'microcells', 'picocells' and even 'personal areas' (Johnston 1998: 51–2). Standards for all these levels are supported by either ETSI or the Third Generation Partnership Project (3GPP), now responsible for UMTS and related standards (Hännikäinen et al. 2002: 84).

At the *macrocell* level, 'GSM 2.5' technologies were developed by ETSI during the 1990s to improve data transmission capacities and thereby further evolution towards UMTS. The first of these was high-speed circuit-switched data (HSCSD), which uses multiple time-slots for data connections 'to reach 28.8, 43.2 and 57.6 Kbit/s data rates' (Pohajakallio 1998: 47-50). It was soon followed by GPRS, which is capable of 'data transmission at rates ranging from 14 Kbit/s to 115 Kbit/s and higher' (Clever 1999: 41). The maximum GPRS rate of 171.2 Kbits 'brings the GSM system much closer to legacy data networks by providing packet access for a GSM terminal and packet switching based routing in the GSM infrastructure'; moreover, it 'facilitates several types of variable data rate services, including IP based applications for mass markets' (Hännikäinen et al. 2002: 84). The latest development has been enhanced data rates for GSM evolution (EDGE), which uses the same TDMA (time division multiple access) frame structure and 200 kHz carrier spacing as GSM to provide up to 348 Kbit/s for HSCSD and GPRS data services, thus bringing GSM bit rates close to the level of third-generation systems. EDGE, because of its architectural compatibility, can be implemented by GSM operators without requiring any major technical investments (Furuskar et al. 1999).

At the *microcell* level, there have been developments in both fixed wireless access and digital cordless telephone systems. ETSI's main contribution to fixed wireless access has been the high performance radio access standard BRAN (broadband radio access network), which meets third-generation multimedia requirements and supports various networks including the 'core network' of UMTS and both ATM- and IP-based networks (ETSI 1998, 1999). In digital cordless phone technology, ETSI has continued to develop the DECT (digital European cordless telephony) standard (discussed in chapter 3, section 4.1). New applications include LAN cards providing DECT with access to a fixed network. However, wireless local access networks (WLANs) are superior for local data communications. (Hännikäinen et al. 2002: 86).

At the *picocell* level, WLANs have been a strong focus of development in the transition to third-generation systems. ETSI's efforts in this area began in 1992 with the HiperLAN-1 standard for wireless ATM short-range access, publishing the functional specifications in 1996 (Taylor 1999). Thereafter, in conjunction with the BRAN project, ETSI initiated HiperLAN-2, to define a radio access network that could be connected with different core networks through specific convergence layers, and would provide high performance in dispersive radio environments such as offices (Khun-Jush et al. 2000). Despite early standardization, no HiperLAN-1 products materialized, since 'in 1996 markets were not ready for wireless data in general' (Hännikäinen et al. 2002: 88). Because of its better timing and support for multimedia quality of service, HiperLAN-2 has met with a different reception, such that 'major companies producing consumer electronics ... are planning video over HiperLAN-2 for home applications' (ibid.). However, it faces strong competition from US-based IEEE 802.11 a and b standards (Garber 2002; Mannings and Cosier 2001).

In *personal area networks* (PANs), the main standard associated with ETSI is Bluetooth, which aims at wireless serial connection of laptops, printers, personal digital assistants (PDAs), cellular phones, headsets, keyboards, and other devices. Bluetooth is a de facto standard originated by two prominent ETSI members, Ericsson and Nokia, in collaboration with a private consortium, whose other core members include major computer and semiconductor firms (Keil 2002). Bluetooth profiles define several ways of using wireless connection in applications that enable 'legacy services', including WAP, to be used over Bluetooth. Recently, a new specification of Bluetooth has been initiated, and 'extensive work is being done on new profiles, such as audio and video (multimedia) communications, in-car communications, and enhancing the PAN support in Bluetooth' (Hännikäinen et al. 2002: 89). The growth of interest in – and, by implication, demand for – Bluetooth has been phenomenal. Beginning with an alliance of five major firms in 1998, the Bluetooth Special Interest Group (SIG) grew so rapidly that the SIG was reorganized, in 1999, to include Microsoft, 3Com, Motorola and Lucent as additional core members or 'promoters'. Further, 'by the end of April 2001 over 2000 companies [had] joined … as adopters' (Keil 2002: 208).

4.2. Rival Standards

The ITU's IMT-2000 decision of 1998 established that there would be a 'harmonized family' of third-generation standards. As a consequence, 'the 3G scene will see more competition on a worldwide basis, than the 2G scene, except in Europe', raising the question of 'how a single-standard Europe will fare in comparison with multiple standard Japan, USA, and other nations/ regions in the 3G era' (Kano 2002: 320). In 2000 there were three main rival standards. In addition to the European–Japanese W-CDMA, adopted by ETSI as the basis of its UMTS standard, there were also the US-based CDMA2000 and UWC-136 standards (the former an evolution of CDMAOne, and the latter an evolution of the digital advanced mobile phone systems: D-AMPS). The discussion below will deal briefly with each of these rival systems.

4.2.1. W-CDMA
W-CDMA was adopted by both NTT DoCoMo and ETSI. The former an-nounced its intention in 1997 to collaborate with Ericsson and Nokia to de-velop W-CDMA as a third-generation standard within the IMT-2000 framework established by the ITU. The latter subsequently decided in 1998 on W-CDMA as the technical basis of its UMTS standard (Funk 2002: 80–84). Until 1997, it was still uncertain what the technical basis for the UMTS would be, and there were a number of European equipment manufacturers who assumed that an enhanced version of GSM would be selected. However, since NTT DoCoMo accounted for nearly 60 per cent of all subscribers in Japan and, moreover, had enlisted a large group of other Asian telecommuni-cations operators, its announcement weighed heavily in favour of the W-CDMA proposal of its collaborators, Ericsson and Nokia. After compromising on the incorporation of a TD-CDMA (time division code division multiple access) proposal within the W-CDMA standard, the proposal put forward by Ericsson and Nokia won out in ETSI (ibid.: 82–3). Since ETSI could define a single standard for the EU market (also influencing Africa and Oceania), and NTT DoCoMo had a commanding share of the Japanese market, their deci-sions 'made W-CDMA to all intents and purposes a global standard' (ibid.: 208). Subsequent developments in the W-CDMA story, including ETSI's formation of 3GPP to include non-European interests in the development of W-CDMA/UMTS (3GPP 2002a), are dealt with in later sections. The remain-der of this section deals with the main competitors to W-CDMA within the IMT-2000 family.

4.2.2. CDMA2000

CDMA2000 will compete directly with W-CDMA in the US, Japan and other countries. In the US, it emerged as a de facto standard – a development consistent with the historically 'pluralistic' (i.e., market-based) approach to standard selection. (For further discussion of the US approach to standard setting and selection, see chapter 3, this volume, section 4.2). In Japan, CDMA2000 has been adopted, along with W-CDMA, as a third-generation standard by both ARIB (Association of Radio Industries and Businesses) and TTC (Telecommunications Technology Committee)[2] (Kano 2000: 318–19).

CDMA2000 is essentially an evolution of the US-based second-generation CDMAOne standard. CDMAOne was developed as a proprietary standard in 1989 by Qualcomm, and was eventually accepted as a US standard in 1994, due to the support of a number of important telecommunications firms, including network operators, such as AT&T and PacTel, and equipment manufacturers such as Motorola (Garrard 1998: 315–17). Although CDMA-1 emerged considerably later than the first major second-generation standard in the US, D-AMPS, it was technically superior in many respects (Paetsch 1993: 179). It therefore rapidly won a major share of the US market, as well as making a strong impact in Asian markets, notably Hong Kong and South Korea (Garrard 1998: 325–8).

In the late 1990s, the technological superiority and increasingly wide market diffusion of CDMAOne was such that '[m]ost Americans in the mobile communication field expected that CDMAOne would become the de facto third generation standard' (Funk 2002: 80). Reflecting this confidence, the US authorities did not actively seek to define third-generation standards but instead assigned the frequencies that the ITU had allocated for third generation systems to personal communications services (PCSs), which had begun to operate in 1995, leaving the award of third-generation licences and the implementation of '3G' services to existing system providers (ibid.: 79). The equipment manufacturers primarily associated with CDMAOne were therefore caught off guard by the 1997 announcement of Japan's NTT DoCoMo that it would co-operate with Ericsson and Nokia (both major GSM suppliers) to develop W-CDMA as a third-generation standard, abandoning its proposed ISDN (integrated services digital network) interface in favour of one based on 'GSM evolution'. These developments were soon followed by NTT DoCoMo's creation of an international development team of major equipment manufacturers and its enlistment of other Asian telecommunications operators in support of W-CDMA (ibid.: 81). Subsequently, Qualcomm, Lucent, Mo-

---

[2] ARIB is responsible for the standardization of radio technologies and systems in Japan, while TTC's mission includes the standardization of non-radio-related technologies and systems.

torola and Northern Telecom hastily announced the development of CDMA2000, but it was by then too late for this standard to rival the 'critical mass' that had already been achieved by NTT DoCoMo's proposal (ibid.).

CDMA2000 nevertheless managed eventually to find important supporters, even in Japan. There, two new entrants into the telecommunications market, the network operators DDI and IDO, announced in 1998 that they would adopt CDMA2000 instead of W-CDMA. Their arguments were that a different standard would enable them to overcome the disadvantage of W-CDMA suppliers' natural prioritization of NTT DoCoMo in filling orders for new equipment and it would also help them to innovate more effectively – since if they attempted to differentiate their products and services within a W-CDMA framework, they would have insufficient tacit knowledge and risk leakages of more codified knowledge to their main competitor. Consequently, the Japanese authorities decided to adopt both CDMA2000 and W-CDMA as third-generation standards (Kano 2000: 318–9). Moreover, CDMA2000's proponents had other important allies in Asian countries where CDMAOne had been widely adopted – notably, South Korea and China. South Korea, during the mid-1990s, experienced the rapid growth of one of the largest CDMAOne markets in the world, and several South Korean firms, notably Samsung, had become important suppliers of handsets and infrastructural components (Funk 2002: 83). Similarly, China had been lobbied with initial success by both Qualcomm and the US government to adopt CDMAOne – a development which caused serious concern to Ericsson, which in 1999 had a 40 per cent share of China's mobile infrastructure market (ibid.: 210). Ericsson, a major proponent of W-CDMA, and a firm that had earlier flatly rejected CDMA (Garrard 1998: 319), considered this a serious threat when resolving its patent dispute with Qualcomm over CDMA/W-CDMA (Funk 2002: 210). Not only in China, but also in South Korea and in established markets of the US and elsewhere, the 'backwards compatibility' of CDMA2000 with CDMAOne ensures that the former will have good prospects for growth as a third-generation standard for mobile telecommunications.

In addition, CDMA2000 has also developed a strong industry forum to represent its members' interests in international standards setting. In 1999, the Third Generation Partnership Project Two (3GPP2) was established to parallel ETSI's creation in 1998 of 3GPP. 3GPP2's members include national standards organizations such as South Korea's TTA (Telecommunications Technology Association), Japan's ARIB and TTC, and the US-based TIA (Telecommunications Industry Association) (Kano 2000: 319). More recently, China's CWTS (China wireless telecommunications standards) group has also joined. 3GPP2, like its sister project 3GPP, 'embodies the benefits of a collaborative effort … while at the same time benefiting from recognition as a specifications-developing body, providing easier access of the outputs into the ITU after transposition of the specifications in a standards development organization (SDO) into a standard and submittal via the national process, as applicable, into the ITU' (3GPP2 2002).

4.2.3. UWC-136

The Universal Wireless Consortium's standard UWC-136 is another US-based response to the IMT-2000 initiative of the ITU. It was originally conceived as a competitor to W-CDMA and CDMA2000 in the US and some other national markets (Kano 2000: 319). However, it now appears that UWC-136 has become strategically aligned with W-CDMA.

UWC-136 is an evolution of the TDMA technology on which D-AMPS, the first major digital standard in the US, was based. D-AMPS, supported by equipment manufactures such as Northern Telecom and Ericsson and a number of large telecommunications operators, including AT&T, was approved in 1990 by the CTIA (Cellular Telephone Industry Association) (Lindmark and Granstrand 1995: 390). A key feature leading to early approval of this standard was its 'backwards compatibility' with the first-generation AMPS standard (Paetsch 1993: 390). Although superior second-generation standards later emerged in the US, D-AMPS had the advantage of having been the first major domestic standard, and even in the late 1990s retained a major share of the US market (Garrard 1998: 324). While backwards compatibility with AMPS acted to some extent as a brake on rapid diffusion, it also meant that D-AMPS could be installed more cheaply than other second-generation standards by US telecom operators (Funk 1998: 434). D-AMPS also fared reasonably well internationally, particularly in Latin America, where all of the national governments eventually adopted D-AMPS as their national standard (Garrard 1998: 327).

As noted previously, NTT DoCoMo's 1997 announcement that it would collaborate with Ericsson and Nokia – and by extension, ETSI – to develop W-CDMA as a third-generation standard within the IMT-2000 framework of the ITU galvanized the proponents of CDMAOne into mobilizing a new CDMA2000 standard. In the case of UWC-136, a similar initiative had begun even earlier, with the formation of the Universal Wireless Communications Consortium in 1996. The mission of UWCC, whose membership eventually included over 100 operators, equipment suppliers, and software vendors, was to develop the TDMA-based UWC-136 standard and promote its acceptance by the ITU as a member of the IMT-2000 3G family of standards (3GPP/OP#7 2002). However, since the standard was based on the same TDMA technology as GSM and, moreover, included Ericsson, a major GSM supplier, this led to a natural convergence of interests with proponents of

GSM – and by extension ETSI and the 3GPP. The convergence with GSM was evident, for example, in the fact that the UWC-136 standard included the EDGE technology referred to in the preceding sub-section (4.1) as a complement to UMTS (ibid.). Ericsson, moreover, was a 'major proponent of these developments', building upon its history as a key infrastructure and equipment provider for D-AMPS networks to collaborate with AT&T and other operators in implementing and testing EDGE in 2000 (Funk 2002: 212).

In early 2002, the UWCC was disbanded, having 'fulfilled the goals and objectives of its five year program' (UWCC 2000). The coalition's members were absorbed into the 3GPP through the formation of a new market representation partner organization, 3G Americas (3GPP 2002b). The membership of 3G Americas includes both TDMA and GSM operators and equipment suppliers. Moreover, the organization is committed to support migration to W-CDMA/UMTS. Its formation 'marks a significant milestone for the advancement of all five technologies and ensures a smooth transition to Third Generation services in North, Central, and South America as well as the Caribbean, where a growing number of leading carriers are committed to the GSM/GPRS/EDGE and UMTS (W-CDMA) technology migration' (3G Americas 2002). Certainly, it greatly enhances the prospects for widespread adoption of W-CDMA/UMTS in the new world. In the continents of North and South America, together with the Caribbean, 'there [were] 108 million combined TDMA and GSM subscribers as of year-end 2001, with TDMA as the leading digital cellular technology in the region' (ibid.).

4.3. Summary and Assessment

This section has dealt with both complementary and rival standards related to UMTS. Due to the comprehensive scope of the UMTS concept, as well as its planned approach to development, only the second type of standards have posed any direct competitive challenge to UMTS. However, so-called complementary standards enabling the further evolution of second-generation standards such as GSM may nevertheless have the effect of delaying the implementation of third-generation standards by stalling market demand.

Section 4.1, on complementary systems and standards, discussed technologies developed in conjunction with UMTS, concentrating on hierarchical levels lower than that of the overall radio access system, – i.e., macrocell, microcell, picocell and personal area network. ETSI has developed successful standards at both the microcell and picocell levels – i.e., DECT and Hiper-LAN 2, respectively – but it now appears that the latter may obviate the former, with the growing corporate use of WLANs. This probability has also been strengthened by the recent development of the proprietary standard for PANs, Bluetooth. 'In the future, mobile phones will support both a cellular network and WLAN or Bluetooth, which means that DECT alone is not viable any longer' (Hännikäineen et al. 2002:15). Another, even more interesting development in complementary technologies concerns the emergence at the macrocell level of new technologies for enhancing data transmission rates. High-speed circuit-switched data, GPRS, and, more recently, EDGE have improved the data transmission capabilities of existing GSM networks to a point where they approach the basic capabilities specified for UMTS, raising the possibility of a market contest between '3G' UMTS and '2.5G' GSM networks (ibid.; Furuskar et al. 1999).

Section 4.2 dealt with rival '3G' standards. It showed that, at least formally, a shift has occurred in competition amongst standards. Whereas standards were regionally defined and competed primarily on a regional basis in the first and second generations of mobile telecommunications (Funk 1998), third-generation standards have been defined in relation to the global framework of the IMT-2000 initiative of the ITU (Kano 2000). Established regional markets, like NTT DoCoMo's, and regional SDOs, such as ETSI, continue to play an important role, but the competitive strategies of firms and firm coalitions that are proponents of one or another standard are oriented towards the global market. Through the construction of international alliances among SDOs and firms representative of the major regional markets, as well as equipment producers backing one or another competing standard, competition within the 'IMT-2000 family' has been narrowed to a contest between two major third-generation standards: W-CDMA (UMTS) championed by the 3GPP alliance, and CDMA2000, championed by the 3GPP2 alliance. Major equipment producers such as Ericsson and Qualcomm have played key roles in the construction of these broad international alliances, as evidenced by the manner in which Ericsson and Nokia engineered the common agreement of NTT DoCoMo and ETSI on W-CDMA, and Ericsson's part in steering the UWC-136 standard and its supporters into strategic alignment with the UMTS standard and the eventual absorption of UWCC into the 3GPP, leading to the creation of the '3G Americas' MRPs (market representation partners). Qualcomm, the main proponent of CDMA2000, has evidently played an equally central role in the creation of the 3GPP2 alliance, relying on both firm coalitions and political lobbying.

5. PUBLIC-SECTOR ACTORS

This section deals with the main public-sector actors engaged in the development of UMTS. Significantly, the list does not include public telephone operators (PTOs) or (post, telephone and telegraph (PTT) operators, due to the privatization and deregulation of EU telecommunications markets during the

1990s. Instead, the discussion begins by outlining the role of the EC and tele-communications regulators – a topic also addressed in section 6. The EU and global SDOs are addressed, as are international alliances that operate in relation to these bodies. Finally, public-sector research programmes are also discussed.

5.1. The European Commission, Liberalization and National Regulators

As discussed in chapter 3 (this volume), the European Commission (EC) made the liberalization of telecommunications markets a top priority during the 1990s. The EC integrated this policy very closely with measures designed to strengthen the EU's competitive advantage in mobile telecommunications (Commission of the European Communities 1994). Accordingly, the EC was also instrumental in hastening the development of UMTS via the 1996 report of a special EC Task Force and creation of the UMTS Forum within ETSI (Garrard 1998: 478–9). Through these measures, and also through extensive programmes of public and corporate research on '3G' mobile telecommunications, the EC provided strong support for UMTS. At the same time, its liberalization policies spelled an end to the key role once played by PTOs in developing new technologies and standards (Pisjak 1994).

The complete liberalization of EU telecommunications markets – i.e., the removal of monopoly privileges for all telecommunications operators – was accomplished by the beginning of 1998. The creation of a competitive tele-communications market spanning all the member states was accompanied by the development of national regulatory authorities (NRAs), which were re-sponsible for, among other things, the award of licences for telecommunica-tions operators (and radio spectrum allocations for mobile operators) (Melody 1999). Some critics of the EU's framework for liberalization pointed out that NRAs had considerable latitude in licensing, which might be used to protect incumbent positions in national markets. This could be done through, for example, the imposition of 'carrier selection' on all operators (thus possibly discouraging investment in local infrastructure by new operators) and pursu-ing broad definitions of 'universal service' that would create severe financial burdens for new entrants (thus raising steep entry barriers to new operators) (Kiessling and Blondeel 1998: 590–91). Others emphasized that such licens-ing policies could seriously affect the post-entry competitiveness of markets, by encouraging 'collusive behaviour' among operators and service providers (Xavier 1998: 484).

In the case of Sweden, these concerns proved to be groundless. As dis-cussed in chapter 3 (this volume) liberalization of the Swedish telecommuni-cations sector, including privatization of the Swedish PTO, Televerket/Telia, proceeded rapidly during the 1990s. By the end of the decade, Sweden led the EU in telecommunications liberalization (OECD 1999a: 11). Moreover, the recently created NRA, Post och Telestyrelsen, did not pursue a policy of favouring incumbents and raising steep entry barriers to new entrants in awarding '3G' mobile telecommunications licences in late 2000. Instead of an 'auction', the Swedish NRA staged a 'beauty contest' based on technical criteria – which was lost by, among others, the major Swedish incumbent, Telia. The four winners included two smaller Swedish incumbents, Europolitan and Tele 2 (Comviq), as well as two large new entrants from abroad, Hi 3G Access (Hutchison-Whampoa) and Orange Sverige (Ovander 2000). As for the issue of investment into local infrastructure, the Swedish government was simultaneously developing a policy of ensuring the installation of broadband infrastructure in all communities in the country, contemplating the provision of public investment where necessary in order to guarantee universal access (Mellander 2000: 9–12).

5.2. Standards Development Organizations – ETSI and ITU

ETSI's role in developing the UMTS standard has been referred to extensively in preceding sections, particularly section 3. Significantly, ETSI has had to rely on organizations with more extensive international coverage in order to accomplish this initiative – a development consistent with the shift from regional to global strategies for standards-based competition in third-generation mobile telecommunications (Kano 2000). In particular, ETSI's UMTS standard has been developed in relation to the IMT-2000 framework defined by the ITU. Compared to the ITU, ETSI is both regionally based (founded and supported by the EU) and relatively young (established in the late 1980s) (Temple 1992). In contrast, the ITU is an SDO that was originally set up as an intergovernmental treaty organization and now operates under a charter from the United Nations (UN). It is, therefore, truly worldwide in coverage. Moreover, the ITU, first established in 1865 as the International Telegraphy Union, is 'not only the oldest specialized international organization in the communications field, but, arguably, the oldest in any field of endeavour' (David and Shurmer 1996: 4). The salient differences between the two SDOs help to explain the division of labour between them with respect to the development of standards for 'third-generation' mobile telecommunications. While the ITU possesses the legitimacy required to arbitrate and settle international disputes, ETSI is able to unify and promote the 'regional' interests of the EU. This also involves arbitration between competing national and corporate interests. ETSI, for example, negotiated the 1998 concession of Ericsson and Nokia which had those firms agreeing to conform to the wishes of other ETSI members (such as Alcatel, Siemens, Italtel, Nortel-Matra and Bosch) by including TD-CDMA in their proposal to Japan's NTT DoCoMo to make W-CDMA the basis of UMTS (Funk 2002: 82). Significantly, though,

ETSI's structure and mandate did not provide adequately for the inclusion and representation of non-European interests – for example, the many GSM network operators based outside of Europe – in its standardization proposals to the ITU. Because of the strategic importance of Japan's NTT DoCoMo, which would become in 2001 the first operator in the world to implement W-CDMA, ETSI sought to resolve this inadequacy. Soon after its 1998 decision on W-CDMA, in the same year in fact, ETSI created an international collaborative agreement with other regional or national SDOs known as the Third Generation Partnership Project or 3GPP (3GPP 2002a).

5.3. Third Generation Partnership Project

The 3GPP is a collaborative agreement established by ETSI in December 1998. The goal is to bring together as 'organizational partners' a number of telecommunications standards bodies including ARIB and TTC (Japan), TI (the telecommunications standards committee of the American National Standards Institute) and TTA (South Korea). 3GPP's mandate is to develop specifications for, and implement, the UMTS standard, in addition to maintaining and developing GSM networks via the further evolution of GPRS and EDGE radio access technologies (3GPP 2002a). 3GPP also includes MRPs such as 3G Americas (see sub-section 4.2.3). Essentially, the organization is a successor to the earlier UMTS Forum within ETSI and performs many of the same functions in relation to UMTS as the ETSI's Special Mobile Group carried out in relation to GSM, in addition to some of the functions of the GSM MoU administration (see chapter 3, this volume). Parallel to the GSM MoU (Memorandum of Understanding) administration, and drawing upon that organization's protracted dispute with equipment manufacturers over IPRs (intellectual property rights), one of the first initiatives of the 3GPP was an attempt to reconcile the potentially conflicting interests of equipment manufacturers and network operators by establishing the UMTS Intellectual Property Rights Association (UIPA) as a mechanism to determine and collect licence and royalty fees for key UMTS patents (Cataldo 1999: 1). This initiative, which was consistent with the ITU's policy requiring either the waiver of patent rights or the reasonable and non-discriminatory negotiation of licences, was delayed by the ongoing patent dispute between Ericsson and Qualcomm over CDMA/W-CDMA, finally resolved in late 1999 at the insistence of the ITU (Funk 2002: 208–11, n. 5 and 9).

5.4 Other Public-sector Actors: EU-supported Research

As noted earlier, the EU provided extensive support for the development of UMTS in the form of extensive programmes of public and corporate research and development. This supply-side approach to the development of new mobile telecommunications technologies was actually initiated during the 'second-generation' period associated with GSM (cee chapter 3, section 5.3). However, most programmes initiated at that time bore fruit only with the development of UMTS. During the early 1990s, the EU initiated the RACE/CODIT programme, which led to the development of W-CDMA and also provided European firms, notably Ericsson, with the testbed for its Ericsson Wideband Testbed technology. Similarly, the FRAMES project provided the technological basis for the radio access network components of UMTS. 'The EU programmes were hence merged and submitted to ETSI as a candidate technology for UMTS' (Glimstedt 2001: 16). A later EU initiative, ACTS, was responsible for developing new technologies for nearly all aspects of the UMTS system, from multimedia applications to the basic building blocks of mobile systems, in addition to developing a strong European command over IPRs essential to the new standard (Infowin 2002).

6. PRIVATE-SECTOR ACTORS

To date, the most important private-sector actors involved in developing UMTS have been telecommunications equipment manufacturers – in particular, the Swedish firm, Ericsson. In Sweden and the rest of Europe, telecommunications operators have yet to play a very important role, mainly due to the fact that '3G' networks and services have not yet actually commenced operation. Internationally, however, the Japanese NTT DoCoMo has certainly played a key role in the development of UMTS. Service providers, including internet content providers, are expected to figure importantly in 'growing' the market for 3G mobile telecommunications, but it is not possible at present to make any direct observations about their performance. It is possible, though, to comment on the growth of 2.5G services such as WAP and I-Mode, which can provide insights into the prospects for 3G services.

6.1. Equipment Suppliers: Ericsson

As noted in section 4.3, telecommunications equipment producers played a major role in the development of UMTS. This is true not only in technological development but also in building coalitions and alliances that were crucial to securing an initial market large enough to make UMTS a truly 'global' standard. Through its engagement in a broad range of coalition-building strategies, the Swedish firm Ericsson has made decisive contributions to the development of UMTS. Some of these coalitions have taken the form of a consortium – i.e., 'an informal alliance of firms, organizations and (sometimes) individuals that is financed by membership fees for the purpose of co-ordinating technological and market development activities' (Hawkins 1999: 161). A case in point (discussed in section 4.1) is the complementary – but proprietary – Bluetooth standard for PANs developed by Ericsson and Nokia, together with IBM, Intel and Toshiba (Keil 2002). Ericsson and Nokia's co-operation agreement with NTT DoCoMo to develop W-CDMA as an IMT-2000 standard, and their successful subsequent lobbying within ETSI to have W-CDMA accepted as the basic radio access technology for the UMTS standard (discussed in sections 4.2 and 5.2) is, of course, an outstanding instance of coalition-building. According to Funk (2002), it illustrates how firms such as Ericsson and Nokia can use their membership in SDOs to influence the character and direction of their private alliances with other firms – and vice versa (ibid.: 80–84). Significantly, this case led to the creation by ETSI of the 3GPP – a consortium-like 'collaboration agreement' whose core members were not private firms but SDOs, although regional coalitions of telecommunications operators and equipment producers were also incorporated as MRPs (see section 5.3). Ericsson also engineered the creation and acceptance into the 3GPP of organizations belonging to this last-mentioned category – particularly, the strategically important 3G Americas alliance (discussed in section 4.2.3). In this case, Ericsson used 'market' and 'committee' relations to complement each other in an overall strategy to promote UMTS.

Competitive relations between equipment-producing firms were also crucial to the consolidation of the UMTS standard. Here, again, Ericsson occupied a position of central importance, due to its ongoing patent dispute with Qualcomm over CDMA/W-CDMA (see section 5.3). Qualcomm, the originator of CDMAOne, claimed to hold a majority of essential W-CDMA patents and demanded not only high licensing fees but also a single worldwide CDMA standard for IMT-2000 that would, unlike W-CDMA, be 'backwards compatible' with CDMAOne, while Ericsson and NTT DoCoMo claimed (questionably) to hold patents that allowed them to bypass Qualcomm-patented technology (Funk 2002: 208–9, n. 3 and 4). The position taken by Ericsson and NTT DoCoMo was arguably weaker than that of Qualcomm in strictly legal terms, but Qualcomm's position was politically weaker – not least because it assumed it could dictate terms to other firms as well as the ITU (Glimstedt 2001: 23–5). This was a serious miscalculation, though Ericsson's bargaining power was also gravely weakened by China's expected adoption of CDMAOne (see section 4.2.2). In 1999 the ITU effectively forced Qualcomm and Ericsson to resolve their dispute through the cross-licensing of patents, Ericsson's purchase of Qualcomm's infrastructure business, and an agreement to achieve a compromise regarding W-CDMA (Funk 2002: 210–11). The agreement reflected a balance between the 'political' pressure marshalled in support of Ericsson within the ITU, based on its alliances in Japan and the US (notably the interoperability agreement that it had brought about between GSM and TDMA operators in the Americas) and the 'commercial' pressure that Qualcomm had mustered, partly through lobbying the US and other governments (Glimstedt 2001: 23–5). In addition to upholding the IPR policies of ITU, 3GPP and ETSI, the agreement required by ITU established CDMA2000 as a major IMT-2000 standard only on condition that it be made 'interoperable' with W-CDMA, promoting in the short term the continuation and convergence of GSM and TDMA services, and in the long term, an 'open architecture' of compatible and interoperable standards – the IMT-2000 'family' (ibid.: 25–6).

During the development of UMTS, Ericsson continued its established technological strategy (see chapter 3, section 6.1) of acquiring and extending a complete 'systems competence' in mobile telecommunications (Hellström 2002). This strategy was interwoven with Ericsson's competitive strategy of outflanking its major competitor, Qualcomm, through the construction of international consortia and alliances. The latter strategy was in fact based largely on Ericsson's technological assets as a leading supplier, along with Motorola and Nokia, to both GSM and D-AMPS (or TDMA) networks for '2G' mobile telecommunications (see, e.g., section 4.2.3). Generally, market alliances were closely related to technological collaboration agreements. The alliance with NTT DoCoMo was an outgrowth of Ericsson's earlier relations with the Japanese firm as a supplier for the '2G' PDS standard, which led to a 1996 invitation to tender from NTT DoCoMo for the construction of a W-CDMA evaluation system (Eldstaåhl and Näsman 1999: 56). During the same period, Ericsson had also invested heavily in Japan's Yokosaka Research Park, home to R&D units of many major Japanese IT companies (*The Financial Times*, 9 October 1997). Thus, when Ericsson's mobile handset operations ran into serious difficulties in 2000, a key element of its response was to enter into a partnership with Sony. Sony Ericsson Mobile Communications was formed in 2001 to develop and market '2.5G' and '3G' mobile multimedia products on an international basis, and brought its first products, including state-of-the-art handsets, to market in early 2002 (Sony Ericsson Mobile Communications 2002). At the same time, Ericsson created a new company, Ericsson Mobile Platforms, to license 'complete mobile 2.5G and 3G technology platforms to manufacturers of mobile phones and other wireless devices' (Ericsson 2001). This strategy, also pursued with Bluetooth, allowed Ericsson to concentrate on the development of complete system architectures (ibid.).

As noted earlier (in sections 3.2 and 3.4), the 'platforms' approach also enables Ericsson to develop new relationships with telecommunications operators and service providers, including the provision of 'consulting, integration

and management services' (Carlgren 1999). Since the UMTS concept pro-
motes a common technological standard as the basis on which telecommunications operators can compete in a liberalized market by differentiating their
service offerings, the operators now require specialized applications software
that can run on the platforms created by systems suppliers. Thus, even though
systems are interchangeable, suppliers' development of proprietary components and software in both terminals and switching/transmission systems
'means that once the operator chooses a technological platform it must establish solid industrial relationships with its supplier' (Lera 2000: 415). Reflecting this shift towards a new technological basis for vertical integration and an
industry structure in which suppliers with the most advanced capabilities in
data communications will dominate (ibid.: 416), telecommunications equipment manufacturers now seek to expand their 'platform' competence in this
area through acquiring or forming consortia with IT firms (Hawkins 1999)
and outsourcing applications-related software development to independent
vendors (Rao 1999). Ericsson has followed these trends, acquiring Advanced
Computer Communications in the late 1990s (Lera 2000: n. 15), building up
the internal software capabilities of the Ericsson Group (Manninen 2002:
section 4.5), and actively promoting the spin-off from Ericsson of entrepre-
neurial 'wireless start-ups' specializing in new applications based on the use
of open source development protocols and connectivity standards originated
by Ericsson. Sponsoring start-ups cultivates a periphery of 'ventures ... working primarily to develop technologies compatible with Ericsson's next-
generation wireless technologies' (Casper and Soskice 2001: 26). Thus, Ericsson's strategy involves both vertical integration with operators and data communications firms and vertical disintegration with software vendors, as well as
licensed terminal manufacturers developing handsets and other devices customized for special applications (see above).

6.2. Network Operators and Service Providers

As observed in section 5.1, the total liberalization of telecommunications
markets within the EU, completed by 1998, greatly diminished the potential
for network operators and service providers to contribute to the technological
development of UMTS. In a number of EU countries, most spectacularly the
UK, '3G' licences were auctioned for astronomical amounts, having the pre-
dictable effect of encouraging collusive behaviour among the bidders in later
auctions (Klemperer 2002; van Damme 2002). Sweden held a 'beauty contest'
instead, in which the largest incumbent, Telia, lost and two foreign-based
operators, Hutchison and Orange, were successful 'new entrants' (Ovander et
al. 2000). The subsequent prolonged downturn in telecommunication markets
(to which, according to some analysts, the '3G' auctions contributed), com-

bined with the fact that UMTS networks were scheduled to begin operation in the EU only in 2002, meant that neither incumbent firms nor new entrants would soon play any important role in the development of UMTS in Sweden apart from purchasing infrastructure and equipment from Swedish suppliers such as Ericsson (ibid.).

Generally, both the regulatory structure of UMTS and trends in technological development spelled a subordinate role for conventional operators in relation to both equipment suppliers and service providers specializing in data communications (Lera 2000: 415–6). The imperative for operators to 'emphasise more their capability of new services provision' greatly increases their dependency on applications software vendors and equipment manufacturers (ibid.: 415). In view of these trends towards market fragmentation, it is a historical irony that the fate of UMTS as a 'global' standard has depended critically on Japan's NTT DoCoMo, a formerly monopolistic telecommunications operator that still holds a 60 per cent share of one of the largest national markets in the world (see section 4.2.1). NTT DoCoMo would also be the first to offer '3G' services, which began in Japan in 2001. Significantly, the incumbent Japanese mobile network operator commands not only a large market but also the capability to combine the roles of operator and service provider. By early 2002, however, it appeared that NTT DoCoMo's '3G' service, first launched in October 2001, had been a slow starter. At the end of March 2002, NTT DoCoMo 'had sold only 80,000 3G handsets, well below its target of 150,000' (Economist 2002a).

Prior to the international 'take-off' of UMTS and other 3G services, the eventual role of new service providers in market development can only be indicated by the performance of the '2.5G' services that have recently emerged. Of these, two are of particular interest: WAP and I-Mode. WAP was developed in 1998 by a 'forum' founded in 1996 by Ericsson, Nokia, Motorola and Unwired Planet to set technological parameters for the wireless Internet access market, based on Unwired Planet's handheld device markup language (HDML) (O'Shea 1998: 24). It used an HTML-compatible open protocol that initially supported GSM networks but would later evolve to support CDMA (Code Division Multiple Access) as well as all other current and digital cellular technologies (Pohajakallio 1998: 48). WAP has met with wide international success, with over 500 telecommunications operators and manufacturers having joined the WAP Forum by 2000, and an estimated 16.5 million users in Europe (Batista 2000). However, WAP only provides access to a limited number of Internet sites, and its new markup language poses special problems to content providers (ibid.). In Sweden, both Telia and Europolitan offer WAP, and some 400 WAP services are available in Scandinavia, most of them providing specialized information such as news, sports, weather and stock market reports, or booking and ticketing services (Erlandson 2000). Yet WAP is expensive and appears to have only limited prospects for growth based on a wider range of services. Its Japanese counterpart, I-Mode is a proprietary technology developed and provided by NTT DoCoMo.

In contrast to WAP, I-Mode can read practically any web-page, based on its use of 'compact HTML', and also offers more affordable access rates, more robust content and higher connection speed (Batista 2000). There were 10 million I-Mode subscribers in Japan by 2000, as compared to only 3 million WAP subscribers. However, I-Mode is a closed standard, available only in Japan, and not accessible to foreign manufacturers and operators (ibid.). Nevertheless, I-Mode's superior market performance in Japan deeply impressed the WAP Forum, and the second WAP specification, released in 2001, involved evolution to a markup language akin to I-Mode's 'compact HTML', with similar capabilities (WAP Forum 2002). In 2002, NTT DoCoMo's competitors, using WAP, among other technologies, were able to report successful wireless Internet services, but I-Mode continues its phenomenal growth. As of December 2001, there were 29.5 million I-Mode subscriptions in Japan (Megler 2002: 1). One of the main lessons drawn from these comparisons is that I-Mode's success is due to a very different focus on entertainment services aimed at young people. In contrast, European and US service providers using WAP have targeted a very different market. 'In their focus on business users and popular fixed line contents, Western services and content providers are in danger of offering mobile Internet services that few people want', leading to 'too little investment in contents, phones, and appropriate services' (Funk 2002: 223).

7. MAIN OUTCOMES

It is extremely difficult to evaluate fully the economic outcomes of UMTS, given the fact that service has not commenced in Europe or elsewhere, except for Japan with the launch in late 2001 of NTT DoCoMo's '3G' network. As reported earlier, the initial results have been somewhat disappointing, with NTT DoCoMo having sold only 80 000 3G handsets by the end of March 2002, rather than the expected 150 000 (*The Economist* 2002a). Europe presents an even more discouraging picture. 'Having paid a fortune for their 3G licences, operators have been hamstrung by huge debts and have delayed building their 3G networks', leading to reduced sales for equipment suppliers and a situation where 'nobody expects much sign of 3G in Europe until 2004 at the earliest' (Economist 2002b). In the meantime, '2.5G' services are being implemented that will in the nearer term compete directly with '3G', resulting in market fragmentation not only in the US but also in Europe. In Japan, where '2.5G' services are flourishing, this is already contributing to slow growth of '3G'. In the longer term, however, installed base in 'backwards compatible' 2.5G networks should provide the foundation for the development of 3G markets. This outlook has been strategically fundamental for all major 3G standards (see sections 4.2, 5.2 and 5.3).

In the long term UMTS should have considerable benefits for the European firms that have invested most heavily in its development, not least because of their substantial share of essential patents (see section 5.3). However, the benefits are more likely to accrue to equipment producers than operators, who will have the burden of paying for 3G licences amounting to over 90 billion Euro (*The Economist* 2002b). In addition, operators are also expected to place orders for infrastructure and equipment amounting to 175 billion Euro, with the greatest share of these orders being placed with 3GPP and ETSI member firms such as Ericsson, Nokia and Motorola (Economist 2000: 98). To date, the Swedish firm Ericsson has captured a substantial share of this potential market. Ericsson has been selected as the main supplier of infrastructure for many of the UMTS networks recently licensed in Europe, and in early 2002 claimed 'an approximately 40 per cent market share in both GSM and W-CDMA globally' (Ericsson 2002).

As emphasized earlier (for example, in section 2), UMTS has already achieved the status, albeit rather anticipatory, of a global standard, and therefore has good growth prospects outside the EU – notably in Japan and throughout the entire international community of GSM and TDMA networks that the 3GPP represents. Here, too, W-CDMA proponents and UMTS supporters, such as the Nordic firms Ericsson and Nokia, stand to benefit from their early involvement in the development of this standard. Earlier, some observers expressed concern that since Japanese networks and service providers would provide the pioneer market, Japanese firms, i.e., Sony and Matsushita (Panasonic), might replace Ericsson and Nokia as the dominant equipment developers, at least in the Japanese context (Dalum et al. 1999). However, the extensive international connections of the Nordic firms, including strong partnerships with Japanese firms – for example, the recently formed Sony Ericsson Mobile Communications (see section 6.1) – should compensate for this possible disadvantage.

8. CONCLUSIONS

The following conclusions address 'key questions' of the research network on European Sectoral Systems of Innovation (ESSY). Since the conclusions drawn here build to a great extent upon those elaborated in Chapter 3, they are much briefer.

8.1. Knowledge Base and Learning Processes

In the development of UMTS, the shift of 'system competence' from formerly monopolistic PTOs to equipment producers and SDOs not only continued but greatly accelerated. Liberalization and the regulatory framework of UMTS instituted a clear division between network operation and service provision, further diminishing the potential of operators to act as system integrators, although both regulatory and technological developments impelled them to develop specialized capabilities and expertise in service provision. The new regime of 'open' standard setting was consolidated, and equipment producers emerged as key system integrators. At the same time, technological convergence compelled firms such as Ericsson to continue expanding their technical competencies, not only through R&D and participation in publicly funded research programmes, but also through a variety of mechanisms, including acquisitions, joint ventures and the development of new, vertically disintegrated relationships with licensed manufacturers and independent software developers.

8.2. Firms, Non-firm Organizations and Networks

In addition to the organizational changes already mentioned, there was a clear shift in standard setting and standards-based competition from the regional to the international level, reflected in the ascendancy of global SDOs, such as the ITU, over regional ones, such as ETSI. A related development was the emergence of consortia among regional SDOs – for example, the 3GPP and 3GPP2 alliances – paralleling and interacting with private consortia created primarily by firms to carry out competitive strategies based on de facto standardization. In the former context, as well as the latter, firms such as Ericsson were the main architects of international alliances, which became increasingly crucial to their competitive strategy. Ericsson and Nokia's alliance with NTT DoCoMo was thus a decisive influence, not only on ETSI's choice of W-CDMA, but also because it led to the construction of the 3GPP, which also built upon the two Nordic firms' ties with other GSM and TDMA suppliers and telecommunications operators.

8.3. Geographical Boundaries

The advent of 'global' standard setting partially diminished the role of regional SDOs, but they continued to play a vitally important role – particularly where, like ETSI, they could define a single standard for an extensive regional market. For the same reason, NTT DoCoMo, because of its command over nearly 60 per cent of the Japanese market, played a critically important role in making W-CDMA/UMTS a 'world standard'. The Chinese and South Korean governments apparently played a similarly important role in providing the CDMA2000 standard sufficient 'market power' to become the main competitor of W-CDMA. Moreover, strong 'home markets' continue to be regarded as important sources of competitive advantage for equipment producers – although the globalization strategies and international alliances of transnational firms such as Ericsson, with its strong Japanese connections, now enable them to develop new technological assets in foreign markets as well as domestic ones. Sectoral governance therefore increasingly depends on international authorities with 'global reach', as in the ITU's resolution of the patent dispute between Ericsson and Qualcomm.

8.4. Long-term Dynamics of the Sector and Co-evolutionary Processes

In certain respects the shift from 2G to 3G mobile telecommunications represented a competence-enhancing technological discontinuity, reflected in the capability of firms to 'evolve' from one generation of technology to another and, in the process, develop '2.5G' technologies. But technological convergence between mobile telecommunications and the Internet was also potentially competence destroying, indicated by the entry of new firms with different technological capabilities – e.g., in data communications – into the formerly closed oligopolistic world of major telecommunications equipment producers. Independent software developers, to whom an increasing share of R&D is now out-sourced, may challenge the dominant role of firms such as Ericsson, which have already begun restructuring their operations in order to accommodate these new partners. Similarly, telecommunications operators are entering new, technologically-based relations of vertical integration with both applications software vendors and equipment manufacturers.

8.5. Public Policy and European International Performance

The development of UMTS marked the completion of the transition to a new policy regime in telecommunications, characterized by market liberalization and a strong 'supply-side' orientation with respect to technological development. Regional SDOs took over the role of articulating market demand from monopolistic PTOs, and in the case of ETSI performed this function well in relation to technology development. However, such organizations cannot play the same role with respect to subsequent market development, and in the case of 3G mobile telecommunications the demands of the marketplace may be a crucially important source for further technological development. The growth prospects of UMTS will depend greatly on the creation of demand for new services based on the application of data transmission and multimedia capabilities. In this respect large telecommunications operators may have a role to play that cannot be easily replicated by any other type of organization. At least that is one hypothesis that might be raised on the basis of NTT DoCoMo's success with I-Mode and the comparatively weaker market performance of WAP in Japan. Trends towards the fragmentation of telecommunications markets might undermine the potential for creating positive feedback between emerging mass markets and investment, R&D and production in new areas of technological development.

REFERENCES

3G Americas (2002), 'About 3G Americas', available: http://www.3Gamericas.org/ 2002 [cited 18 May 2002].

3GPP (2002a), 'About 3GPP', available: http://www.3GPP.org/ 2002a [cited 18 May 2002].

3GPP (2002b), 'Membership of 3GPP', available: http://www.3GPP.org/ 2002b [cited 18 May 2002].

3GPP/OP#7 (2002), 'Cancellation of Status for the Universal Wireless Connection Consortium, April 7, 2002', available: http://www.3GPP.org/ 2002 [cited 18 May 2002].

3GPP2 (2002), 'About 3GPP2', available: http://www.3GPP2.org/ 2002 [cited 18 May 2002].

Andermo, P.-G. and L.-M. Ewerbring (1995), 'A CDMA-based Radio Access Design for UMTS', *IEEE Personal Communications* **2** (1), 48–53.

Batista, E. (2000), 'WAP or I-Mode: Which is Better?', *Wired News*, 17 May.

Buitenwerf, E., G. Colombo, H. Mitts, and P. Wright (1995), 'UMTS: Fixed Network Issues and Design Options', *IEEE Personal Communications* **2** (1), 30–7.

Carlgren, B. (1999), 'Professional Services – Meeting the Changing Needs of Network Operators', *Ericsson Review* (2), 94–100.

Casper, S. and D. Soskice (2001), 'Patterns of Innovation and Varieties of Capitalism: Explaining the Development of High-technology Entrepreneurialism in Europe', Paper presented at Final Conference of ESSY (European Sectoral Systems of Innovation) research network, at Milan, Italy.

Clever, M. (1999), 'Mass Market Solutions for Mobile Data', *Telecommunications* **33** (6), 40–9.

Commission of the European Communities (1994), Towards the Personal Communications Environment: Green Paper on a Common Approach to the Field of Mobile and Personal Telecommunications in the European Union, CEC Communication – COM (94) 145, 27.4.1994, Brussels-Luxembourg: CEC.

Dalum, B., C. Freeman, R. Simonetti, N. Von Tunzelmann and B. Verspagen (1999), 'Europe and the Information and Communication Technologies Revolution', in J. Fagerberg, P. Guerrieri and B. Verspagen (eds), *The Economic Challenge for Europe: Adapting to Innovation-Based Growth*, Cheltenham, UK: Edward Elgar.

DaSilva, J.S. and B.E. Fernandes (1995), 'The European Research Program for Advanced Mobile Systems: Addressing the Needs of the European Community', *IEEE Personal Communications* **2** (1), 14–19.

David, P.A. and M. Shurmer (1996), 'Formal Standard-setting for Global Telecommunications` and Information Services: Towards an Institutional Regime Transformation?', Stanford, California: Stanford University Center for Economic Policy Research.

The Economist (2000), 'Nokia: A Finnish Fable', *The Economist*, 11 October, 97–103.

The Economist (2002a), 'Japanse Telecoms – Foreign Adventures', *The Economist*, 11 May, 64.

The Economist (2002b), 'Mobile Telecoms: The Tortoise and the Hare', *The Economist*, 11 May, 63.

Ekudden, E., U. Horn, M. Melander and J. Olin (2001), 'On-Demand Mobile Media – A Rich Service Experience for Mobile Users', *Ericsson Review* (4): 168–77.

Eldståhl, J. and A. Näsman (1999), 'WCDMA Evaluation System – Evaluating the Radio Access Technology of Third Generation Systems', *Ericsson Review* (2), 56–69.

Emmerson, B. (1998), 'On the Move', *Communications International* **25** (4), 40–4.

Enderin, M., D. LeCorney, M. Lindberg and T. Lundquist (2001), 'AXE 810 – The Evolution Continues', *Ericsson Review* (4), 10–23.

Ericsson (2001), 'Ericsson Accelerates Licensing of Mobile Phone Technology', 31 August, Stockholm: Ericsson Press Releases.

Ericsson (2002), 'Telefonica Mobiles Names Ericsson as Supplier for UMTS Launch Phase in Spain and Germany', 15 April, Stockholm: Ericsson Press Releases.

Erlandson, Å. (2000), 'Vad? Hur? WAP!', *Aftonbladet-IT*, 20–21 March, 4–5.

ETSI (1998), 'Broadband Radio Access Networks (BRAN): Requirements and Architectures for Broadband Fixed Radio Access (HIPERACCESS)', Technical Report 101 177 (1999–01), Sophia Antipolis: ETSI.

ETSI (1999), 'Broadband Radio Access Networks (BRAN): High Performance Radio Local Area Network (HIPERLAN) Type 2 – Requirements and Architectures for Wireless Broadband Access', Technical Report 101 031 (1999–01), Sophia Antipolis: ETSI.

Farjami, P., C. Görg and F. Bell (2000), 'Advanced Service Provisioning Based on Mobile Agents', *Computer Communications* **23**: 754–60.

Friis-Hansen, S. and B. Stavenow (2001), 'Secure Electronic Transactions – The Mobile Phone Evolution Continues', *Ericsson Review* (4), 162–7.

Funk, J.L. (1998), 'Competition between Regional Standards and the Success and Failure of Firms in the World-wide Mobile Communication Market', *Telecommunications Policy* **22** (4/5), 419–41.

Funk, J.L. (2002), Global Competition Between and within Standards: The Case of Mobile Phones, Basingstoke, Hampshire/New York: Palgrave.

Furuskar, A., S. Mazur, F. Muller and H. Olofsson (1999), 'EDGE: Enhanced Data Rates for GSM and TDMA/136 Evolution', *IEEE Personal Communications* **6** (3), 55–66.

Garber, L. (2002), 'Will 3G Really be the Next Big Wireless Technology?', *IEEE Computer* **35** (1).

Garrard, G.A. (1998), Cellular Communications: Worldwide Market Development, Boston: Artech House.

Glimstedt, H. (2001), 'The Competitive Dynamics of Technological Standards: The Case of the Third Generation in Cellular Communications', paper presented at Seminar for the Systems of Innovation Research Programme, Department of Technology and Social Change, Linköping University, Linköping, Sweden, December.

Gustås, P., P. Magusson, J. Oom and N. Storm (2002), 'Real-time Performance Monitoring and Optimization of Cellular Systems', *Ericsson Review* (1), 4–13.

Hagen, L., J. Mausberger and C. Weckerle (1999), 'Mobile Agent Based Service Subscription and Customization Using the UMTS Virtual Home Environment', *Computer Networks* **31** (19), 2063–78.

Hameleers, H. and C. Johansson (2002), 'IP Technology in WCDMA/GSM Core Networks', *Ericsson Review* (1), 14–27.

Hawkins, R. (1999), 'The Rise of Consortia in the Information and Communication Technology Industries: Emerging Implications for Policy', *Telecommunication Policy* **23**, 159–73.

Hellström, K. (2002), 'R&D Strategy is Key to Success', *Industry Week*, April, 24.

Hännikäinen, M., T. Hämäläinen, M. Niemi and J. Saarinen (2002), 'Trends in Personal Wireless Data Communications', *Computer Communications* **25** (1), 84–99.

Infowin (2002), 'ACTS Results', available: http://www.cordis.lu/infowin/ 2002 [cited 19 May 2002].

Johnston, W. (1998), 'Europe's Future Mobile Telephone System', *IEEE Spectrum* **35** (10), 49–53.

Kano, S. (2002), 'Technical Innovations, Standardization and Regional Comparison – A Case Study in Mobile Communications', *Telecommunication Policy* **24**, 305–21.

Keil, T. (2002), 'De-facto Standardization through Alliances – Lessons from Bluetooth', *Telecommunication Policy* **26** (3–4), 205–13.

Khun-Jush, J., G. Malmgren, P. Schramm and J. Torner (2000), 'Overview and Performance of HiperLAN Type 2', paper presented at IEEE Vehicular Technology Conference at Tokyo, Japan.

Kiessling, T. and Y. Blondeel (1998), 'The EU Regulatory Framework in Telecommunications', *Telecommunication Policy* **22** (7), 571–92.

Klemper, P. (2002), 'How (Not) to Run Auctions: The European 3G Telecom Auctions', *European Economic Review* **46**, 829–45.

Lera, E. (2000), 'Changing Relations Between Manufacturing and Service Provision in a More Competitive Telecom Environment', *Telecommunication Policy* **24** (5), 413–37.

Lindmark, S. and O. Granstrand (1995), 'Technology and Systems Competition in Mobile Telecommunications', in D.M. Lamberton (ed.), *Beyond Competition: The Future of Telecommunications,* Amsterdam: Elsevier Science B. V.

Manninen, E. (2002), 'Quantitative Employment Effects of Product and Process Innovation: The Case of Mobile Telecommunications in Sweden', Doctoral dissertation, Department of Technology and Social Change, Linköping University, Linköping, Sweden.

Mannings, R. and G. Cosier (2001), 'Wireless Everything – Unwiring the World', *BT Technology Journal* **19** (4).

Megler, V. (2002), 'I-Mode: From Bandwidth Problem to Internet Phenomenon', *Developer Works*, February.

Mellander, C. (2000), 'Broadband – In Broad Terms', Department of Technology and Social Change working paper 227, Linköping: Department of Technology and Social Change, Linköping University.

Melody, W.H. (1999), 'Telecom Reform: Progress and Prospects', *Telecommunication Policy* **23**, 7–34.

Nilsson, M. (1999), 'Third Generation Radio Access Standards', *Ericsson Review* (3), 110–21.

Novak, L. and M. Svensson (2001), 'MMS – Building on the Success of SMS', *Ericsson Review* (3), 102–9.

O'Shea, D. (1998), 'WAP: The Sound of Data Progress?', *Telephony*, 24–5.

OECD. (1999), *Communications Outlook – 1999*, Paris: OECD.

Ovander, P., O. Castelius and Å. Erlandson (2000), '3G licenserna', *Aftonbladet*, 17 December, 6–8.

Paetsch, M. (1993), Mobile Communications in the US and Europe: Regulation, Technology and Markets, Boston/London: Artech House.

Pisjak, P. (1994), 'Interdependence Between Regulation and Technological Innovation in the Telecommunications Sector', *Technology Analysis and Strategic Management* **6** (3), 289–303.

Pohajakallio, P. (1998), 'Casting the Cellular Net', *Telecommunications* **32** (4), 47–50.

Rao, P.M. (1999), 'Convergence and Unbundling of Corporate R&D in Telecommunications: Is Software Taking the Helm?', *Telecommunication Policy* **23**, 83–93.

Rapeli, J. (1995), 'UMTS: Targets, System Concept and Standardisation in a Global Framework', *IEEE Personal Communications* **2** (1), 20–8.

Rapeli, J. (2001), 'Future Directions for Mobile Communications Business, Technology and Research', *Wireless Personal Communications* **17**, 153–73.

Samukic, A. (1998), 'UMTS Universal Mobile Telecommunications System: Development of Standards for the Third Generation', *IEEE Transactions on Vehicular Technology* **47** (4), 1099–104.

Sony Ericsson Mobile Communications (2002), 'About Us: The Company', available: http://www.sonyericsson.com/ 2002 [cited 19 May 2002].

Taylor, L. (1999), 'HIPERLAN Type 1 Technology Overview – White Paper', Sophia Antipolis: ETSI.

Temple, S.R. (1992), 'The European Telecommunications Standards Institute – Four Years On', *Electronics and Communication Engineering Journal* **4** (4), 177–81.

Urie, A., M. Streeton and C. Mourot (1995), 'An Advanced TDMA Mobile Access System for UMTS', *IEEE Personal Communications* **2** (1), 38–47.

van Damme, E. (2002), 'The European UMTS Auctions', *European Economic Review* **46**, 846–58.

WAP Forum (2002), 'WAP Forum Releases WAP 2.0 Specification for Public Review', available: http://www.wapforum.org/ 2002 [cited 19 May 2002].

Xavier, P. (1998), 'The Licensing of Telecommunication Suppliers', *Telecommunication Policy* **22** (6), 483–92.

Öhrlings-Coopers & Lybrand (1998), *Internetmarknaden i Sverige*, Stockholm: National Post and Telecom Agency, available: http://www.pts.se/Aktuellt/final. pdf [cited 6 June, 1999].

5. Data Communication: Satellite and TV Subsystems

Bent Dalum

1. INTRODUCTION

The telecommunications sectoral system of innovation consists of several highly related segments, which have escalated over time, due to the increasing convergence of basic technologies, especially digitization of signals. Some segments act as substitutes, others are complementary, and these roles may change over time. The development of each segment is often mutually dependent; and all are heavily influenced by trends in generic technologies put forward by the semiconductor and computer industries.

The focus of this chapter is on satellite communications related to telecommunications networks, whether wireless or wired. The emergence of satellite communications networks was, however, not only influenced by demand for long-distance telecommunications. Efforts to land man on the moon triggered large investments in space technology and made a satellite-based communication system a necessity. Later, the main economic stimulus was a rapidly increasing demand for broadcasting TV over long distances.

Satellite communication systems may either be directly linked to or supplement 'ordinary' telecommunications networks. The systems are based on communications satellites, which technically may be combined in various configurations and managed in different economic and institutional contexts. A communications satellite is basically a microwave repeater station revolving around the earth in a specified orbit.[1] Satellite communications are, as telecommunications in general, focused on handling – sending, transmitting, receiving, etc. – electromagnetic signals, in this case radio waves. Usually the latter are called microwaves when the frequency is larger than 1 GHz. Many basic physical laws apply, whether we focus on satellite communications or terrestrial mobile communications (mobile phones). The latter term refers to a

[1] For an introduction to various technical and institutional characteristics, see Elbert (1999).

telecommunications system based on an infrastructure divided into hexagons (a 'cellular' configuration) with a 'base station' in the centre. The latter consists of an antenna and 'box' of electronic devices creating the connection between wireless signals and the traditional wirelined telecommunications systems. This structure is knit together by large 'public switches', which basically can be compared with huge mainframe computers. While terrestrial mobile telephony signals are transmitted near the surface of the earth and require a large number of base stations distributed on the physical landscape, the number of 'earth stations' that satellite communications require depends on the configuration of the satellites. If there are very few satellites the earth stations may consist of large telescope antennas, while direct-to-home satellite TV (DTH) may require only very small 'dishes' on each house.

The basic principles for handling the signals, e.g., principles of 'modulation', may have a good deal in common with various subsystems of telecommunications. Abbreviations such as time division multiple access (TDMA) – and later code division multiple access (CDMA) – entered the vocabulary of satellite as well as mobile communications two decades ago. Such duplications in the knowledge base imply interchanges in labour markets for engineers, scientists and technicians. Skilled workers may move between the subsystems without excessively large transition costs. The same kind of phenomenon may apply to overlaps in wirelined and mobile communications. Fixed wireless access (FWA) technologies may act as substitutes for high-speed Internet connections, e.g., asymmetric digital subscriber line (ADSL) equipment. Diffusion of this technology may be hampered by the incumbent wirelined telecommunications operators, and new solutions such as FWA may enter the market.

One way to better understand the dynamic development of the entire telecommunications innovation system is to focus on the co-evolution and complementarities of the different subsystems. The 1990s and early 2000s have witnessed dramatic examples of commercial failures in the satellite communications industry, caused by significantly underestimating the vigorous growth of cellular mobile communications. The establishment of a de facto world standard for European second-generation mobile system (GSM) – and even more clearly in the case of the coming third-generation UMTS (universal mobile telecommunications systems) standard – was not foreseen by the forces behind the huge global mobile satellite systems, such as Iridium, Motorola and Boeing. The present analysis will focus on these complementarities, which are of technological as well as institutional nature.[2]

---

[2] The application of satellites for *positioning* purposes has not been treated in this context. The opening of the US global positioning satellite (GPS) system for commercial use after the Gulf War in 1991 has been the main carrier of many new types of business, some of which are linked

2. SATELLITE COMMUNICATION TECHNOLOGIES AND INSTITUTIONS AT THE GLOBAL LEVEL

There are two main configuration principles of the satellite communication systems. They may revolve around the earth in a fixed orbit in the plane of the equator. The simplest system covering almost all locations consists of three satellites revolving around the equator once per 24 hours, each separated by 120 degrees of longitude. Such a configuration is called a geo-stationary earth orbit system, or GEO. The 24–hour restriction defines GEO satellites to re-volve with an altitude around 36 000 km, which sets restrictions on techni-cally feasible solutions. The circular orbit is not stable over time; there is a 'natural' and accumulating propensity to deviate from this 'clean' kind of orbit. The inclination of the satellite increases over time; some energy is re-quired to keep the satellites on track.

The other main group of systems is termed non-GEO, and is confined to revolution periods shorter than 24 hours, which make altitudes shorter than 36 000 km possible. By increasing the number of satellites, global coverage is possible with much shorter altitudes, which is important for the technical pos-sibilities of decreasing the size of terminal equipment – a feature of signifi-cant importance for demand. Two main groups on non-GEO systems are usually distinguished, depending on distance from the earth. *LEO* is a con-figuration of low orbit satellites at altitudes between 500 and 1000 km and with an orbit period (i.e., one trip around the globe) of slightly less than two hours. *MEO* consists of medium orbit satellites with an altitude around 10 000 km and an orbit period around 6 hours.

The satellite communications field emerged in the late 1950s. The launch of Sputnik in 1957 accelerated demand for space activities in the western world, communications included. Military efforts through large government-sponsored programmes were the main drivers behind early technological de-velopments. In 1959 Hughes Aircraft developed the first prototype GEO sat-ellite (SYNCOM) to be launched by NASA, the US National Aeronautics and Space Administration. In 1963 the first operational GEO satellite (SYNCOM II) to provide intercontinental communications was launched. The Kennedy administration also encouraged and created a regulatory framework for civil-

---

to telecommunications. Such diverse areas as integration of truck fleet management by transport companies and taxis with mobile communications, application in precision agriculture, etc., have emerged. The influence of these technologies is, however, touched upon in section 5 on maritime communications. At the institutional level a major EU initiative, the Galileo project, is still under consideration as a counterpart to (but compatible with) the US Navstar GPS system. If realized, there will be three positioning systems based on satellites, including the Russian GLONASS. For an overview see OECD (2000: Chapter 8).

ian use of satellites. The Communications Satellite Corporation (COMSAT) was set up in 1962 as a private company to organize service provision.

To initiate an internationally workable communications system, in 1964 the US government and COMSAT established INTELSAT, which in 1973 formally became the predominant global satellite communications operator (INTELSAT 1999). INTELSAT started operations with the Early Bird satellite in 1965 and the first global satellite communications system was established in 1969. These initiatives were very much driven by the NASA (National Aeronautics and Space Administration) Apollo project of landing man on the moon. The integration of military demand and the large commercial potential of transmitting TV signals globally was visibly demonstrated when the entire western world watched Neil Armstrong's first step on the moon in 1969 on their TV screens at home.

Satellite technology was fundamentally dependent on the development of the launch carrier 'vehicles', i.e., on rocket and aviation technology. During the emerging phase of satellite communications in the 1960s the quest for bringing a manned spacecraft to land on the moon gave an enormous boost to the industry. As has been the case in the computer and semiconductor industries demand gradually moved from being primarily of military nature to become more driven by dynamics of the non-military sector. INTELSAT launched a series of satellites during the late 1960s and onwards (until now series I-VIII) for telephone and TV links.

In 1984 INTELSAT Business Service was introduced for private communications networks typically used by multinational corporations. The 1980s also saw the flourishing of US TV networks using satellite communications as a complement to their domestic cable infrastructure, such as CNN, Home Box Office (HBO) and Disney Channel. New satellite operators emerged in the US, such as PanAmSat in 1984 to be merged with Hughes in 1995. Another private US operator, Orion, emerged in 1982 involving some European firms in joint ventures, such as British Aerospace and more recently the French Matra. In general the 1980s was a decade of industry expansion, fuelled largely by the boost of military activities, not least space oriented, created by the Reagan administration.

The dismantling of the AT&T monopoly in 1985 by the US antitrust authorities also gave a boost to the 'domestic' US satellite communications sector. The split-up of AT&T into seven regional Baby-Bells and a long-distance company (preserving the AT&T brand name), which gradually experienced competition from other players, gave large US companies an impetus to use satellite communications, even for their domestic communications networks (as was the case for the large department store chain Wal-Mart). The fragmented character of the new set-up for the US domestic telecommunications system from the mid-1980s appeared to encourage application of satellite communications-based solutions for intrafirm communications networks, even domestically.

During the 1990s TV transmission continued to be a major driving force for INTELSAT activities. The emerging digitization of the cable/satellite based TV networks has, however, opened the way for increasing applications of this infrastructure to non-TV data communications. Measured as shares of revenue the profile of the present INTELSAT business is grouped in three main segments, serviced by a total of 19 GEO satellites. Maintaining and expanding corporate networks represented 25 per cent of INTELSAT activities in 1999; and this segment is considered to have a high growth potential. Revenue from satellite broadcasting of TV amounted to nearly 20 per cent; this segment had been larger, before the spin-off of many TV contracts to an independent company, New Skies Satellites N.V., at the end of 1998. The largest segment, 45 per cent, represented the 'international carrier market' for interconnection of public switched voice and data networks; this field, however, is characterized as 'mature'.

When INTELSAT was founded its members consisted of representatives from national governments. This structure is currently changing. Previously governments were represented by their telecommunications regulating bodies and/or the national telecommunications operators, which in most countries acted in a highly co-ordinated manner. The deregulation and privatization of many public service provider monopolies has required a change in the organization of international bodies, such as INTELSAT. The decision rules were formalized in a treaty, based on consensus decision making among 144 governments and nearly 300 authorized 'customers' in 210 countries.[3] INTELSAT was privatized during 2001, with previous telecommunications service providers becoming shareholders, and this was supplemented by a stock exchange listing (an initial public offering).

While INTELSAT has the role of an umbrella for all satellite operators, the necessary global regulation of telecommunications at large has been co-ordinated by the International Telecommunications Union (ITU), which has been a specialized agency under the auspices of the United Nations since 1947.[4] ITU was founded in 1865 because it was necessary to co-ordinate telegraph procedures across borders, since the first systems were nationally based and could not communicate internationally.

ITU has constantly adapted to the new technologies developed and at the same time has been a central institution in forming them. After the breakthrough of, initially completely unregulated, sound broadcasting (consumer

---

[3] Based on INTELSAT data from November 2000.
[4] A brief summary of the ITU history can be seen at http://www.itu.int (ITU 2002).

radio) at improvised studios of the Marconi Company in the US in 1920, the International Radio Consultative Committee (CCIR) was created as an ITU body in 1927. Marconi has been the leading innovator in the wireless communications field since the turn of the 20th century. The first two decades of the 20th century were focused on maritime communication, not least for the British and German marines.

As radio frequencies naturally became a scarce good during the 1920s international regulation became a simple necessity. ITU managed through CCIR to allocate frequencies for the existing wireless services at the time: fixed, maritime, aeronautical (emerging demand from aeroplanes), broadcasting and amateurs with the launch of Sputnik and plans for the first western GEOs to be launched in the early 1960s, CCIR set up a study group for dealing with space radiocommunication in 1959. That resulted in the First World Radiocommunication Conference in Geneva (the site for ITU's headquarters) in 1963 to deal with allocation of frequencies for the various emerging space services.

The continuously fast-paced technological developments in various fields relevant to telecommunications has constantly required an adaptation of the ITU structure. A major reorganization was implemented in 1993. The activities of satellite communications, broadcasting as well as mobile communications have been merged into the ITU Radiocommunications Section (ITU-R) in order to create an institutional framework that can match the increasing degree of convergence between these technologies.[5]

3. EUROPEAN SATELLITE COMMUNICATIONS DEVELOPMENT – EUTELSAT

A European satellite organization was initiated by the formation of EUTELSAT in 1977 as a regional service provider, but with the explicit aim of supporting an indigenous European manufacturing base for the space industry. The European Space Agency (ESA), formally founded in 1985 by 17 Western European countries, launched the first EUTELSAT satellite in 1983. EUTELSAT, based in Paris, is a treaty-based organization with 48 member

---

[5] The fast development of the Internet in the 1990s has raised new challenges for ITU. ITU-T takes care of 'telecommunications networks'. New co-ordination requirements are emerging especially with third-generation mobile communications systems which make integration of mobile and satellite communication with the Internet possible. Under the umbrella of IMT-2000 considerable effort is going into harmonizing as much as possible the various standards of 3G (UMTS, CDMA2000, etc.).

countries.[6] With 18 GEOs[7] in operation EUTELSAT has entered the group of the largest international operators.

Its core business is transmission of TV and radio broadcasting with a total of 750 digital and analogue TV channels and 450 radio channels at the end of year 2000.[8] This generated 80 per cent of EUTELSAT's revenue in 1999. Twenty per cent of EUTELSAT's capacity was in 1999 used for a range of broadband services, including Internet backbone and access as well as corporate networks. In comparing the profiles of the INTELSAT and EUTELSAT fields of business it is, however, important to recognize that the former is intended to be a truly global – although US-dominated – organization. EUTELSAT cannot be considered a direct challenger to that position. It is rather a parallel to the domestic US situation, where COMSAT initially was the national counterpart. The EUTELSAT capacity and revenue profile is more in line with the operators of the US domestic market. According to Elbert (1999) two-thirds of the domestic US satellite capacity is occupied by TV transmission.

Given that the size of each participating European country is small, co-operation is essential to create a regional player as part of the international systems of satellite operators, which INTELSAT co-ordinates. Aside from radio and TV transmission, however, there is no doubt that European activities have been directly aimed at encouraging and supporting the fragmented European space industry. The French government and French firms have been especially active in the entire value chain of the industry – from satellite construction (Alcatel and Aerospatiale), building and operating the launching vehicles (Ariane rockets from Arianspace) to design of the communication networks (Alcatel).

As with INTELSAT, EUTELSAT is in the process of being privatized. By mid-2001 the structure will be divided into two tiers: a private company based in Paris and an intergovernmental regulating organization. The general liberalization of telecommunications services has also influenced the organizational set-up in Europe. While the US set-up was dominated by private companies from the beginning, this has become the case in Europe to an increasing extent.

---

[6] Based on December 2000 data. See www.eutelsat.com. Membership is still growing, especially from Eastern European countries.

[7] These are so-called Ku-band satellites operating in the 11–14 GHz frequency interval.

[8] Of the 81 million homes in Europe, Asia and Africa that receive signals form the EUTELSAT's five HOT BIRD satellites, 58 million are connected to cable networks and 23 million are equipped with small receivers and 'dishes'. See EUTELSAT *Annual Report 1999*.

4. DATA COMMUNICATIONS THROUGH SATELLITE AND CABLE TV NETWORKS

The strong French position in satellite launching in the late 1980s was temporarily bolstered in the aftermath of the severe accident in the US launching industry with the destruction of the manned Challenger space shuttle in 1986. But the entrance of new players for satellite operators in European consumer TV led to inroads by US space firms. Société Européenne des Satellites (SES) of Luxembourg, founded in 1985, was the first private satellite operator in Europe. SES is operating the Astra satellites, which were launched in 1988, and in 1999 it had eight satellites in operation. Since 1995 the Astra satellites have been oriented towards digital satellite broadcasting. The media mogul Rupert Murdoch's News Corporation's Sky TV marked in 1987 the start, in a European context, of the so-called DTH principle of broadcasting TV directly to individual receivers (i.e., small 'dishes'). In 1990 Sky was merged with the British Satellite Broadcasting venture as B-Sky-B. These companies opened for US deliveries of satellites from Hughes (the dominant US firm in the industry) and RCA. The organizational set-up for radio and TV broadcasting has, not surprisingly, in itself been of importance for the choice of technologies.

As early as 1977 ITU organized a World Administrative Radio Conference (WARC) on DTH at a time when only the national broadcasting company NHK in Japan had initiated such a project. The assignments of Ku-band channels and GEO positions were decided. The initial DTH projects failed in the US in the early 1980s. The real rush in DTH TV in the US came when some of the large cable TV networks (CNN, HBO and Disney) sought to increase their existing revenues by adding 'backyard dish subscribers' in remote areas without cables. In that perspective the satellite-based TV was a supplement to the cable TV networks. TV primarily based on DTH first became a major business in the US with the establishment of DIRECTV, a subsidiary of Hughes, in 1994. The European development was, surprisingly, in front of the US.

On the Asian scene, Murdoch's News Corporation has also been very active in the 1990s by taking over the Hong Kong-based Star TV covering various Asian countries, except Japan. Along with Japan's NHK, the Hughes-owned DIRECTV is among the leading players in that market.

What makes these TV networks relevant to data communications is the emerging digitization of the TV signals as well as the transmission technologies whether they are based on cables, satellites, more traditional terrestrial networks or, as often is the case, various combinations of these. Application of digital technology in broadcasting has increased significantly because of progress in compressing technologies, developed by the computer industry. According to Henten et al. (2000) there are basically four categories of digitized TV:

- low definition TV (LDTV) requires 2 Mbit/s. Same quality as VHS (ordinary videotape quality);
- standard definition TV (SDTV) requires 5–6 Mbit/s. Same quality as analogue PAL TV, which is the ordinary TV standard in Denmark;
- enhanced definition TV (EDTV) requires 8 Mbit/s; and
- high definition TV (HDTV) requires 20 Mbit/s. High resolution TV on big screens.

Europe has chosen SDTV as a standard for digitized TV, while the US has chosen HDTV in the first round for terrestrial broadcasting. Digitized TV will make it possible to transmit TV over the Internet leading to convergence from both sides – so to speak.

Another factor is the digitization of the existing cable TV networks. The cable operators have been increasing the capacity of the existing networks and preparing for the coming digitized TV by digitizing their networks. In Denmark the two largest cable operators are Tele Denmark and Swedish Telia (STOFA) – i.e., the two previous monopoly telecommunications service providers in Denmark and Sweden, respectively. According to Henten et al. (2000), in mid-1999 1.1 million households in Denmark had at least technically – the option of using digitized telecommunications services through these cable TV networks. The number of households with a TV (nearly 100 per cent) in Denmark in 1998 was 2.4 million of which 1.3 million had access to cable TV. Approximately 50 per cent of all Danish households apparently already have potential access to high-speed data communication. According to Henten et al. (2000) around 30 per cent of the US households had the same option in 1998 – either through cable or satellite.

EUTELSAT has carried digital video based (DVB) TV since 1996 for such broadcasters as Canal+, the BBC, RAI, Viacom and Bloomberg. EUTELSAT claims to have 'spearheaded' the development of the DVB standard by being the first operator to introduce an on-board processing technology called SKYPLEX.[9] The standardization efforts for digital TV in Europe led to the formation of the DVB consortium in 1993, which at present comprises nearly 300 broadcasters, manufacturers, network operators, software developers and regulatory bodies in 35 countries.

In the autumn of 2000 this consortium released a DVB-MHP standard for so-called multimedia home platforms.[10] This standard has been adopted by the European Telecommunications Standards Institute (ETSI). The latter is the main EU body for standardization in telecommunications, established in

---

[9] Developed in co-operation with the European Space Agency and built by the Italian space company Alenia.
[10] For further details, see http://www.dvb.org (DVB 2000).

1987, which has been highly successful in creating the second-generation GSM and third-generation UMTS standards for mobile communications at the European level.[11] From a data communication perspective the development of such so-called 'set-top boxes' may facilitate high-speed Internet access in remote areas. They may also represent an alternative solution if incumbent telecommunications operators are too reluctant in making high-speed access available. In addition, they make it easier for people without computer skills to reach the Internet through their TV screen. Telecommunications convergence can in this context be illustrated by a recent (September 2000) introduction of a DVB-MHP set-top box by Nokia, initially destined for the German cable and satellite TV market.[12]

The importance of the TV networks lies in the potential but not yet used capacity for data communications (other than TV). The digitization of these networks, which in many EU countries is at a fairly advanced stage, *and* the coming introduction of digital TV, which at the moment is primarily at the experimental stage,[13] open an enormous capacity for Internet applications. The technical possibilities are within reach, but one main barrier appears to be the lack of dynamism among incumbent telecommunications operators to introduce high-speed Internet access to consumers and firms. If the cause is that the revenues of the existing – slow – Internet traffic are very high, then increased competition from alternative suppliers and/or technologies (such as FWA, DTH TV combined with set-top boxes) may be recommendable solutions.[14]

5. THE MARITIME SECTOR – INMARSAT

The need to co-ordinate the application of satellite communication at sea for ship management as well as distress and safety purposes led in 1979 to the establishment of INMARSAT, the International Maritime Satellite Organisation. The organization is based in London and refers to the UN International Maritime Organisation (IMO) and the ITU. It operates a system of nine GEOs and 40 land earth stations (LESs) in 31 countries (INMARSAT 2002).

---

[11] The two most outstanding European success stories in the post-war history of telecommunications.

[12] The product to be released before summer 2001 is based on the IP (Internet protocol) standard, Linux operating system, a Mozilla browser in co-operation with Intel. It is to be a combination of Internet access, ADSL-based 'streaming' and digital TV. Whether the product is successful remains to be seen; the point is to illustrate convergence among different technologies embedded in fairly realistic products rather than figments of science fiction.

[13] In Denmark terrestrial field trials are at the early stages, while Sweden is more advanced.

[14] And not just ideological exercising, as is often seen in debates of how to manage general infrastructure projects.

Until around 1990 ships depended basically on high frequency (either VHF or UHF) radiocommunications equipment. From 1992 and before the start of the new millennium all ships above a certain size (300 gross tons) were obliged, according to an IMO decision, to have installed a global maritime distress and safety system which used the INMARSAT C-band system as their 'workhorse'.[15]

The organization has, however, also managed to establish the only mobile communication system, which can provide service (voice, fax, e-mail) globally. The Mini-M system is operating by the INMARSAT 2 and 3 satellites, of which the latter is the most recent generation. The necessary terminal equipment has the size of a laptop computer and weighs around 2 kg. The 'screen' on the 'laptop' is the antenna and the user may need to move outside and change the direction of the terminal to get connected, but the service is highly reliable.

Although the Mini-M system is able to perform data communication (other than voice) the speed is quite slow – up to 64 Kbit/s. The future perspective is the service provided by the next generation INMARSAT 4 satellites. Their launch is scheduled for 2004. The new system may thus be in operation parallel to the third-generation mobile communications system, which will start in Europe one or two years before but probably will not be wide spread until around 2004. The planned system will have a maximum of 423 Kbit/s. Third-generation mobile communications are planned to support data transmission in the range of 144 Kbit/s to 2 Mbit/s. The maximum rate can be reached in low mobility indoor environments.

On this basis, it is not completely out of touch to say that Mini-M services may very well have a considerable, but complementary, market – even if 3G mobile communications were to be an outstanding success. However, behind this statement are some very hard paid experiences for the satellite communications industry, INMARSAT included. The great visions of the global mobile satellite systems (GMSSs) of the 1990s have suffered a hard landing (although *not literally* at the time of writing).

6. GRANDIOSE SATELLITE PHONE MEGA PROJECTS OF THE LATE 1990s – THAT FAILED

At the beginning of the 1990s as many as four large consortia announced plans for mega projects in satellite communications, based on either LEOs or MEOs, which both (but decreasingly) require a rather large number of satellites in operation. At that time the US was the only existing real superpower. The Soviet

---

[15] User no. 50 000, an Australian tuna vessel, was registered at the end of March 2000.

system had collapsed and the Gulf War was won. The considerable investments by the Reagan administration in such systems as the Strategic Defense Initiative (SDI or 'Star Wars') was to be scaled down – the 'peace dividend' was to be reaped. In that context the space industry and other industries strongly oriented towards defence experienced difficult economic conditions. Added to this context was a lack of vision of the coming substantial growth for second-generation mobile communications systems, not least caused by the deliberate European effort to create the common GSM standard.

In this context several large, mainly space industry-driven consortia launched huge GMSS projects, characterized as satellite phone systems compatible with terrestrial public mobile phone systems. The vision for the longer term was not just transmission of voice data, but in principle e-mail, fax, Internet access, video, etc.

Motorola and Boeing were the first to publish their mega ambitions in terms of the Iridium project in 1990. The Iridium configuration consisted of 66 LEO satellites with an altitude around 1 000 km.[16] The satellites pass the single user only every few minutes. For the user the satellites may, in a sense, have the same kind of function as the base stations of a terrestrial cellular mobile phone system – users may shift from one satellite to another in the middle of a message without noticing. The terminals were planned to be fairly small and multimode – i.e., able to switch from Iridium to terrestrial mobile communications systems. When Iridium started to operate in late 1998 the terminal was triple mode, including GSM and D-AMPS (digital advanced mobile phone system) (Motorola developed the US second-generation mobile communications system). Investments were in the area of $5–5.5 billion.

Table 5.1 contains an overview of the three GMSSs, as their consortia perceived the situation in December 1998. The term 'dual mode' indicates an integration of satellite and mobile communications. The second LEO-based consortium was Globalstar with Loral (the major competitor to Hughes in the US satellite industry) and a group of large telecommunications operators as well as Alcatel, the French telecommunications hardware and space firm, and Dasa, the German aerospace company (then Daimler-Benz – now Daimler-Chrysler). The Globalstar configuration contains 48 LEOs. The third player was the INMARSAT spin-off ICO backed by Hughes and the Japanese NEC, with a configuration of 12 MEOs.

During the first half of 1999 both Iridium and ICO went bankrupt and Globalstar's plans were significantly adjusted downwards.[17] Iridium had never more than 63 000 subscribers, although its declared break-even point

---

[16] Originally a configuration of 77 satellites was planned, hence the name Iridium which is number 77 in the Periodic Table.
[17] Summarized in *Financial Times Survey*, 'The Business of Space Survey', 10 December 1999.

was 750 000. Severe technical problems with the system, some malfunction-ing satellites and a call rate of around $8–9 per minute added to its problems. Iridium was rescued at the end of 2000 by a former president of PanAm Air-lines. He has raised $25 million to buy the company, which has been awarded a military contract of $36 million per year for three years. Ambitions have been cut drastically. Data transmission rates will start at 2.4 Kbit/s in early 2001 and will be increased to 10 Kbit/s within half a year.

Table 5.1: Satellite phone ('dual-mode') systems, operators, prices, 1998

Systems/ operators	Launch date	Handset manufacturers	Handset prices	Cost per minute + users
Iridium/ Motorola 66 LEOs (TDMA) $5 billion	1/11 1998	Motorola (300 gram 5.5 hours talk 48 hours standby) Motorola, Kyocera ECI (maritime)	At least $3 000	$3–5 (2–8) US/Europe 4.5 Developing countries: 1–2. Break even: 750 000 (2002?)
Globalstar/ Loral + Vodaphone, France Telecom, Alcatel, Dasa, Hyundai, China Telecom 48 LEOs (CDMA) $2.6 billion	3rd quarter 1999 (32 LEOS)	Qualcomm Ericsson (Q+E $321 million + Telital $32 million)	$750–1 000	$1.25–1.50 3 million users 2002
ICO spin-off from INMARSAT 12 MEOs (TDMA) $4.5 billion	Late 2000 (First launch Dec. 1998)	NEC, Samsung Mitsubishi (Initially 270,000). + Panasonic, Ericsson [NEC, Hughes + Ericsson: ICONET]	$700–1 000	$1–1.70 Max. $3 Developing countries $0.5

Notes: LEO = low earth orbit satellite. MEO = medium earth orbit satellite. Dual mode = traffic routed to terrestrial cellular systems, where roaming agreements are made. Multimode will be normal, e.g., satellite + D-AMPS/GSM.

Source: Overview given by B. Dalum at the NorCOM association for wireless communications firms and research institutes NOVI, Aalborg, 8 December 1998.

In September 1998 Globalstar lost 12 satellites on a malfunctioning Ukrainian Zenit launcher. In mid-2000 all the Globalstar satellites were func-tioning due to the Franco-Russian Stårcem venture, which managed to use an old but workable Soyuz satellite launcher. The Globalstar system thus started to operate during 2000 with service in 25 countries via 11 gateways. Global-star has demonstrated a capacity to carry Internet data at 9.6 Kbit/s; but it was not yet in service by summer 2000. In September 2000 it was announced that the company was testing low-cost broadband services plus Internet and e-mail at speeds up to 200 Kbit/s, and it had plans to go to 1 Mbit/s in 2003 with a new generation of terminals.[18] Geographically, operation has focused on areas where there are no terrestrial mobile communications systems available, which scales the amount of potential customers significantly down compared to the data presented in table 5.1.

The ICO consortium, spun off from INMARSAT in 1995, went bankrupt in 1999 at the same time as Iridium. In 2000 it was taken over by Teledisc, which originally was the fourth and most ambitious of all the consortia. The ideas of Teledisc were put forward in the early 1990s by Greg McCaw, a US pioneer of operating analogue mobile communications networks who earned a fortune by selling his network to AT&T. Teledisc was planned as a 288-LEO project that would start operations in 2002. The basic vision was Internet-in-the-sky. The other two big players were Boeing and Bill Gates. Teledisc was postponed in time, but has so far, though, chosen Motorola technology. During the bankruptcy process McCaw considered taking over Iridium, but that plan has been dropped.

'New ICO' and Teledisc are now wholly owned subsidiaries of the new ICO-Teledisc Global company. During summer 2000 plans for 'New ICO' were adjusted to start service in 2003 at the earliest with maximum rates of data transmission at 144 Kbit/s. However, these plans are still unclear.

7. THE EARLY 2000s – BUSINESS AS USUAL?

By the beginning of the new millennium the huge ambitions of the global mobile satellite systems for broadband communications had been drastically scaled down. The success of second-generation (digitized) mobile communications in the 1990s was not expected, especially in the US. Coverage of the European GSM system had been extended to a group of Asian countries as well as the emerging market economies of Russia and Eastern Europe. Data communication would reach non-negligible speeds with the so-called 2+ systems of GSM that were introduced in early 2001 in Europe. While data could be transmitted at the speed of 9.6 Kbit/s in GSM (or 2G), the new general packet radio switched (GPRS or 2.5G) solutions could offer 30 Kbit/s in late 2001. For the user this requires a new mobile phone at fairly low expense.

With third-generation mobile communications within reach in the next two or three years, the context for GMSS will be even more clearly defined as

---

[18] See *Financial Times Survey* 'Telecommunications', 20 September 2000.

complementary. The UMTS variant of 3G has been chosen by Japan and Europe. Recently AT&T Wireless of the US announced that its 3G solution will be based on W-CDMA, which is the UMTS solution. The latter decision was announced shortly after NTT DoCoMo had acquired a large shareholder position in AT&T Wireless. NTT DoCoMo, part of the previous Japanese monopoly operator NTT, started operation of the first UMTS-based system in the world in Japan in late 2001. Third-generation mobile communications may therefore become dominated by UMTS to a significantly larger degree than has been the case for GSM in 2G.[19]

Satellite communications will thus preserve a role as a complementary transmission channel in areas with weak coverage of terrestrial mobile communications networks. These areas are by no means small, but the purchasing power of their citizens is limited. However, satellite communications appear to have a prominent role in maritime and aircraft communications through the INMARSAT services, which also include a highly esteemed service for the professional market in a 'closed' mobile communications context (Mini-M). The latter has evolved gradually without being 'contaminated' with the huge ambitions of the failed GMSS ventures. The future role of the GMSSs is difficult to judge; but they are no doubt playing against hard odds. The final area where satellite communications will continue to play a significant role is as a carrier of data in broadcasting networks.

REFERENCES

DVB (2002), Digital Video Broadcasting, available: http://www.dvb.org.

Elbert, B.R. (1999), *Introduction to Satellite Communication*, Boston and London: Artech House.

EUTELSAT (1999) *Annual Report 1999*, available: http://www.eutelsat.com.

Financial Times Survey 'The Business of Space Survey', 10 December 1999.

Financial Times Survey 'Telecommunications', 20 September 2000.

Henten, A., K.E. Skouby and R. Tadayoni (2000), 'Fremtidens broadcasting – marked, public service og finansiering', ('The Future of Broadcasting – Market, Public Service and Finance'), Copenhagen: Centre for Tele-Information, Technical University of Denmark.

INMARSAT (2002), available: http://www.inmarsat.org.

INTELSAT (1999), *Annual Report 1999*, available: http://www.intelsat.org.

International Telecommunications Union (2002), available: http://www.itu.int.

OECD (2000), *Communications Outlook*, Paris: OECD.

---

[19] The major competing 3G standard is Qualcomm's CDMA2000 with a strong (but diminishing) foothold in the US. In South Korea, CDMA has been preferred for 2G mobile communications; but the results of the 3G auction published in December 2000 indicate that UMTS (W-CDMA) may become important, if not dominant, in South Korea as well.

6. The Internet Services Industry: Sectoral Dynamics of Innovation and Production

Nicoletta Corrocher

1. INTRODUCTION

The rate of technical change characterizing the telecommunications and computer industries has been a major driver in transforming a closed, stable system into an open and dynamic one. The introduction of a cluster of new technologies over the last twenty years brought dramatic changes within the telecommunications system and the economy as a whole. Significant technological breakthroughs, culminating with the Internet, created a new environment characterized by the convergence of knowledge and competencies, as well as industries and users, previously belonging to separate sectors.

In addition to technological change, the new industry has experienced major regulatory changes worldwide. A wave of privatizations in the 1980s, the recent deregulation of the European telecommunications industry and a process of liberalization initiated by the 1997 World Trade Organization agreement are driving an increasing globalization of telecommunications carriers and stimulating a high entry rate of new operators. This process increased competition not only between companies already existing in the industry but also between start-ups and incumbents previously belonging to different sectors. At the same time, the market is starting to consolidate, as shown by the increasing number of mergers and acquisitions, partnerships and strategic alliances, now occurring around the world.

A new multimedia industry has emerged characterized by a specific knowledge base and learning processes, as well as a significant degree of interactions between firms, non-firm organizations and institutions. It is possible to identify a sectoral system of the multimedia sector as a collective outcome of the interaction among its various elements. In this respect, one of the major features of this sectoral system is the co-evolution between technical change, organizational structure and institutional framework. Institutional pressures from outside the traditional system have supported the development and diffusion of new technologies, products and services. The process of technological convergence and the transformation of the regulatory framework have been responsible for a high degree of turbulence in the market. Knowledge boundaries and geographical boundaries are blurring and this phenomenon is driving the emergence of global-scale competition.

However, the spatial dimension maintains great importance and national factors still play a relevant role in affecting the overall dynamics of the system. The networking nature of this sector affects both the industrial dynamics (in terms of entry/exit, growth and performance of firms) and the innovative activity of different operators. As convergence proceeds, it is poss-ible not only to offer new products and services but also to find new and innovative ways to provide existing ones.[1] We know from theory that the transformation of sectors may involve the emergence of new clusters (of technologies and products, industries and users) that cut across several sectors (Malerba 2000). In the case of the Internet industry, integration between the software sector, the telecommunications sector and the media and broadcasting industries has occurred.

This chapter considers the convergence and merger of previously separated knowledge and technologies and the new relationships among different types of users, firms with different specializations, non-firm organizations and sectoral institutions. The emphasis is on the innovation processes and sectoral dynamics of the Internet services industry, where services include both access and content. Before analysing the specificity of the Internet service industry's sectoral system (sections 4 and 5), two introductory sections are provided. The first (section 2) concerns the process of convergence in the communications industry, while the second (section 3) illustrates the technical and economic characteristics of the Internet. These sections are important for understanding sectoral dynamics in the industry, in that they analyse the knowledge base of the sector and the economic consequences of the relevant technology. Section 6 provides a view on the US and Japan. Concluding remarks are made in section 7.

2. TECHNOLOGICAL CONVERGENCE IN THE TELECOMMUNICATIONS INDUSTRY

The pattern of technical change in the telecommunications industry has been characterized by two successive processes: first, a fragmentation of the under-

---

[1] Video service over telephone networks, Internet access over cellular telephones and voice applications over the Internet constitute some important examples of this trend.

lying technologies (the separation of the radio spectrum for use in one-way broadcasting and two-way telephony); second, a phenomenon of technological convergence (Kavassalis et al. 1996; Rabeau 1999). As far as the latter is concerned, it is important to distinguish between two separate processes, which differ both from a technological and an economic perspective.

The first process relates to the convergence between information and communication technologies (ICTs), which occurred in the 1980s and allowed for linking computers that were based on different operating systems. This process was furthered by the digital electronics revolution, which brought about radical transformations in telecommunications equipment. Much of this innovation was autonomous and could be integrated into the network if it met compatibility standards. In some cases, however, the innovation was systemic and required substantial investments throughout the network, as with common channel interfacing signalling (Davies 1996; Kavassalis et al. 1996).

The second phenomenon identifies what is usually referred to as 'convergence,' i.e., the convergence between ICTs and broadcasting/audiovisual technologies. This second process occurred in the 1990s and constituted the starting point of the multimedia revolution. Four major factors have characterized this convergence. First, the digitization of all types of information, which allows any type of signal – voice, data and video – to be represented by the same unit (bit).[2] Second, the compression of numeric broadcasting signals, which reduces redundancy so that less bandwidth than before is necessary for the same amount of information or, put another way, more information than before can be transmitted over the same bandwidth. Third, the introduction of packet-switching technology, which allows for breaking information into packets that share the same network and making efficient use of existing bandwidth. Finally, the emergence of the transmission protocol, TCP/IP (transmission control protocol/Internet protocol), as the universal standard for communication between computers based upon different local protocols. The combination of these factors has generated a new technological paradigm, which has revolutionized the telecommunications system and changed its economic rationales. Even more, we could arguably say that these phenomena have paved the way for a new 'techno-economic regime,' usually referred to as 'the digital economy' (David 1999).

Before providing a more detailed description of the Internet from a technological and economic perspective, we need to further consider the notion of convergence. When conceptualizing this industry's innovation processes, it is possible to talk about convergence in three different ways: convergence of

---

[2] This process implies the transformation of any type of information into a binary number.

voice, video and data applications; convergence of service providers; and convergence of customer premises equipment (Katz 1996; Sears 1996).

The emergence of a common Internet protocol (IP) for the implementation of different applications is a well-established reality in today's telecommunications.[3] Although many services still run on the traditional public switched telecommunications network (PSTN), increasingly value-added applications of voice, video and data are exploiting the new network. This is largely invisible from the end user's perspective, although the existence of multimedia services is an indirect manifestation of this phenomenon. At the same time, there is convergence of service providers – to be investigated in detail in the next sections: companies belonging to traditionally distinct industries have entered one another's domains, offering integrated solutions and products.[4]

The convergence of customer premises equipment is more complex. Some customer premises offer packages of services that were previously provided on different appliances, but the phenomenon is at an early stage, its potential is still not clear and will likely depend on the diffusion of different appliances in different countries. Third-generation cellular phones, for example, offer Internet connection and narrow-band services. Similarly, desktop computers can be used to make telephone calls or to watch a video, and set-top boxes are becoming an alternative device for Internet access.[5] In this respect the demand for Internet services and Internet appliances will play a significant role. Users differ remarkably among one another, and their preferences together with firm strategies are going to determine the market for the diffusion of Internet appliances. Furthermore, in sectors with heterogeneous demand and competing products and technologies, network externalities may arise as well as a very fragmented market structure (Shapiro and Varian 1999).

Beyond technical differences between various appliances, which seem likely to favour their co-existence more than the emergence of a single solution, there are strong uncertainties over the rate of adoption and acceptance of a universal, single display for voice, data and video. The demand for integrated multimedia applications is still at an early stage, despite the impressive diffusion of the Internet, as well as the adoption of single Internet appliances for voice, video and data. In this respect Europe is still far behind the US, and within Europe, there are significant inter-country differences. It is more likely that in the future

---

[3] However, an alternative packet-switched transmission protocol, the asynchronous transfer mode (ATM), is currently utilized by some telecommunications companies in combination with IP.
[4] This is shown by the activity of major telecommunications and cable operators in the provision of Internet services and by the role of software companies in the field of voice applications and Internet consulting services.
[5] A recent and quite interesting phenomenon is the possibility of accessing the Internet through the consoles of video games.

there will be a variety of customer premises equipment that integrate with one another and with the network. This scenario would be consistent with a 'system of systems' configuration of the new industry (Noam 1994; Davies 1996).

3. THE INTERNET AS A MAJOR TECHNOLOGICAL DISCONTINUITY

Until the advent of the Internet, the telecommunications service industry had not experienced major technological disruptions and the process of innovation had been highly cumulative. Even after the advent of digitization, the structure of the telecommunications system remained hierarchical and vertically integrated, with network resources controlled at a central level. Technical change was incremental, and even when innovations were more radical – such as the introduction of computerized switching technologies or the development of fibre optics networks and advanced transmission techniques (e.g., asymmetrical digital subscriber line: ADSL) – they tended to reinforce the existing monopolistic structure. The development of the integrated services digital network (ISDN) constitutes the major example of an innovation developed to protect the interests of incumbent operators (Mansell 1993; Davies 1996).

The Internet, however, can be perceived as a major technological discontinuity generating 'creative destruction' and modifying the existing technological trajectory (Noam 1994; Davies 1996; Kavassalis et al. 1996). One important outcome of this revolution has been the emergence of an open network architecture, with modularized components and distributed intelligence. Two technological breakthroughs have contributed to qualify the Internet as a new technological paradigm: the introduction of packet-switching technologies and the development of the Internet protocol (Einhorn 1996).

3.1. Packet-switched Networks and the Internet Protocol

The Internet is a network of networks of computers that use a common communication protocol, which enables interoperability of computer networks running on different local transmission protocols (e.g., Ethernet, Netware). The Internet's architecture is open and characterized by distributed intelligence, modularized components, interoperability and general-purpose functionality. Since this model separates components into four layers – bearer services, transport services, middleware services and applications – it allows flexibility in introducing new standards that can compete with existing ones (Sears 1996).

The Internet utilizes a packet-switching technology, by which 'packets' of information share network lines, thus optimizing the use of existing bandwidth. The development of packet-switched transmission protocols has radically changed the technical features of communication networks, bringing substantial benefits in terms of quantity of information deliverable simultaneously on the same network, but at the same time causing congestion. In packet-switched transmission protocols any type of information (data, voice or video) is broken into packets, which are sent from one computer to another in no chronological order: a 'header' on each single packet directs the routing from sender to receiver. These networks do not dedicate a path between sender and receiver; instead, each packet of information shares the available bandwidth with other packets, each with its own content and destination. In this way, different applications can run simultaneously over the same network and this generates congestion, which in turn results in low-quality service (Einhorn 1996; Babbage et al. 1997; Mason 1998).[6]

In comparison, traditional circuit-switched networks ensure fixed bandwidth constraints, pre-allocations of network resources and the establishment of an end-to-end communication path before the communication begins, which stays open during the connection. With the conventional telephony network, each conversation uses a fixed amount of bandwidth for the duration of the call, and the available bandwidth is dedicated to a call even if no information is transmitted (e.g., during silences in a voice conversation). Since circuit-switched networks dedicate a fixed portion of available bandwidth to each user, network resources are not efficiently utilized. In this way, the quality of service for the users is high, because each call has a dedicated circuit and does not share available bandwidth with other packets. It is important to underline that the problem of congestion is caused not only by the technical characteristics of the technology but also by the intense variance in Internet use, which distinguishes it from other resources subject to congestion.

Notwithstanding these problems, which are being solved through several technical and pricing mechanisms, the packet-switching technology is more efficient for variable traffic, since it aggregates data from many users and allows a higher average utilization of available network capacity. This in turn translates to better network behaviour from a provider's perspective, since information is transmitted at much lower cost than over telephone lines (Einhorn 1996; Kavassalis et al. 1996; Cawley 1997). This feature makes packet-switched networks particularly suitable for hosting multimedia applications.

The first packet-switched network was terrestrial (ARPANET), then the concept was extended to satellite and radio communications networks. The ARPANET project was developed by the Advanced Research Projects Administration (ARPA), a division of the US Department of Defense (DoD),

---

[6] The low service quality ranges from simple information delivery delays to the loss of information packets.

and its aim was to link universities with contractors working on high-tech research funded by the DoD. The TCP/IP was introduced as the standard protocol for ARPANET communications. Later, the National Science Foundation (NSF) developed the NSFNET to connect its supercomputer centres. This network provided a high-speed infrastructure for the future development of the Internet (MacKie-Mason and Varian 1998).

Technological advances interact with shifts in the existing knowledge base and changes in market structure. Technological opportunities may derive from major scientific breakthroughs in universities, or advancements in R&D, or interactions between users and suppliers (Freeman 1982; Rosenberg 1982; Lundvall 1993). Other characteristics such as the decentralized nature of knowledge and skill distribution and the kinds of firms and non-firms in possession of the requisite knowledge and skills also affect the rate of technological advance. In its early years the Internet's knowledge base was embodied in scientists and researchers working at universities and government-funded research centres, and the major source of innovation was represented by research projects jointly carried out by the DoD and academic units. As soon as the Internet was privatized and firms became involved in the sector, the main sources of knowledge became firms' R&D efforts and feedback from users and suppliers of the firms' products, services and technologies.

3.2. The Economics of the Internet

The Internet was originally characterized by a subscription-based, distance-independent 'all you can eat' tariff structure, which made the service effectively free at the margin. In order to impose some limitations on the use of the network and reduce congestion, other pricing mechanisms have been implemented, which alternatively rely upon a usage-based structure or bandwidth reservation (MacKie-Mason and Varian 1998). However, what is really valuable about the Internet is not the network itself, but the information put on the network. Unfortunately, it is still very difficult to establish a price for the information, since in this new context information is easily and freely reproducible and marginal cost cannot be used as a proper parameter for setting prices (Shapiro and Varian 1999).[7] This is why the economic sustainability of Internet services providers (ISPs) (who combine both access and content provision) is put under great pressure: because of the scarce value of the connection and the difficulty of evaluating content. Efficient utilization of available

---

[7] Nonetheless, the combination and customization of different types of information according to the users' preferences represents a significant value-added offered by the providers and could constitute the base for setting some form of pricing.

bandwidth has allowed for significant gains in transmission costs, substantially lowering the economies of scale and facilitating the entry of new operators (Clark 1996; Babbage et al. 1997; Mason 1998; OECD 1998).

The Internet's technical characteristics lead to a very flexible and competitive market, with rapid innovation, low barriers to entry and exit, and distributed costs. In contrast, the traditional PSTN leads to a vertically integrated market, with high barriers to entry and low competition. Table 6.1 illustrates these distinctions.

Table 6.1: The Internet and the PSTN: architecture and market differences

Architecture	
Internet	*PSTN*
Distributed intelligence	Centralized intelligence
Hardware dependence	Software dependence
General-purpose functionality	Optimized for voice service
Congestion problems	Guaranteed quality of service
Packet-switched transmission protocol	Circuit-switched transmission protocol
Modularized components	Integrated network
Interoperability with other networks	Limited interoperability
Market	
Internet	*PSTN*
Distributed equipment costs	Centralized equipment costs
Economies of innovation	Economies of scale
Flexible market	Vertically integrated market
Flat-rate billing	Usage-based billing
Competitive environment	Oligopoly
Low barriers to entry/exit	High barriers to entry/exit
Bottom-up development	Top-down development

Source: Sears (1996).

As the table indicates, the advantages of a vertically integrated network mostly stem from the avoidance of possible inefficiencies of local access duplication (Sears 1996; Cawley 1997). However, the development of incentive structures with respect to technology, investments and prices can solve this problem and, at the same time, allow more competition. In this context, the outcome of the competition between different networks for the provision of Internet services depends upon not only the specifications of the Internet itself but also future technological development in the old network and the characteristics of demand.

4. SECTORAL DYNAMICS IN THE PROVISION OF INTERNET SERVICES

4.1. New and Old Actors in the Internet Marketplace

In this complex sectoral system, competition is stimulated by continuous technical change, which drives the innovative entry of different companies that propose alternative business models, implement different strategies and apply innovative approaches for the processes of innovation and production. We can distinguish three types of firms in the sectoral system of the Internet service industry.

1. *Internet access providers (IAPs)*. These companies provide access to the Internet through a proprietary or leased backbone. Within this category we can include:

    - incumbent telecommunications operators;
    - new entrant telecommunications operators;
    - cable TV operators; and
    - 'pure' Internet access providers.

2. *Internet content providers (ICPs)*. This category identifies companies such as portals and specialized content providers (news, financial sites). ICPs include traditional media and publishing companies as well as new firms. Usually these operators derive their revenues from advertising, but sometimes they can charge a fee for the provision of content, especially if the content is highly customized and/or specialized. Within this group it is also possible to include e-commerce companies, i.e., new companies that have developed an activity of electronic commerce, either business-to-business or business-to-consumer (Amazon is a typical example). Companies that promote on-line financial and banking services (e.g., Egg in the UK) and auctions (e.g., e-Bay) are also included.

3. *Software and Internet-specialized consulting companies*. These companies offer various Internet services (web design, web hosting and development of platforms for electronic commerce) to companies that want to develop an on-line commercial activity and even to private users. Although these firms are not precisely Internet service providers, they represent relevant actors in the Internet service sectoral system and should be therefore taken into consideration.

The IAPs started offering free Internet access in most European countries (Freeserve in the UK, Tiscali in Italy, Terra Networks in Spain, Libertysurf in

France), in order to attract more users. It is interesting to note that this phenomenon has taken place almost exclusively in Europe, where the metered phone tariffs and the scarce familiarity (except for Scandinavian countries) with information technology were hindering the diffusion of the Internet, especially among residential users. Furthermore, pure IAPs implemented this strategy well before incumbent operators in almost all European countries, because they needed to build a customer base. However, the profitability of those companies has been seriously undermined by the provision of free services. Consequently, in order to gain revenues from sources other than Internet connections, older IAPs have been forced to develop new business models, and will probably have to restore some pricing schemes. Currently, most of their revenues derive from the advertising of various companies, although in some countries – e.g., in Italy and in the UK – the so-called 'reverse interconnection charge' guarantees some profits.[8]

The incumbent telecommunications operators need to broaden the scope of their activities towards Internet service provision and management. They have to diversify further back along the Internet supply chain, offering value-added content, in order to compete more directly with satellite and digital TV operators, media conglomerates and content owners, all of which already possess advanced technological and managerial competencies. However, one has to consider that the incumbents in Europe still retain a nation-wide subscriber base and possess expertise in managing and distributing complex networked services. Even if the local access market is now liberalized in most countries, these operators have the opportunity to capitalize on their existing advantages to position themselves as the most important distributors of Internet services to the consumer market.

New entrant telecommunications operators can also exploit the increasing diffusion of Internet services, even if they are less stable than the incumbents. These operators have two alternative options to compete in the marketplace. They can either adopt a strategy of free Internet access provision in order to build a substantial customer base, or concentrate on the business segment of the market and develop customized applications for a particular sector (e.g., the banking sector) or market niche (e.g., small and medium-sized enterprises).

Cable TV operators in many European countries are in a weak position compared to other network providers, either because the subscriber base is fragmented, or because the incumbent operator holds a dominant position, or

---

[8] The reverse interconnection charge is a percentage (variable from country to country) of the telephone tariff paid by the users during an Internet session, which is given by the telephone operator to the IAP, as a premium for the generation of telephony traffic.

even because of a lack of physical infrastructure.[9] With the advent of Web TV, these operators have a concrete opportunity to extend their existing range of entertainment services to include Internet services. Cable modems are now available at competitive prices and this gives cable TV operators the opportunity to fully exploit their networks.

ICPs can gain significant benefits from the development of enhanced Internet services. An immediate advantage stems from their capability to distribute products to subscribers at a national and international level. Like telecommunications operators, traditional media and publishing companies that go on-line can rely upon a large user base. The big firms can use their extensive resources to expand their activity into content packaging and access provision. Most of these players are already implementing such a strategy through the development of portals, which allows them to deal directly with consumers instead of using third parties.

While technological development initially drove a phenomenon of innovative entry in the Internet value-chain, recent market trends and innovations have made specialized competencies and specific knowledge a key asset. Thus a process of market consolidation has started, with big companies and specialized content operators emerging as key players. Since most of the value of Internet services for customers is embedded in content rather than access to the Web, the basic function of pure IAPs – Internet access – is likely to become a commodity provided by a few companies – usually the first movers – beyond the telecommunications operators. In order to survive and grow, IAPs will have to diversify their supply and develop value-added Internet services such as e-commerce applications, on-line advertising and customized search services (following the model of portals).

4.2. Competition between Incumbents and New Entrants: Critical Factors of Success

The process of technological convergence of ICT and media has generated a very turbulent marketplace, in which success depends on owning both the physical infrastructure and the content. While these two assets have long been separated and owned by different operators, market segments are now coming together and firms are competing on a global scale in many market niches. The pure ISPs are struggling to position themselves in a market where Internet access is becoming a commodity. A key competence seems to be the ability of bundling content and services in order to offer customized solutions to

---

[9] The Benelux countries and the UK represent a relevant exception as far as the role of cable companies is concerned.

different categories of users. The market opportunities to achieve a high level of performance come from three main activities:

- targeting the existing market for business and consumer terminals and ICT equipment for new value-added applications and services;
- substituting traditional distribution methods and product formats with cheaper and more convenient networked applications; and
- exploiting economies of scale and scope deriving from the provision of a wide range of applications over the same infrastructure.

With reference to the last point, it is worth pointing out that the advent of the Internet has created a series of innovative services in the telecommunications sector. Table 6.2 represents a possible taxonomy of the telecommunications value-added services.

Table 6.2: Telecommunications value-added services

International telephony	Messaging	Internet services
Call-back	Proprietary e-mails	Internet access
Prepaid cards	Fax broadcasting	Web hosting
Satellite telephony		IP telephony – call centres
		Intranets – extranets
		Platforms for electronic commerce

Source: Assinform (1999).

The first two columns of table 6.2 – international telephony and messaging – represent enhanced telephony applications, while the third column includes more specific and advanced Internet services. Beyond simple Internet access, there are more complex services such as Web Hosting (the development of Web pages for enterprises), voice applications over the IP (e.g., for international calls or for call centres), Intranets (virtual private networks for the computers of a local area network), Extranets (networks linking a virtual private network and some external computers) and platforms for electronic commerce (including security systems for financial transactions).

A major driver for the successful diffusion of the Internet has been the accumulation of knowledge and competencies within the scientific and Industrial community of data communication and internetworking. In this new environment, however, the combination of different firm-specific competencies is emerging as a key factor to be competitive. Equipment and software design, programming and network management are important skills, which need to be combined (Rao 1999). This is a fundamental aspect in the overall sectoral dynamics of the Internet industry.

Telephone companies have strong capabilities in network management; cable companies have broadband transmission capabilities; software companies have sophisticated software development skills; media/publishing companies have significant resources in terms of content; ISPs have well-developed marketing capabilities. The development of such a complex knowledge base has undermined the 'knowledge advantages' of the incumbent operators. New entrants such as ISPs and content providers (portals) have better exploited this potential compared to the traditional telecommunications operators, at least in the early stage, and have accelerated the diffusion curve of the Internet. These companies are competing with traditional operators using the telecommunications carriers' facilities but for this reason are still dependent on the existing network. However, recent developments in the market seem to suggest the existence of a core of homogeneous firms and a fringe of more heterogeneous firms, with Internet backbone providers reigning supreme (including incumbent telecommunications operators and cable TV companies) and content providers playing a significant role.

Firms are looking for ways to acquire new competencies in order to exploit the potential offered by the development of the IP network and to accelerate the Internet diffusion curve.[10] They offer new and relatively low-cost services never available before (Internet access, hosting, e-mail and World Wide Web browsing) as well as more traditional telecommunications services including fax, voice services and video transmission (Einhorn 1996; Kavassalis et al. 1996; Ono and Aoki 1998).

The exploitation of new technological opportunities requires not only the accumulation of new technical and organizational capabilities but also the development of a market view, which helps to identify the critical needs of the users (Utterback 1994; Shapiro and Varian 1999). In particular, a careful segmentation of the market and a selective provision of new services to prioritize those applications which build on familiarity with access devices such as personal computers (PCs) or televisions are necessary. The operators should take into account the differences that exist between the consumer and business market segments. The Internet represents a widespread and cheap mechanism for distributing value-added services and multimedia applications, and it provides an efficient link between content and customers. The combination of network and content is therefore a fundamental asset, and the main task for different firms is to exploit their specific competencies, while at the same time, coupling them with new capabilities.

---

[10] Due to the converging technological trajectories in telephony and computers, a network of alliances and cross-ownership arrangements has emerged among companies who want to harness the new technological opportunities, but do not possess all the necessary competencies to do so.

New technologies have to deliver innovative services with an attractive price/quality mix for the users. In this respect, the best solution will not win just on its technical and economic merit, but also on its ability to be deployed commercially and on the possibility of supporting technological applications that respond to users' specific requirements (Shapiro and Varian 1999). In such a complex and changing sectoral system, it is quite difficult to assess the demand for new applications: each technology may be capable of delivering a set of services but these services must add some value to the user. As a consequence, innovation in this area identifies not only the development of new services, but also the provision of the same services at a lower price, or the provision of more/better services for the same price (Katz 1996; Kavassilis et al. 1996).

With the dismantling of national monopolies and the emergence of IP technology, many companies have discovered new specialized market niches and have deployed high-performance, low-cost networks. Having no technological heritage, these new operators can implement IP solutions without incurring losses. On the other hand, the incumbents find themselves locked-in. having heavily invested in the existing network and in the technology already in place, even if this technology was not the optimal solution. But they have a competitive advantage in terms of user base, financial resources and brand. and can promote value-added services to corporate customers. As a conesquence, they can implement a strategy to aggregate services and charge a flat rate for them, so that customers can obtain all the services they need through a single point of contact with the provider (Rabeau 1999).

In the early stages of Internet market development, there was a trade-off for the incumbents related to their entrance into the market. On the one hand, they risked reducing their revenues in traditional services, by stimulating the development of the Internet and its value-added services.[11] On the other hand, their entry opened interesting market perspectives, due to their advantageous position in terms of existing infrastructure. Currently, almost all existing companies have invested in the provision of Internet services, and it is worth pointing out that they derive considerable income from leased capacity for transporting IP traffic. With the distributed network being the dominant future paradigm for the telecommunications system, the fixed costs for telecommunications operators, which represent the greatest part of their expenditures, are spread across different companies and this allows them to gain greater profits.

The new entrants have some advantages from a regulatory perspective. They are not subject to many of the same regulations imposed on traditional telecommunications operators – such as the universal service obligation – and can

---

[11] The case of Internet telephony is representative in this respect, since it constitutes a new service over the IP network, which competes with the traditional telephony service.

benefit from market-discriminating pricing strategies that consist of serving profitable customers in densely populated areas or in the business sector (Clark 1996 and 1997; Ono and Aoki 1998). However, the need to build a customer base either by using attractive price/quality offerings, or by focusing on a specific market segment (business vs. small or home office market), or forming alliances with an established operator makes them subject to great pressure. Some of these companies not only commercialize new products using the existing infrastructure but also invest considerable resources in building proprietary fibre optics networks which support the IP technology: firms such as Oxygen, Qwest, Level3 and Global Crossing are particularly active in this area.

In this phase, increasing competition in telecommunications markets is driven by the interaction between supply and demand. New and old providers are offering innovative services and exploiting new technological knowledge and skills; on the other hand, customers – mostly business customers – are utilizing Intranets to exchange, distribute and process information internally, and Extranets to improve communications with the external environment – suppliers, partners and users. They require an increasing number of specific value-added technological solutions that will allow them to reduce costs and facilitate network management.

Incumbents and new entrants face each other in a very turbulent marketplace, where long-term structural dynamics appear highly uncertain. The traditional telephone companies that typically deploy costly technologies but have a large customer base are moving towards the implementation of IP-based networks and providing value-added services on them. Newcomers that already use IP technology are trying to expand their customer base, offering value-added products and services instead of simply transmitting over the IP.

It is precisely this uncertainty, together with the need for advanced integration capabilities, that is driving the emergence of alliances and partnerships among heterogeneous agents. In a very unstable environment, the creation of a tight web of relationships with other firms and non-firm organizations helps firms acquire key competencies and achieve a high level of competitiveness. The more the knowledge is tacit and firm specific, the less market mechanisms are suitable for an efficient exchange of knowledge between companies. On the other hand, an integrated structure such as the existing telecommunications sector may generate asymmetries of power and may not be a proper solution for providing the best combination of services to end users (Carlsson and Stankiewicz 1995; Katz 1996).

5. THE PROVISION OF INTERNET SERVICES IN EUROPE

A recent empirical analysis of Internet telephony showed that new value-added services over the IP network were not very popular, especially among residential users (Corrocher 1999). However, most ISPs are currently invest-ing in building a proprietary IP infrastructure for the provision of combined voice, video and data services. This section examines the sectoral system of innovation and production in the Internet industry with particular attention to the role of the ISPs. How does Internet service provision differ from country to country? What are the characteristics of the demand in different countries? How do the various providers position themselves in the new converging market of communications? The section begins by examining Internet ser-vices in Europe and is followed by a look at Japan's accomplishments.

5.1. European Trends and Country-specific Features

The features of the European sectoral system of innovation and production in the ICT industry, and in particular in the Internet sector, are not only remarkably different from the US but are also extremely heterogeneous *per se*. This is because of the technological, economic, social and political diversity among various European countries, which translates to substantial differences in local Internet markets. Table 6.3 shows the number of Internet users in some European countries.

Table 6.3: Internet penetration in selected European countries, 2000

Country	Internet Users/Total Population
Norway	49.0
Sweden	45.6
Finland	40.3
Germany	29.2
United Kingdom	25.8
France	14.5
Italy	10.5
Spain	13.3

Source: ITU (2001), 'Telecoms at a Glance', www.itu.org.

As the table indicates, Norway and Sweden have the highest proportion of Internet users of the total population (although Germany and the UK register the highest number of Internet users). Even if most users reach Internet ser-vices through their PC, in the near future the wireless application protocol

(WAP) and cable modems are likely to drive the emergence of new access devices to the Internet, such as third-generation mobile phones and Web TV. In this respect, geography matters a lot. Users in Nordic countries and Italy may connect through mobile phones (where penetration rates are over 50 per cent), while users in the Benelux region, where cable infrastructure is highly developed, prefer digital TV and cable access. Table 6.4 shows the penetration of mobile phones and cable TV in Europe.

Table 6.4: Mobile phones and cable TV penetration in selected European countries, 1999

	Mobile subscribers per 100 inhabitants	Cable TV subscribers per 1000 inhabitants	PCs per 100 inhabitants
Finland	72.64	181	39.61
France	49.41	052	30.48
Germany	58.59	255	33.64
Italy	73.73	007	20.94
Norway	70.26	183	49.05
United Kingdom	66.96	056	33.78
Spain	60.93	023	14.29
Sweden	70.32	221	50.67

Sources: ITU (2001), 'Telecoms at a Glance', www.itu.org, and EITO (2000).

Even if the Internet is supposed to eliminate time and space boundaries, the European countries represent a clear example of the importance of national characteristics. Considering the low diffusion of the English language in some major European countries (e.g., France, Italy and Spain), it is estimated that in order to reach 70 per cent of the audience in Europe, content will need to be translated into five languages.[12] The social and cultural context of the specific countries make it necessary not only to translate on-line contents into the national language but also to adapt the content itself to country-specific characteristics.

Local regulatory regimes also have an increasing relevance both for the development of electronic commerce (e.g., taxation and content regulation) and for the diffusion of the Internet (legislation on interconnection fees). The recent liberalization of the telecommunications market will help new companies enter the Internet sector: in some countries the relationship between incumbents and new entrants is conducted according to the principle of fair

---

[12] At present, 96 per cent of all global domain names are in English.

competition. In Italy and the UK, for example, the ISPs are deriving part of their revenues from reverse interconnection charges.

Although this analysis takes as its starting point the theoretical framework of sectoral systems of innovation and production, national and even regional factors matter significantly in determining the rate of technical change, as well as the diffusion of innovations and the market dynamics. This is evident in the case of the Internet sector and is due to the specificity of the industrial structure and the role of national institutions (Nelson 1993; Breschi and Malerba 1997).

Beyond country-specific characteristics, there are however some *common features* of the European Internet sectoral system, which allow us to identify some invariant patterns of technological and market developments across countries. First, the rise of *free access*, a model that is solely European, has shaped the competitive landscape. This phenomenon was initiated in the UK by Freeserve and has been followed by an increasing number of IAPs within many European countries. Its main effects have been to lower the access costs (traditionally much higher than in the US), and as a consequence, to double the Internet usage. As mentioned before, however, the sustainability of this business strategy is fading. A second characteristic shared by European countries is the significant *decline in telephone tariffs*, which has contributed to diminishing access costs and has brought a significant number of users on-line. Third, there is the *lack of loyalty of consumers*, whose costs of switching to a new provider is zero, because of the availability of many ISPs offering standardized packages of services. As an example, one should note that around 40 per cent of the UK users who signed on to Freeserve in 1998 have moved to another Internet service provider. This is less true for business users, since the services they get are less standardized and of higher quality than those residential users get and therefore business users require a stable source of technical assistance. Fourth, *technical problems* are features of a great number of European web sites. Those problems testify to the lack of technical skills in the business sector as well as the youth of many web sites. In this respect, there is need to stimulate the training of human resources in order to harness the benefits deriving from the Internet. Finally, the *metered use* of the Internet is hindering its development. This problem mostly relates to the complex pricing/interconnection regimes which still characterize most European countries.

Generally speaking, one could argue that despite a highly differentiated and developed supply, and although Internet usage has substantially increased, the demand for Internet services in Europe is not very sophisticated. This is due to the low PC penetration as compared to the US (see table 6.4) and to a scarce familiarity with multimedia applications, which may be attributed to the users' lack of technical skills as well as their attitudes and behaviours. Furthermore, the demand for Internet services is quite heterogeneous and this implies that enhanced applications have to be tailored to specific user needs. Consumers are interested in free, easy-to-use services mostly for entertainment purposes, while businesses prefer high-quality services, which facilitate network management and help the development of electronic commerce.

5.2. The Phenomenon of Mobile Internet Services: Lessons from Japan

We have underlined that mobile phones are likely to become one of the most diffused Internet access mechanisms, since mobile handsets are upgraded on an average of every 12 months and are set to launch the next generation of mobile Internet terminals. Demand for Internet services via mobile phones will be driven by an increase in the number of mobile subscribers, the availability of new equipment and the number and quality of applications. An interesting development is that the mobile phone of the future will become a personalized information portal, offering a series of value-added services beyond communications (short messaging services and e-mail) and information (news, weather, finance and timetables) services already available. Future services will include organization (personal organizer functions), electronic commerce (electronic wallets, tickets, gambling), advertising (TV-style, full screen 'flash' adverts) and entertainment (games, video, music). As customers become more familiar with the enhanced functionality of mobile handsets, they will demand more high-value services, moving up in the value chain.

At present, the most diffused and advanced data application for mobile phones is short-text messaging services, which have been operational in most cellular networks for the last three years. The next stage in data products is the development of information services, which ultimately leads to the creation of mobile portals that will allow users to access a full range of services, comparable to those accessible from the fixed network. According to EITO (2001), mobile commerce users as a proportion of total cellular subscribers were 3 per cent at the end of 2000. It is foreseen that more than one-third of the total Western European subscriber base will be active users of mobile e-commerce by the end of 2005. Although Western Europe will be the key region for the growth of mobile services, the success of Japan's I-Mode gives the Asia-Pacific region an early advantage.

The Japanese NTT DoCoMo has pioneered technological developments in mobile services with the launch of I-Mode in February 1999, answering at the same time the content provider's dilemma of how to generate content and get paid for it. This operator has gained a considerable competitive advantage in the Japanese market, not only by benefiting from being the first mover, but also by achieving a strong position in the mobile Internet market before the introduction of WAP. NTT has established a 9 per cent surcharge to provide content to end users on third-generation phones by using a reduced set of compact HyperText markup language (HTML). Subscribers make use of a series of on-screen menus to buy customized content on news, sports, financial and weather reports. The Japanese operator has stimulated usage levels by providing users a combination of 'pull' and 'push' options: 'pull' services allow subscribers to choose one-off options and pay for them directly, while 'push' services are those delivered to customers on a regular basis. Content-based services are a core component of I-Mode and there is a strong focus on mobile electronic commerce services. On-line transactions such as mobile banking, ticket reservation, travel reservation, mobile trading and book purchasing are highly popular and other services are being added at a fast pace. According to the company, 48 per cent of the over 30 million users of I-Mode are paying for content and those users subscribe to an average of 2.2 content services. Both subscription and free content services are available from official sites, which are authorized by NTT DoCoMo for inclusion in I-Mode.

I-Mode is competing with WAP technology, but it requires a different content format. WAP needs wireless markup language (WML) for its browser and since most web sites are written in HTML, it is not possible to access most web sites available in the world today. In contrast, I-Mode does not require a special language for mobile units and can access all existing web sites using compact HTML. Furthermore, although WAP can be accessed by either a circuit-switched or a packet-switched network, while I-Mode is only accessible by a packet-switched network which means users are always on-line, mobile providers for WAP prefer to use the slower and more expensive circuit-switched network. This might be due to the limitation of their network's infrastructure, but it is quite likely that they enjoy making more money from airtime charges, while there is no competing I-Mode in the European market. On the other hand, I-Mode users pay only for the amount of information they download to the I-Mode unit and therefore the service is obviously cheaper than WAP. Once again, the key factors that will determine the winner in the mobile Internet competition are service rates and the quality and availability of content.

The development of I-Mode represents an interesting issue for the future growth of the Internet in Europe. Apparently the reasons for the overwhelming acceptance of I-Mode in Japan are somewhat paradoxical and cultural. First, the country records one of the lowest rates of computer literacy in Asia, resulting from an antiquated educational system, and this is common to at least some central-southern European countries. Second, on average people commute approximately 90 minutes and in this context communications mobility becomes quite important. Third, the cost of a new fixed phone line is quite high in Japan, while a new mobile phone costs nothing and the monthly fee starts at quite a low rate. Mobile phones are also becoming cheaper in Europe, and as their diffusion constantly increases over time, users will progressively demand more sophisticated services over their handsets. The I-Mode could constitute an important technological opportunity for European operators to boost Internet usage and generate revenues from content. There are already some signs of European market involvement in the I-Mode business. NTT DoCoMo, the company that runs the service, is set to enter the European wireless market through a new UK subsidiary and alliances with several European companies. NTT DoCoMo has taken a number of steps to ensure that I-Mode will be just as successful in Europe as it is in Japan. The company will focus its European operations through a UK-based subsidiary, DoCoMo Europe, which will work closely with the company's European partners, Dutch operator KPN Mobile and Hutchison 3G UK Holding Ltd. NTT DoCoMo is planning a joint venture with KPN Mobile to provide I-Mode based and third-generation wireless services in Europe. The company also plans to set up a research lab in Munich to examine mobile security technologies and network infrastructure in Europe.

6. A VIEW ON THE US AND JAPAN

This section briefly deals with the Internet sectoral system of innovation and production in the US and Japan in order to identify the main characteristics of the sector in those two countries and assess their industries' performance in comparison to that of Europe.

6.1. United States

The US is currently the major market for the Internet in absolute terms, while in relative terms (number of users over total population) it is just behind Norway and Sweden. This condition is likely to remain stable over the next few years as a result of supply- and demand-side elements. As far as supply-side factors are concerned, it is worth noting that the main players on the global Internet stage will be US companies, since these actors have been engaged in a substantial number of acquisitions worldwide in the last few years. The most innovative Internet solutions – except for mobile Internet technological developments – will originate in the US and will be pushed by the supply side of the market, since the process of deregulation and the enhancement of local competition has stimulated the entry of different operators, and it will be pulled by the demand from both consumers and business users. The former are interested in multimedia services, whereas the latter are willing to implement business-to-business and business-to-consumer on-line transactions. The majority of users already demand broadband services, so that web transactions, video-on-demand and video-conferencing are becoming successful value-added applications. Moreover, alternative Internet access devices such as set-top boxes and network computers will cost much less than most personal computers and their diffusion will contribute to lowering the costs of Internet access.

The Internet infrastructure in the US consists of more than fifteen major backbones, which are operated either by an inter-exchange carrier (e.g., MCI-Worldcom) or by an independent IAP (e.g., UUNet). The R&D activity of network developers is the most significant source of innovations, since these firms are strongly committed to the development of innovative technical solutions and business models as well as the design of new pricing structures, in order to offer high-quality and reliable services. In this respect, the deployment of new fibre capacity and the upgrading of the speed and interoperability of Internet routers and switches constitute two important areas of significant technological investments.[13] The market for backbone providers is quite competitive, but the increasing demand for bandwidth as well as the growing outflow of Internet traffic (as most servers are based in the US) will allow several operators to exist in the sector. At the ISP level, there are about 4 000 companies operating in the US and no restrictions on who can provide services. However, as in the case of most European countries, the US is experiencing consolidation, especially in the business segment of the market, witnessed by several mergers between ISPs and telecommunications operators in recent years. Because the US has a mature Internet market, its firms are focusing more on the development and provision of content. New partnerships between ISPs and content owners – typically big media players – are emerging (e.g., AOL and Times Warner) and multimedia applications are offered in the market, stimulated by the increasing broadband capacity of the networks. Furthermore, IAPs in the US have not adopted the free access business model, used in some European markets, and therefore can rely upon significant revenues from Internet access fees.

US public policy strongly supports the Internet sector because it generates new jobs and new export revenues. In particular, the government sustains the implementation of international regulations for e-commerce and, more specifically, a clear definition of taxation for the Internet environment. The rapid changes characterizing the technological trajectory of the Internet and the telecommunications system as a whole have convinced public authorities that the new Internet-based services should not be subject to the regulatory constraints that are imposed upon traditional services.

---

[13] However, in the development of wireless Internet access, the US is still behind the Scandinavian countries.

6.2. Japan

Japan has the second highest number of Internet users in the world, but still substantially less than the US, and is well behind major European countries in terms of infrastructure and human resources development for Internet use. At present most Japanese people access the Internet at work or at the university, but the number of home users is also increasing. A relatively even distribution of wealth across the population and a high level of urbanization have contributed to an enormous growth in Internet diffusion.

From a technological point of view, Japan's infrastructure is generally very advanced, with NTT – the former telecommunications incumbent – still the dominant operator in terms of network development. Most ISPs need to interconnect with NTT's network in order to reach the end users, at least for the last mile of the local loop. However, some of these companies do not own a backbone and must lease the lines from NTT to provide long-distance and international services. In order to reduce the ISP's dependence on NTT, the government is encouraging alternative players to improve the existing infrastructure. In this context, utility companies will play an increasing role in backbone provision, as will the Japan Information Highway. While fixed wireless technologies will be of limited use, mobile services will become increasingly important and will boost the development of multimedia services, especially via the I-Mode technology. In recent years, digital television has become an interesting alternative Internet access platform. JskyB and Perfect TV represent the major players, while cable television companies are already offering high-speed Internet access via cable modems.

The Japanese government is stimulating the completion of the national fibre-to-home network, in order to accelerate the development of the national broadband infrastructure. Since Japan is currently experiencing a financial downturn, for the time being the main operator in the industry – NTT – has adopted an alternative system, installing fibre-optic cables as far as the local trunk lines without connecting every home. There will be connection-on-demand services for consumers, and end users who want to be connected by the fibre-to-home network will have to pay for this value-added service.

As far as demand is concerned, it is interesting that Internet use in Japan has been somewhat slow because PC penetration has been minimal relative to the US and some European countries. This phenomenon occurs in the consumer and business segments of the market. PC penetration is particularly low among employees (27 PCs per 100 employees compared to a European average of 81.4 and 135 in the US), but it is also quite limited in the residential market (31.5, compared to a European average of 34 and 58.5 in the US). However, the development of mobile-based Internet services will give Japanese users an alternative way to access the Web. Furthermore, it is worth underlining that the driving force in the consumer sector is probably going to be a cultural one, i.e., the fascination for the newest and most advanced technologies that most Japanese share.

There are over 3 000 ISPs in the Japanese market, most of which are small, with fewer than 1 000 subscribers. Fierce competition in the industry coupled with the financial and market power of the most successful operators such as NTT, Internet Initiative Japan and Nifty are likely to provoke a shake-out in the market, at least as far as the business-user segment is concerned, where a few big players have considerable leverage to provide professional Internet services on a nation-wide basis. Some ISPs are forming partnerships with cable operators to offer high-speed connections, both to avoid the threat from cable operators themselves and to bypass NTT's interconnection charges for the local loop. Access charges for Internet services are quite high compared to the rest of the world, but competition among different operators will contrib.- ute to reducing connection rates and rentals and this in turn will reduce the final price for end users. In this respect, it is interesting to note that a significant role will be played by Internet telephony, which is likely to be quite successful, due to the slow decline in Japan's expensive telephone rates.

7. CONCLUDING REMARKS

The theoretical framework of sectoral systems of innovation focuses on how the characteristics of a specific sector affect its innovative performance and puts emphasis on the interaction of firms, non-firm organizations and institutions, as well as on the processes of competition and selection within the industry (Breschi and Malerba 1997; Malerba 2000). However, this should not lead us to think that sectors show similar patterns of development and performance across countries. As the literature emphasizes, the role of country-specific factors in influencing the growth and performance of sectors cannot be underestimated. Social, cultural and institutional contexts in which the actors of a sectoral system operate contribute to determining the rate and direction of technical change, as well as the level of competitiveness (Lundvall 1993; Nelson 1993).

7.1. Knowledge and Learning Processes

Recent technological developments in the telecommunications sector have brought about significant changes in the knowledge base. The process of convergence between telecommunications, computing and broadcasting technologies is responsible for the widening range of competencies necessary to survive and grow in the market. In this new environment, the combination of different firm-specific skills is becoming a key factor to successfully compete in the industry. Equipment design, software programming, network management, content development and assembling are relevant assets that need to be combined. Telecommunications companies have strong capabilities in network management, cable companies have broadband transmission capabilities, software programming skills lay mainly outside current boundaries of the industry, while content development – traditionally belonging to companies in the media and publishing industries – now constitutes a crucial asset for all firms to emerge in the market. As pointed out, ISPs possess strong marketing capabilities and can take advantage of their ability to commercialize new products and services, while relying upon external technological skills to build infrastructure. All these companies need to be looking for ways to acquire new competencies in order to exploit the potential offered by the development of the IP network and the diffusion of Internet value-added services.

Learning is fundamental in a complex environment. Research shows that the learning process occurs most efficiently and effectively in a collective and interactive way that involves firms, their users and suppliers (Malerba 2000). There need to be more relationships between firms and non-firm organizations. Private companies, the academic world and public research organizations need to interact in ways that will create synergies of knowledge and skills, improve the quality of existing human resources and expand opportunities for joint ventures.

The Internet can be perceived as a major technological discontinuity that has generated 'creative destruction' along the existing technological trajectory of the telecommunications sector, leading to the emergence of a new paradigm. This revolution is attributable to two technological breakthroughs: the introduction of packet-switching technologies and, related to this, the development of the Internet protocol. This wave of radical innovations has caused relevant changes to the structure of markets and the internal organization of firms. Technological convergence has generated a tension between integration and specialization of knowledge and skills. The empirical evidence as well as part of the literature (Katz 1996; Shapiro and Varian 1999) suggest that specialization is an efficient and profitable strategy for small companies that do not possess the infrastructure (which requires substantial financial investments to develop). Similarly, it is believed that network owners can successfully integrate all their activities and become full service providers, offering both access and content. There is also a parallel tension between the exploration of new technological opportunities and the exploitation of the existing competencies. This constitutes a problem especially for the incumbent operators, whose innovative activity in the sector has so far been characterized by a high degree of cumulativeness. Those companies have strong competencies in the field of traditional network management, but lack specific skills for Internet access and content provision. If they want to become leaders in the new industry they will have to acquire new competencies and integrate them with their own accumulated skills. They will also need to invest in the provision of new products and services which could cannibalize existing resources.

7.2. Long-term Sectoral Dynamics

How can access providers and content providers survive and grow in this changing and competitive environment? What are the critical factors of success? What is the role of demand in affecting firms' strategies? How will companies adapt their innovative and business strategy to the new sectoral structure?

We have seen that the convergence of different types of demand and competing technologies has created a new sector with continuously expanding boundaries. The companies that come from the various industries constituting the multimedia sector have to implement new strategies more in tune with the features of multimedia. The process of convergence has created a new group of users with specific requirements which differ significantly from the previously existing demands facing the telecommunications, software and broadcasting industries (Mansell and Silverstone 1996; Shapiro and Varian 1999). Demand will develop along more innovative ranges of products, and in particular towards enhanced applications over the Internet. Packages of combined services, such as data, video and voice services over the Internet will be required.

The incumbent telephone operators face the greatest challenge, as their largest source of revenues – voice service – is being seriously threatened by new competitors who develop innovative services, employing targeted price/volume discounts to attract new customers. For this reason, incumbents need to adopt an aggressive business strategy, to undertake substantial investments in new technologies, and to modify substantially their internal organization. Yet we have also seen that ownership of the Internet backbone constitutes a key resource in the industry and, in this respect, the network owners – such as telecommunications and cable operators – are likely to play a significant role in the future, especially in the provision of Internet access. For new entrants, new technologies offer a way to attack existing monopolies and provide greater scope for service differentiation. The main challenge for these operators is to choose which technology to invest in, which market segment to target, and which type of services to provide (OECD 1996 and 1998).

Utilizing the notion of technological regime (Malerba and Orsenigo 1997), we can say that the Internet industry is rapidly evolving from a Schumpeter Mark I to a Schumpeter Mark II model. This means that, from being an Industry with a high rate of entry and exit, a high level of competition, and the existence of multiple innovative trajectories, the Internet service sector has changed towards a structure in which the selection process tends to favour the established technological leaders and innovation is proceeding along an existing trajectory. The emerging industrial structure is composed of a stable core of consolidated companies and a turbulent fringe of smaller, more innovative firms. However, the structural changes occurring in the industry, particularly this shift from innovative entry to the reinforcement of advanced integration capabilities, is leading to the formation of partnerships among agents, more than to a highly concentrated industrial structure. As underlined by some theoretical contributions (Lundvall 1993; Nelson 1993; Edquist 1997), networks emerge in unstable environments not because agents are similar, but because they are different. In this way, firms may integrate complementarities in knowledge capabilities and specialization and have a higher opportunity of survival.

Once they have established themselves in the market, companies need to adopt an aggressive business strategy in order to seize the opportunities and to manage growth in a turbulent and rapidly evolving sector. First-mover operators that have expanded their offerings by providing innovative services and technologies will have a competitive advantage over latecomers. Furthermore, the ability to focus on a niche market is considered a fundamental asset to compete in the Internet sector. Having easy access to external funding and a strong financing position provides a certain degree of flexibility and enables firms to undertake innovative activity. In the new multimedia sector, the role of venture capital is becoming more important. There is a growing number of start-up e-commerce companies (especially for e-commerce applications), whose survival and growth strongly depend upon the availability of external funding. At the same time, venture capital organizations are emerging in Europe, while the stock exchange market is seen as an opportunity for fund raising. As services become more standardized, companies pay more attention to marketing, service quality, reliability and customer care. Providing value-added applications and differentiated combinations of services is becoming a relevant factor for operators who need to expand their customer base while exploiting new technological opportunities.

In the early years, the services offered by ISPs were complementing the services of telecommunications operators, who in turn tried to slow the entry of new companies in the market by charging high access rates. Eventually incumbents understood the potential of the Internet and started providing Internet services. They have recently invested in high-speed networks for Internet traffic and improved the existing network by developing new transmission techniques (e.g., ADSL) for broadband applications. The importance of an advanced infrastructure for Internet services and the growing demand for content put the 'pure' IAPs in an uncertain position. Smaller firms are being absorbed by larger companies, while large IAPs are concentrating their efforts on business users because that proves to be the most profitable market and allows firms to price their services according to the quality they offer.

7.3. Institutions, Non-firm Organizations and Public Policy

Notwithstanding the relevance of firms in the development of the Internet sector as producers and users of technologies, products and services, in a systemic perspective there is the need to emphasize the role of non-firm organizations and institutions as an important source of innovation and change (Nelson and Rosenberg 1993; Edquist 1997). These agents are responsible for the processes of variety creation and selection which characterize the long-term dynamics of the industry.

As far as the Internet sector is concerned, the development of innovations and the outstanding growth which characterizes the industry have been greatly affected by some major regulatory changes. Sectoral competition authorities either have acted as supportive agents for the innovative activity and for the creation of a competitive market structure – as in the UK – or have long hindered the emergence of such an industry – as in Italy. Recently some governments have sponsored and promoted the diffusion of innovations by encouraging the growth of educational web access and by developing web sites for public administration. Even among latecomers such as Italy, the public sector is undertaking a noticeable effort in connecting local and national public institutes to the Internet.

However, the role of regulatory authorities has not been accompanied by a parallel effort among other non-firm organizations. This seems to be a common characteristic of European countries and affects the performance of Europe as a whole compared to the US. Particularly worrying is the phenomenon of the skill shortage in the ICT industry. This is partly due to the historical development of the Internet industry, which significantly involved the academic community in the early years, but subsequently relied on private firms as the major developers of innovation. Firms now complain about the mismatch between their requirements and the availability of qualified human resources. The creation of new departments and degrees in universities in response to new technological developments in the industry is a crucial component in the process of innovation (Arora et al. 1999). The growth and competitiveness of the Internet sectoral system strongly depends upon the participation of academic institutions for innovative activity and the diffusion of innovations.

Regulators need to manage the complexity of a world where previously separate sectors – telecommunications, computing, broadcasting and media industries – are converging. In developing a competitive infrastructure for service provision, the implementation of a sector-specific regulatory framework represents a critical step. This constitutes a serious challenge for public authorities that need to revise existing regulatory frameworks and implement new regimes. The Internet sector relies upon the regulation of the telecommunications industry and its evolution has greatly benefited from the process of liberalization. Issues such as degree and conditions of network unbundling and licensing, tariff structure and re-balancing have been taken into account by regulators. The harmonization of rules at the EU level has also allowed greater transparency in the management of the Internet.[14] It is interesting to note that technological and market developments may anticipate and thus constrain regulators' decisions. This process is very much dependent upon country-specific characteristics.

As mentioned, former monopolists have an advantage over their competitors because they own much of the infrastructure and have benefited from being monopolists in the local loop. However, incumbent telecommunications operators have also been subject to significant constraints in terms of universal service obligation. With the convergence of voice, video and data, it is difficult to determine the type of regulation most suited to new operators offering integrated solutions. The confusion raised by the introduction of voice service over the IP, whose providers are subject to different regulatory frameworks in geographical markets around the world, is an example of the difficulties in dealing with this new system.

7.4. Geographic Markets

Despite an emphasis on existing similarities across countries for the same industries, the sectoral system approach recognizes the ability to generate and exploit technological opportunities is less similar across different nations (Nelson 1993; Malerba 2000). Country-specific factors remain very important in determining the technological and market dynamics of a sectoral system of innovation and production. Notwithstanding some common and invariant sector-specific trends, national characteristics strongly influence the rate and di-

---

[14] Some issues remain to be clearly defined, especially with reference to content regulation. Among these, the revision of intellectual property rights legislation appears to be a major priority.

rection of technical change and the economic performance of the Internet sectoral system in each single country. Even more, we have observed some peculiarities of the European Internet market, which make it quite different from the US and Japan.

Competition between different operators combined with processes of interaction between firms, users and suppliers, non-firm organizations and institutions have resulted in different developments across geographical markets. For example, recent developments in Europe, in particular the advent of free service, have seriously undermined the position of IAPs, while strengthening the position of content and network providers. This is unique to Europe, where the metered usage of the Internet, in contrast to the flat-rate structure of the US market, traditionally represented an obstacle to its diffusion, although recently some alternative ISPs have started providing Internet access at flat rates. In Japan, the incumbent telecommunications operator still has a significant market share for the provision of the Internet services, despite efforts from governments to promote competition. The process of standardizing protocols for mobile communications has also played out quite differently in Europe and the US and partly explains the leadership of European countries in this market. This is particularly important as far as the future of the Internet is concerned, since the possibility of accessing the Web through mobile phones represents a concrete opportunity for Europe to catch up and even overtake the US along an alternative technological trajectory.

In markets with a well-developed network and high levels of competition such as the US, Japan, the UK and Scandinavian countries incumbents and new entrants compete on traditional communications services and more enhanced services over the Internet. In those countries, the development of new access technologies and increasingly efficient transmission protocols stimulate the introduction of value-added services, which can be customized to the specific requirements of users. Telecommunications firms, pure IAPs and alternative Internet backbone providers, cable companies and content providers have great opportunities to succeed, providing that they find a way to differentiate their activity from that of competitors, offering innovative combinations of services and targeting particular market niches.

On the other hand, countries such as Italy, Spain and France have a less-developed Internet market, not only in terms of diffusion of services among potential users, but also in terms of infrastructure and competition among providers. Those countries generally do not have a wide installed base of cable TV infrastructure. For this reason, the introduction of broadband services could be slower, although the utilization of ASDL technology over the existing network constitutes an important step in this direction. The development of broadband infrastructure is particularly important if one considers that new

Internet appliances such as Web TV are emerging and represent an important catalyst for the widespread diffusion of the Internet. Despite the delay in the process of opening up competition for the provision of Internet services, these countries are now catching up with technological leaders.

The most interesting technological opportunity for Europe as far as the Internet trajectory is concerned is the development of mobile Internet services, which will become available as soon as third-generation mobile phones diffuse in the market. In this area, European countries are much more technologically advanced than the US, as far as both the supply and demand sides are concerned. The Scandinavian equipment producers Ericsson and Nokia have for long overtaken the biggest US player – Motorola – in terms of technological innovations and market shares. Most European countries have a well-developed demand for mobile phones, which is likely to grow and become more sophisticated. In this respect, convergence between the Internet and mobile telecommunications technologies will meet the demand for value-added services, while stimulating the development of innovative solutions. This represents a relevant window of opportunity for Europe. But according to the major operators in the industry, the most important and sensitive issue is going to be the design of appropriate pricing schemes for consumers and business users. In this respect, the role of public policy is going to be crucial, since it may contribute to the definition of efficient pricing. Since free access will disappear, firms need to find new sources of revenues, while making sure that users are willing to pay for new value-added applications. As the market matures, there is need for an increasing differentiation of supply from different providers, who have to customize services to meet the heterogeneous preferences of end users. This is more true as the degree of technological advancement embedded in services grows.

REFERENCES

Arora, A., R. Landau and N. Rosenberg (1999), 'Dynamics of Comparative Advantages in the Chemical Industry', in D. Mowery and R. Nelson (eds), *The Sources of Industrial Leadership*, Cambridge: Cambridge University Press.

Assinform (2000), *Report on Information Technology and Telecommunications*, available: http://www.assinform.it.

Babbage, R., I. Moffat, A. O'Neill and S. Sivaraj (1997), 'Internet Phone: Changing the Telephony Paradigm?', *BT Technology Journal* 15 (2), 145–57.

Breschi, S. and F. Malerba (1997), 'Sectoral Systems of Innovation: Technological Regimes, Schumpeterian Dynamics and Spatial Boundaries', in C. Edquist (ed.), *Systems of Innovation*, London: Pinter.

Carlsson, B. and R. Stankiewicz (1995), 'On the Nature, Function and Composition of Technological Systems', in B. Carlsson (ed.), *Technological Systems and Economic Performance: The Case of Factory Automation*, Dordrecht: Kluwer.

Cawley, R.A. (1997), 'Internet, Lies and Telephony', *Telecommunication Policy* 21 (6), 513–32.

Clark, D. (1996) 'Adding Service Discrimination to the Internet', *Telecommunication Policy* **20** (3), 169–81.

Clark, D. (1997), *A Taxonomy of Internet Telephony Applications*, available: http://www.itel.mit.edu:/itel/pubs/ddc.tprc97.pdf.

Corrocher, N. (1999), *Prospects for Internet Telephony: Toy for Multimedia Hobbyists or Next-generation Technology?*, SPRU Electronic Working Paper Series.

David, P. (1999), 'Understanding Digital Technology's Evolution and the Path of Measured Productivity Growth', in E. Brynolfsson and B. Kahin (eds), *Understanding the Digital Economy*, Cambridge (MA): MIT Press.

Davies, A. (1996), 'Innovation in Large Technical Systems: The Case of Telecommunications', *Industrial and Corporate Change* **5** (4), 1143–80.

Edquist, C. (ed.) (1997), *Systems of Innovation*, London: Pinter.

Einhorn, V. (1996), 'Internet Voice, "Cyberbypass", Competitive Efficiency', *Industrial and Corporate Change* **5** (4), 1067–77.

European Information Technology Observatory (2000), EITO, Frankfurt.

European Information Technology Observatory (2001), EITO, Frankfurt.

The Financial Times (1999), *Different Issues*.

Freeman, C. (1982), *The Economics of Industrial Innovation*, London: Pinter.

Katz, C. (1996), 'Remarks on the Economic Implications of Convergence', *Industrial and Corporate Change* **5** (4), 1069–75.

Kavassalis, P., R.J. Solomon and P.J. Benghozi (1996), 'The Internet: A Paradigmatic Rupture in Cumulative Telecommunications Evolution', *Industrial and Corporate Change* **5** (4), 1097–126.

Lundvall, B.A. (ed.) (1993), *National Systems of Innovation*, London: Pinter.

MacKie-Mason, J.K. and H.R. Varian (1998), 'Economic FAQs about the Internet', in L.W. McKnight and J. Bailey (eds), *Internet Economics*, Cambridge (MA): MIT Press.

Malerba, F. (2000), *Sectoral Systems of Innovation and Production*, Working Paper ESSY.

Malerba, F. and L. Orsenigo (1997), 'Technological Regimes and Sectoral Patterns of Innovative Activities', *Industrial and Corporate Change* **6**, 83–117.

Mansell, R. (1993), *The New Telecommunications*, London: SAGE Publications.

Mansell, R. and R. Silverstone (eds) (1996), *Communication by Design: The Politics of Information and Communication Technologies*, Oxford: Oxford University Press.

Mason, R. (1998), 'Internet Telephony and the International Accounting Rate System', *Telecommunications Policy* **22** (11), 931–44.

Nelson, R. (ed.) (1993), *National Innovation Systems: A Comparative Study*, Oxford: Oxford University Press.

Nelson, R. and N. Rosenberg (1993), 'Technical Innovation and National Systems', in R. Nelson (ed.), *National Innovation Systems: A Comparative Study*, Oxford: Oxford University Press.

Noam, E.M. (1994), 'Beyond Liberalisation: From the Network of Networks to the System of Systems', *Telecommunications Policy* **18** (4), 286–94.

OECD (1996), *Alternative Local Loop Technologies: A Review*, Paris: OECD.

OECD (1998), *Internet Voice Telephony Development*, Paris: OECD.

Ono, R. and K. Aoki (1998), 'Convergence and New Regulatory Frameworks', *Telecommunication Policy* **22** (10), 817–38.

Rabeau, Y. (1999), 'The World Telecom Industry: In the Eye of Change', *Forces*, (124), 18–27.

Rao, P.M. (1999), 'Convergence and Unbundling of Corporate R&D in Telecommunications: Is Software Taking the Helm?, Telecommunications Policy **23**, 83–93.

Rosenberg, N. (1982), *Inside the Black Box*, Cambridge: Cambridge University Press.

Sears, A. (1996) *Innovations in Internet Telephony: The Internet as the Competitor to the POTS Network:* http://itel.mit.edu:/itel/Docs/INNOVATE/INNOVATION%20IN%20INTERNET%20TELEPHONY.DOC.

Shapiro, C. and H.R. Varian (1999), *Information Rules: A Strategic Guide to the Network Economy*, Harvard Business School Press.

Utterback, J. (1994), *Mastering the Dynamics of Innovation*, Boston: Harvard Business School Press.

7. The Internet Services Industry: Country-specific Trends in the UK, Italy and Sweden[1]

Nicoletta Corrocher

1. THE INTERNET SECTORAL SYSTEM IN THE UK

1.1. Introduction

If we exclude the Scandinavian countries, the UK is the most advanced European nation in terms of Internet development. The early process of liberalization of the telecommunications market has been a major driver for the development of value-added communication applications, in particular of Internet services. The shift in the attitude of policy makers towards the telecommunications industry has opened the way for a wide range of large and small players to compete for different groups of customers. The Telecommunications Act in 1984 introduced a licensing system based on service categories, so that for each service category a duopoly was created, whereby a new entrant could compete with the incumbent British Telecom (BT). Since 1991 over 200 licences have been issued to new operators, including cable TV companies with local franchises, metropolitan operators and long-distance operators. As a result, more than 30 per cent of households have a real choice of telecommunications operator, a situation unique in Europe.

In the UK the relationship between technical change and the regulatory framework has had a significant impact on market structure. However, one could arguably say that in the UK the role of institutions has been crucial in determining the rate of technical change itself, since it has allowed the entry of new companies and forced incumbents to engage in the development of innovations. Therefore, at least in the early years, changes in the regulatory

---

[1] The analysis of the Internet services industry in the UK and Italy is largely based upon a series of interviews with Internet service providers, conducted between June 1999 and March 2000.

regime have determined the generation of new technologies and the achievement of high levels of competition.

This story represents a clear example of how much timing and policy intervention matters for sectoral growth (Nelson 1993). This case represents more than a process of co-evolution between technical change and regulation – aside from a certain degree of temporal alignment in the dynamics of the two events, a more cause–effect link can be observed. In particular, one could conclude that the liberalization and the deregulation of the telecommunications sector have constituted a fundamental determinant for the UK in achieving leadership in the European Internet industry. However, the shifts in the institutional regime have been a necessary but not sufficient condition to achieve a high level of economic and technological performance. The overall structure of the system has been supportive and has exploited the windows of opportunity by stimulating innovative activity.

Once the technological opportunities deriving from the convergence of different technological trajectories became available, the UK was ready to take advantage of them and a very competitive supply of Internet services emerged. Traditional telecommunications companies, dedicated Internet access providers (IAPs), Internet content providers (ICPs) and cable TV operators are exploiting the coming together of previously separate technological trajectories, even though they still rely on their existing competencies. The competition among different operators and the entry of new companies have generated significant changes in the knowledge base of the sectoral system. Interestingly enough, so far the role of the public research system in shaping the knowledge base has been quite irrelevant.

1.2. Technological Development and Innovation

The UK represents one of the most advanced countries in terms of Internet infrastructure. According to recent estimates (EITO 2000; OECD 2001), in 2000 there were 50 Internet hosts per 1 000 inhabitants, which is quite a relevant number, compared to 30 in Germany and 19 in France. In January 1998, the number of hosts per 1 000 inhabitants was 17.0, while in July 1998 this number was 20.5. The number of Web servers has also increased at a rate of 25 per cent. Here the UK is second only to Sweden. As a technological pioneer in the Internet industry, the country has developed one of the largest fibre optic networks in the world, with over three million miles of cables, as well as an optically-based communication infrastructure. However, due to the large and growing demand for Internet services, this network is still not sufficient to transmit the increasing volume of data, voice and video traffic. BT has the largest network in the UK and has recently formed an alliance with

AT&T in order to deliver voice and data services to multinational corporations over an Internet protocol (IP) global network.[2]

Notwithstanding its advanced infrastructure, it is important to note that BT has heavily invested in a packet-switched network based upon asynchronous transfer mode (ATM) technology instead of investing directly in IP technology. This is consistent with the technological base of the company, with its core competencies in the field of traditional telecommunications infrastructure. The use of ATM technology may indeed be considered as a way to upgrade the existing network and is the outcome of a cumulative process of technical change (Davies 1996; Kavassalis et al. 1996). As is well known from evolutionary theory, it is quite difficult for a company with an established set of competencies and routines to acquire a new ensemble of skills and modify its internal organization (Nelson and Winter 1982; Teece and Pisano 1994). In the traditional telecommunications industry, and to a lesser extent, the software sector, technical change has been characterized by a high degree of cumulativeness. Existing operators tended to follow well-determined technological trajectories, mostly because of significant switching costs. This has resulted in a high degree of inertia at the level of firms, which has considerably slowed down the process of innovation (Mowery 1996; Shapiro and Varian 1999). Subsequently, a major technological disruption occurred with the advent of the Internet, which generated a new technological paradigm and lowered the degree of cumulativeness in technical change.

The competitors of BT are also investing heavily to upgrade the network. Cable companies in particular are quite active in the telecommunications and Internet markets and are likely to become important players in the near future, when set-top boxes become common Internet appliances, competing with other devices for Internet access. Telewest and NTL have already developed an activity of Internet service provision through the creation of proprietary Internet service providers (ISPs). Due to the need for an advanced network, the R&D activity of the ISPs is quite considerable. However, interviews with ISPs in the UK reveal a clear-cut separation between two categories of companies in terms of innovative effort. On the one hand, there are technological pioneers such as BT, Demon Internet, Level3, Cable and Wireless, which perform R&D in-house and consider cost efficiency a crucial driver for innovation. Their core competencies are in network development and management. These companies exploit fibre optics to build efficient backbones and utilize new transmission techniques (xDSL, ADSL: asymmetrical digital subscriber line) to offer high-quality service to end users. On the other hand, there are

---

[2] The company has also planned to build a European network with its European partners.

companies whose core competencies are in content provision. These operators aim at satisfying customers' needs, and their innovative activity is directed at generating customized services for different categories of users. They usually outsource the R&D function to an external company – often to their backbone provider – and concentrate on assembling and providing value-added content.

All interviewees participating in this study agreed that technological development in the sector is proceeding along two parallel paths. There are firms working to improve the quality of the infrastructure to provide more advanced services, to lower the level of congestion, and to allow networks to add functionality incrementally, without restructuring the entire backbone. Then there are firms developing visual communication in the belief that long-distance electronic commerce and video conferencing are going to be quite popular over the next few years. ISPs seem to agree convergence at the network level will soon lead to convergence at the customer premises equipment level.[3]

Another interesting point raised by the interviewees is that technological change is accompanied by change in the internal organization of firms, which tend to 'disintegrate' and form strategic partnerships with other providers. Strategies of vertical/horizontal integration are very difficult to implement in the Internet market. As far as vertical integration is concerned, the problem relates mostly to the technical architecture of the system, which encourages a decentralized structure (see section 3.2). Furthermore, the competencies required in each segment of the market are quite specific, making it difficult for a single operator to accumulate all the knowledge and skills to compete in the market as a fully integrated company. With reference to horizontal integration, the problem is that having specialized companies offering different services requires great co-ordination between providers to ensure that the best combination of services get to end users. This is difficult to achieve in an ever changing environment, where new technologies, products and services are introduced on a constant basis.

The ISPs in the UK are forming partnerships with providers of network components such as Cisco Novell and Sun, although some companies state they are willing to form alliances with media companies and content providers. The absence of any mention to universities and publicly funded research institutes as possible partners signals the poor links between firms and non-firm organizations in the development of innovations. In the UK's sectoral innovation system of the Internet industry non-firm organizations are not participating in the innovation and production processes. They are not involved

---

[3] Some literature however questions this (Katz 1996).

with firms' R&D projects and they do not provide qualified researchers and technicians. This seems to be an invariant sectoral pattern across countries in Europe and is quite different from North America where in the early years of Internet development innovation took place mostly in public-sector research centres and universities (McKnight and Bailey 1998).

Some interviewees remark upon having significant interactions with customers and stress the relevance of user feedback as a major source of innovation. The feedback comes from highly heterogeneous categories of users and appears to be fundamental in the development of customized technological solutions. In a context where differentiation is emerging as a key strategy for companies that cannot be system integrators but tend instead to address niche markets with specific requirements, building a strong relationship with the users assumes great relevance. However, even the dominant players in the industry, which are able to offer their services to different categories of users – both businesses and consumers – consider their customers a major source of innovation. However, contacts between users and producers are not always easy and there are often mismatches between user requirements and firm offerings. The role of user–producer interaction in the development of new technologies, products and services seems to be particularly relevant in determining the relative efficiency of the innovation process and in affecting the overall sectoral dynamics of the Internet industry.

1.3. Users and Providers in the Internet Market: The Free Service Phenomenon

The Internet backbone market in the UK is dominated by telecommunications operators. However other companies are playing a significant role in the provision of the IP network, carrying out substantial investments in bandwidth, a key resource for the future development of the Internet, since bandwidth needs increase as customers use more for new applications. Demon Internet, a pioneer in the UK Internet access market, launched its service in 1992. The company provides a standard set of Internet services for home and small and medium-sized enterprise (SME) users, currently including voice and fax over IP and Internet access through mobile phones.[4] UUNet, the Internet services division of MCI WorldCom, is a global leader in Internet communications solutions, offering a comprehensive range of Internet services to business customers and ISPs worldwide. Providing Internet access, web hosting, remote access and other value-added services, UUNet is active in 114 countries, with

---

[4] This has been possible because of a recent collaboration with Orange.

more than 70 000 businesses, and owns and operates a global network in metropolitan areas throughout North America, Europe and Asia-Pacific.

The Internet's diffusion in the UK has been boosted by the phenomenon of free access initiated by Freeserve and immediately followed by other operators, which has contributed to making the country an Internet leader in Europe and has helped consumers become familiar with new communications services. There are approximately 300 ISPs in the UK, of which more than 10 per cent are 'free ISPs'. Around 200 ISPs have full UK coverage, while others are either regional ISPs or specialized business providers. Beyond basic Internet access, almost every ISP offers some forms of content and other enhanced services such as web hosting, Intranet and platforms for electronic commerce.

Freeserve has played a crucial role in the UK market by attracting considerable numbers of users on-line and stimulating other competitors to imitate and find new ways to compete. The emergence of free ISPs has also been responsible for significantly differentiating demand, revealing how the strategy of Internet operators can impact the behaviour of users (Shapiro and Varian 1999). In particular, the possibility of accessing the Internet for free attracted an older and less rich audience than the previously existing user community.[5] Furthermore, the decrease in personal computer (PC) prices and the development of innovative access solutions (e.g., Web TV, screen telephones and palmtops) is widening the boundaries of the on-line users' base. Following this trend, some companies traditionally belonging to other sectors have started a proprietary business unit for the provision of Internet services. Mirror Group and News International, for example, owners of the UK's popular newspapers, have moved into the market through the launch of competitive Internet offerings.

The customer base of each ISP is homogeneous: some companies target residential users with low-priced basic services, while others provide business users high-quality expensive services. Only the most profitable companies that own a network can target heterogeneous groups of users with customized services for different categories.[6] The UK represents one of few European countries where the former incumbent telecommunications operator is not the leader in the provision of Internet services – Freeserve, not BT, has the biggest market share. The country's history in telecommunications indicates that competition was first pursued in the telecommunications market and subsequently extended to the new sector. Figure 7.1 illustrates the market share of top UK ISPs.

---

[5] A 1999 survey from NOP suggests the majority of UK Internet users are still affluent males under age 45.
[6] This strategy of providing different versions of products and services is a winning one, since it allows firms to derive the highest profits from each category of users (Shapiro and Varian 1999).

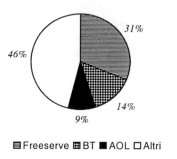

☲ Freeserve ⊞ BT ■ AOL □ Altri

Figure 7.1: UK top 3 ISPs' market share, June 1999
Source: Merrill Lynch (1999).

While BT competes on an equal basis in the Internet services market, it dominates most telecommunications areas (controlling 85 per cent of the local call telephony market and 84 per cent of the digital leased lines market). Due to the breadth of its offerings and the technological advancement of its underlying infrastructure, BT has been able to offer a range of innovative applications, and has made substantial investments to upgrade its network to provide broadband integrated solutions. Among the telecommunications and cable operators that have entered the Internet service industry, Cable and Wireless and Telewest are now active players in Internet service provision for corporate and consumer markets. Other companies, such as COLT Telecom and INS, are instead concentrating on the business sector and the provision of wholesale IP bandwidth for ISPs.

The ISPs in the country include companies that exploit other operators' infrastructure to provide high-quality content to niches of consumers as well as backbone providers. AOL, Compuserve, MSN, LineOne and Which?On-line fall in this category. In particular the last two operators are very interesting examples of national companies that have implemented an innovative strategy for the provision of content and Internet access services. LineOne utilizes BT's network, while Which?On-line relies upon NTL's infrastructure. Both are focusing on the residential users' market and consider it a segment with significant market potential, even though they agree that SMEs also represent an important market to address, especially now that the free service phenomenon is undermining the economic sustainability of companies that exclusively target the market for residential users.

1.4. Competition and Co-operation in the Internet Market

Notwithstanding the high rate of penetration of the Internet in the UK, ISPs face significant challenges to survive. One major problem is that users show little loyalty to service providers. A recent study indicated that 83 per cent of subscribers to the free ISP X-Stream have more than one account; the figure is 71 per cent for AOL, 55 per cent for BT Click Free, and 32 per cent for Freeserve (Merrill Lynch 1999). This tendency has serious implications for ISPs needing to find innovative ways to provide services and investing in the development of value-added content, which appears to be a valuable resource especially for firms that do not own the infrastructure. Specialized content providers have started operating in the UK with generalized content providers (portals). The entry of Which?Online in the Internet sector witnesses the emergence of such a phenomenon: this company was originally a consumer association that subsequently decided to offer on-line content-on-demand and Internet access to existing subscribers. This strategy could be appealing to media and publishing companies, which are latecomers in the Internet industry, but have strong skills in providing traditional communication media content. They could exploit their core competencies to harness the new technological opportunities and quickly catch up and succeed in the Internet sector.[7]

According to the interviewees, the main barriers to entry are related to financial constraints, technology and human resources management. The difficulty in operating a flexible network is also seen as a potential obstacle to the entry of new companies. There is a compelling need to create a strong customer base, since in the future it will not be possible to provide Internet for free and therefore ISPs will not be able to attract new customers with this offer. This means that they must have an established user base to survive in the market. One of the interviewees also stressed that the small ISPs could be successful if they concentrated on a particular market niche, since the market will tend to be vertically separated.

The process of technical change has both positive and negative effects on the level of competition. New technologies open windows of opportunities to many existing companies and increase demand for new services and applications, opening the market for entry of new companies. However, there is extreme pressure on ISPs, especially in terms of human resources training and management. This is shown by the fact that in the early years of Internet development, entry was very high, then it slowed and gave way to a process of consolidation. As a consequence, companies now try to differentiate from one

[7] As a sign of the growing importance of content provision, even BT has invested in content, with its 50 per cent ownership in Excite UK.

another by offering different combinations of Internet services. A process of shakeout is now characterizing the UK market. A possible outcome may be that ISPs will be run by retail companies that act as an electronic commerce conduit (e.g. Dixons). Another possibility is related to the different values placed on two segments: the Internet infrastructure is highly valued and will always be needed, while the access segment is much less stable. This is reflected in the market structure where there are about 300 ISPs (including access and content providers) and about 20–25 major backbone providers (companies that own the infrastructure). Instead of a general shakeout, it is likely that in the UK there will be significant consolidation at the level of network providers and a process of differentiation in the market for access and content provision. Telecommunications operators and cable companies are going to play a considerable role as ISPs in the future, and among these firms, BT will be an important competitor.

1.5. Future Prospects for the Internet's Sectoral System in the UK

The UK was the first country to liberalize the telecommunications industry and this represented an important step in the development of the Internet sector, due to the strong links between the two markets. The telecommunications market is going to become even more competitive, as the combination of data, voice and video emerges as a critical resource for companies. All the interviewees agree that competition is quite high in the country but they also notice that BT still retains a monopolistic position in the local loop. The situation is worsened by the fact that many traditional telecommunications operators are also ISPs, so that survival in the market is quite difficult for 'pure' IAPs.

The liberalization of the telecommunications market had the consequence of substantially reducing the charges of telephone calls, which are among the lowest in Europe. Another interesting point concerns the role of cable TV operators. The interviewees believe that those companies are in a very advantageous position to compete in the Internet service market, because of their broadband distribution channels and because of the potential for Web TV applications. OFTEL, the national regulatory authority for telecommunications, in principle does not allow unfair competition, but one has to consider that the cable market is basically a duopoly with NTL and Telewest owning a large share of it and that these companies can provide telephony services. Despite the early deregulation of the telecommunications market, OFTEL is seen as protecting the incumbent operator. This raises some interesting issues with respect to the role of public organizations and institutions in affecting the market structure. The institutional context of the UK seems to favour the incumbent, while giving few opportunities to new entrants.

The UK Internet sectoral system will soon experience important changes due to the development of digital television. Set-top boxes will soon become a very popular Internet appliance and will compete with many other customer premises devices such as screen telephones, digital mobile phones, new digital television sets and PCs. The cable television industry will develop its own Internet services with cable modems. Cable companies and newly licensed telecommunications operators already provide telephone calls at lower prices than BT and, unlike the incumbent, they are not tied to the Universal Service Obligation. Content will play a fundamental role in the near future for the development of the Internet and, as a consequence, new alliances between content developers (traditional and new media companies) and ISPs will emerge.

Companies in more traditional sectors have also entered the business of Internet provision. The most relevant example is Dixons, a consumer electronics retailer, whose strategy has been to offer a free Internet service (Freeserve) through its distribution channels to users with experience in consumer electronics goods, in order to create a strong brand and to build a substantial customer base. Interviewees agree that these free services can play a significant role in the future. As one stated,

> You cannot ignore these free services, but you have to choose a mix of price/quality service. The market will split up. On-line retailers will address niche markets; cable operators are potentially important, because they have the technology to offer more bandwidth, but there are lock-in problems for people to shift from a PC/telephone to a TV. Again, early adopters will probably be the drivers.

Being the most saturated market in Europe, the UK represents a point of reference for future trends. This is particularly important for the successful development of a strong demand. Free PC and innovative use of toll-free connections constitute two significant tendencies that are likely to shape the future diffusion of Internet services.

2. ITALY: LATECOMER IN THE INTERNET LANDSCAPE

2.1. Introduction

> Italy is a country of fashionable trends and the Internet has certainly become fashionable. (OVUM 1998: 100)

This quotation illustrates well the situation of the Internet market in a country, which has only recently entered the 'digital era'. Italy has registered a significant delay in the development and diffusion of the Internet, not only compared to the US, but also compared to other European countries. Consequently it now faces significant opportunities but also considerable risks as far as the development of the Internet industry is concerned. The country's interest in the Internet and in new communication applications generally has grown from 1999 to 2000, following the advent of free service in the consumer market and the recognition of the enormous potential of the World Wide Web (WWW) in the business market. However e-mail and Internet access are still the most utilized applications and will probably remain dominant in the next few years, due to the lack of technical skills, the low familiarity with multimedia applications and the inappreciable diffusion of the English language among the Italian population. Unlike the UK, one of the major obstacles to the development of the Internet market in Italy has been the slow process of deregulation of the telecommunications sector, which in turn has been caused by the lack of a strong regulatory framework and an independent regulatory authority. This has hindered not only the development of a competitive industry, but also the diffusion of new technologies and applications.

It is reasonable to argue that as soon as Italy's 'digital literacy' increases, users will become familiar with value-added Internet services and with new communication applications other than e-mail and WWW surfing. National operators have initially focused on the corporate segment of the market, but are now making considerable efforts to meet the growing demand for consumer Internet usage. The development of new Internet access devices – in particular portable terminals (cellular phones using the wireless applications protocol and palmtops) and set-top boxes – are likely to boost the diffusion of Internet services in Italy over the next five years. Telecom Italia, the leader in the provision of Internet services and leader also in the telecommunications market, is already offering multimedia services through its subsidiary STREAM, while Omnitel, the major competitor of Telecom Italia in the mobile market, is providing Internet access through cellular phones.

A quite notable phenomenon in Italy has been the rapid diffusion of cellular phones. Together with the Scandinavian countries, Italy's mobile phones penetration is the best in Europe. This is quite relevant if one considers the technological complementarities that are arising between wireless technologies and the IP network. Third-generation mobile telephones may act as a catalyst to diffuse the Internet in Italy. In this respect, one could say that the process of convergence is occurring at the level of customer premises equipment.

2.2. Innovation and the Diffusion of New Technologies

Following the growing diffusion of the Internet, Italy's telecommunications operators have been forced to build a corresponding infrastructure to provide high-speed connections and broadband services. Although the transition from traditional narrow-band to real-time multimedia applications is occurring slowly in the country, there are strong pressures on existing operators to build advanced networks. The quality of Internet backbones in Italy is in line with the EU standards, even if the South is lagging behind the North in terms of Internet infrastructure. Telecommunications operators are investing in ATM-based networks and are building integrated services digital networks (ISDNs), but they are also developing asymmetric digital subscriber line (ADSL) techniques for large businesses and small office, home office (SOHO), which would significantly upgrade existing networks (OVUM 1998; EITO 2000).

As emphasized, the Internet constitutes a technological breakthrough in the telecommunications trajectory and has generated significant changes in the pattern of innovation and production processes of firms. This is particularly evident in a latecomer country like Italy, where ISP innovative activity does not concern purely technological aspects (an exception being represented by telecommunications operators), but rather relates to the combination of new value-added services and to the development of customized solutions for business users. All interviewees stress that user needs have a major role in affecting the rate and direction of innovation in the Internet services industry. Some also stress the importance of monitoring the activity of European competitors, in order to be able to follow the major technological trends.

In describing the determinants of innovation, the theory of sectoral systems emphasizes the role of non-firm organizations such as universities and research centres in providing skilled human resources and in developing R&D activity (Nelson 1993). However, as in the case of the UK, Italian ISPs seem to have no relationship with the academic world and complain about the gap between the knowledge and competencies provided by the university sector and their own requirements. The skill shortage in the information and communication technology (ICT) sector is a common phenomenon across European countries, but it is particularly worrying in Italy, because of the specificity of the Italian educational system and the late development of the Internet industry, which has not given enough feedback to the public research and educational system as far as skills and knowledge requirements are concerned.

The process of technological convergence has also been responsible for a process of market convergence. In particular, telecommunications and media companies are positioning themselves in a market formerly dominated by pure Internet access providers, stimulating intense competition and a wave of important technological, market and organizational innovations. Table 7.1 illustrates the activity of selected companies.

Table 7.1: Internet activity of selected ICT operators

Company	Traditional business	Recent business expansion (except in Internet services)	Internet activity
Telecom Italia	Fixed telephony	Mobile telephony (TIM) Digital TV (Stream)	ISP: Consumer mkt – TINIT Business mkt – Interbusiness
Infostrada	Long-distance fixed telephony	Local fixed telephony service	ISP: Consumer mkt – Libero/IOL Business mkt – Infostrada
Gruppo Espresso	Publishing Radio service	Fixed telephony	IAP & ICP (portal) – Kataweb
Wind	Mobile telephony	–	IAP
Mediaset	Broadcasting	–	IAP & ICP (portal) – Jumpy
Tiscali	IAP (first to offer free access)	Fixed telephony; plans for mobile telephony	IAP

Particularly interesting is the development of Internet activity by Gruppo Espresso and Mediaset, which demonstrate that the boundaries of the industry are changing and content is becoming a highly valuable asset to compete in the market. Content owners are destined to play an important role in this industry, but they need to set agreements with network providers, so that they can run multimedia services on the existing infrastructure. This need is stimulating a growing number of alliances in the sector, as the importance of sharing key competencies and resources is increasingly understood.[8] In this respect co-evolution between market structure and technological change is occurring in this sectoral system (Malerba 2000). This sector's processes of innovation and production involve an increasing number of firms, which contributes to the development of new combinations of knowledge and competencies and has introduced new business and organizational models to the sector.

---

[8] The recent agreement between TIN – the ISP of Telecom Italia – and Seat Pagine Gialle, an Internet company (formerly publishing) of Gruppo Espresso, is the most distinct example of this phenomenon.

Even though the Italian Internet market for service provision is competitive, there remain great obstacles to full competition at the level of network providers, where Telecom Italia has a dominant role. However, other companies have built an infrastructure for the provision of both telephony and Internet services. Infostrada has a 3 700 km fibre optics backbone, with some urban networks in the North and ambitions of covering the whole territory. Wind and Albacom rely upon ENEL and Snam for the provision of communication infrastructure, while Tiscali has started covering an increasing number of areas in the country.

In the Italian ISP market there are around 300 companies, including content providers. The Italian system is characterized by a sharp distinction between companies that provide Internet services at a national level and operators that focus their activity at a regional level and usually operate in the northern regions. This symbolizes the substantial diversity between different regions not only in terms of industrial structure but also in institutional, social and cultural aspects, which suggests the existence of regional systems of innovation even in a 'global' sector such as the Internet industry. It is important to note that most ISPs (with the notable exception of Telecom Italia and a few other firms like Infostrada) are relatively young companies that were born at the beginning of the 1990s on the wave of the technological changes that were occurring in the industry.

The process of liberalization has recently stimulated the entry of additional operators, increasing the number of competitors in the sector. Even though there is a tendency towards specialization, ISPs still offer a standard range of services, with particular attention to consulting and helpdesk services.[9] Interviewees agree that the development of customized services for SMEs – in particular Intranets – is a very profitable business. There seems to be little interest in the consumer segment, mostly because the free service phenomenon has undermined the economic sustainability of ISPs, who now count on the reverse interconnection agreement and advertising as the main source of revenues. First-mover ISPs see free service as a means of advertising the Internet and increasing interest in new communication services, but some interviewees consider this phenomenon poor advertising for the Internet, since free service is often associated with low quality. The low penetration of the Internet in Italy has caused insufficient utilization of existing infrastructure, with serious consequences for the economic efficiency of network providers. Nevertheless, the possibility of accessing the Internet for free eliminates one of the most relevant barriers to its usage – the cost of access – and stimulates

---

[9] This reflects a lack of technical skills among users.

an increasing number of users to go on-line, so that operators can achieve an efficient use of their infrastructure.

All interviewees agree that the major difficulty for ISPs does not relate to the existence of barriers to entry, but to the low opportunities of survival. Start-up investments in the Internet industry are not very high, but the rapid disappearance of initial competitive advantages causes the exit of many small ISPs and induces specialization among surviving companies in providing Internet services to business users. The lack of qualified human capital represents a substantial barrier to the entry and survival of new operators and reflects the lack of synergy between firms and non-firm organizations for the growth and competitiveness of the system.

It has been underlined that knowledge embodied in people and organizations constitutes a core component in the development of innovations and that innovation itself is the result of an interactive and collective process which involves the different parts of a sectoral system (Lundvall 1993; Malerba 2000). Firms can acquire technical and scientific competencies through a continuous exchange of knowledge and skills with the educational system, in particular with universities and research centres, whose activities should include providing qualified human capital, proposing guidelines for future R&D, and collaborating on existing research projects with private companies. In the case of the Internet, however, one could argue that universities are looking at the evolution of the market to gain insights in the future directions of research and to investigate the needs of firms in terms of technical competencies. The role of human capital is even more important when knowledge is highly specific and technical change rather cumulative in nature. This appears to be the predominant characteristic of the Internet sector's technological evolution, where a high degree of specialization in various segments of the system – network/infrastructure, services and content – requires the development of specific skills.

Most interviewees agree that it is necessary to implement a strategy of diversification by providing customized services with valuable content to users, since content is going to constitute the value added for final users, while transport is going to become a pure commodity. This is why, as mentioned before, telecommunications operators, which are weak in terms of content, are forming alliances with content providers. Pure ISPs are also entering partnerships, some with network providers to exploit the infrastructure in place and provide broadband services, others with software providers to develop customized software packages for business users, and still others with hardware providers to obtain the best network components for the implementation of integrated technological solutions. Integrated services for businesses – in particular platforms for electronic commerce and Intranets – are seen as most profitable. The trend is towards an increasing integration of voice, data and video, and in the near future voice applications will lose importance relative to data and visual communications.

Italian ISPs consider the system uncompetitive at present, observing that the ex-monopolist still retains a considerable power. The interviewees identify their competitors according to geographical area and targeted market (business or consumer). Telecom operators owning the infrastructure see one another as direct competitors, while cable TV operators are not viewed this way, which reflects the limited role of these companies in the industry compared to the UK. The free ISPs may find it difficult to compete in the market, once the competition becomes better organized. These firms are now going through a difficult stage of trying to survive in a market where content and conduit are emerging as key complementary assets to simple Internet access and basic service provision.

2.3. The Demand

The Internet's penetration of Italy is low by European standards and this can be attributed to the historic pricing structure of Internet connections, the lack of Italian language content and the low level of PC penetration. However, these constraints are easing considerably and this should help the diffusion of Internet usage across the country, although the lack of familiarity with multimedia applications will hinder the growth of demand. Improving the situation involves acquiring technical skills to utilize Internet services, as well as changing personal habits and behaviours.

Italy's Internet services market has experienced significant growth in the last two years, with the business segment, and especially large firms, accounting for 70 per cent of the total Internet market (Assinform 2000). The major driving force behind this trend is that an increasing number of companies see the Internet as an effective marketing channel and an opportunity to gain a competitive edge over competitors that are not on-line. Furthermore, the free access phenomenon has significantly lowered the margins in the consumer market, casting doubts over the economic sustainability of ISPs that focus exclusively on the residential user segment. More corporate users for whom Internet access becomes business critical will install leased line connections. Recent estimates show that the number of corporate Internet users will reach 3.2 million in 2005, and that among business users, the number of Internet subscribers will grow to 704 000 in 2005.

The business market has experienced a process of development and consolidation in Internet use between 1999 and 2000. According to recent estimates (Federcomin 2001), in June 2000, 80 per cent of the local business units of Italian firms that use ICT have an Internet connection, compared to 66 per cent in 1999. In terms of size, all large and medium-sized companies have at least one Internet connection, while 79.3 per cent of SMEs access the Web. This is significant, considering that in 1999 the percentage of SMEs with an Internet connection was 65.4 per cent. Looking at the patterns of adoption across sectors, the banking industry appears to be the most active, with 90.9 per cent of banks currently using Internet services. Within the public sector, 72.2 per cent of institutions access the Web, although this figure is affected by the inappreciable performance of the health system, where just 67.9 per cent of organizations have an Internet connection.

In the consumer market, we observe a similar situation to the UK's, although Internet penetration among households is considerably lower in Italy. The demand for Internet services has been strongly stimulated by the possibility of accessing the Web for free. Furthermore, the low price for modems together with the decrease in telephone tariffs has contributed to attracting large numbers of consumers to the Internet market. As already underlined, however, there are two main barriers to the diffusion of the Internet. The first relates to the insignificant penetration of PCs in households and workplaces. Since PCs are still the most diffused Web access device, their diffusion provides a good indication for the diffusion of the Internet.[10] Another important indicator is the ratio of users per device, which shows the number of users sharing a device to access the Internet. Table 7.2 presents a national comparison of this ratio.

Table 7.2: User per device ratio in selected European countries, year-end 1998

Country	Ratio
Germany	1.6
UK	1.7
France	2.0
Italy	2.2
Sweden	1.5
Spain	2.2
Finland	1.8
Norway	1.5
Europe (average)	1.8

Source: Warburg Dillon Read (2000).

As the table shows, Italy's ratio is very high, which is quite common for latecomer countries: this indicates that a demand-side pull rather than a sup-

---

[10] However, the proportion of Web-enabled PCs is currently 34 per cent.

ply-side push is currently driving Internet penetration. Since PCs are still relatively expensive, most of the demand is coming from individuals and businesses with a specific need or desire to get on-line, with the Web penetration itself acting as a catalyst.

A second barrier to Internet use is the minimal knowledge of English among the Italian population. Since almost 90 per cent of the Internet content is currently in English, ISPs stress the need for greater diffusion of the English language, yet they agree that the development of Italian content may act as an incentive for consumers to go on-line, at least in the short term. The recent increase in Italian language content has added values for existing on-line users, while giving incentives to potential users to go on-line.

With the advent of free service, a major barrier to Internet usage – the cost of access – was eliminated. Furthermore, increased competition among telephone operators have resulted in call charges that are now among the lowest in Europe (OECD 2001). Recent estimates suggest that there will be 3 million residential subscribers by 2002, which corresponds to almost 15 per cent of total households: this is quite significant when compared to 400 000 subscribers in 1998. All interviewees criticize the education system for not contributing to the diffusion of a multimedia culture and providing the necessary training for using the new technologies. As we have seen, in some countries – including the UK – the government is directly involved in the sponsorship of the new Internet economy. In particular, several administrations are encouraging the growth of educational Web access by offering subsidies to companies that give employees home PC access and by moving key public institutions on-line.

ISPs know there are risks involved in expecting increased Internet usage in Italy. Low PC penetration might be slow to change because it requires Italians to change the ways they spend their time and money. Furthermore, the modest amount of Italian content may slow acceptance of the Internet, although the provision of local content on web sites is now expanding rapidly. Some doubts also appear to remain with regard to the market potential of business-to-consumer electronic commerce in Italy, as empirical evidence shows a low diffusion of on-line transactions. For cultural reasons, Italian consumers are not keen on using the Internet as a means of conducting commercial transactions, especially because they feel unsure about the security of on-line financial operations.

2.4. Institutions, Market Potential and Future Prospects for the Internet in Italy

As underlined at the beginning of this section, the regulatory regime in the telecommunications sector in Italy has been characterized by the absence of clear and well-defined guidelines for the implementation of an appropriate competition policy. The slow acceptance of European laws has caused a significant delay in the process of liberalization, which has hindered not only competition, but also the exploration and exploitation of new technological opportunities. The late deregulation of the fixed lines telecommunications business in Italy took place on January 1, 1998, when competitors were granted the right to apply for licences. The first interconnected services were offered by Infostrada in July 1998. A subsequent step in the deregulation process has been the unbundling of the local loop on 1 January 2000. This delay was also due to the lack of a telecommunications authority, which was established just at the end of 1997, with the task of governing the telecommunications and broadcasting markets according to the rules and principles of the European Union.

The liberalization of the telecommunications sector is fundamental for the development of the Internet, since it implies lower tariffs for end users and lower prices of leased lines for ISPs.[11] Furthermore, liberalization in the licensing regime allows both for the emergence of several new operators in the telecommunications and Internet markets and for the participation of companies traditionally belonging to different sectors in the Internet services market. All interviewees agree that a higher level of competition in the Internet market has occurred as a consequence of liberalizing the telecommunications sector. They also stress that there have been significant changes in the typology of their competitors. In particular, Italy has experienced a relevant rate of entry of media and publishing companies, while cable TV operators do not play as great a role as in the UK.

It is possible to identify a similar pattern between Italy and the UK in the evolution of market structure, which is also found in many European countries. After a period of high innovative entry, the sector is now characterized by a gradual diminishing of the number of ISPs. It seems that firm size matters a lot, since the process of consolidation occurs through the acquisition of small companies by big operators. This phenomenon has not so far concerned telecommunications operators that are also network providers, since they can exploit economies of scale stemming from a more efficient utilization of the network, by offering Internet as well as telecommunications services.

The characteristics of Italian users not only in terms of skills and requirements but especially in terms of culture, habits and behaviours have a relevant impact on firms' future strategies. The market dynamics in Italy are developing along two parallel paths. Along one path, network providers (telecommunications operators) and media/publishing companies that have entered the

---

[11] Interestingly enough, according to recent estimates the telephone tariffs in Italy are among the lowest in Europe (OECD 2001).

Internet sector address the consumer segment, offering a wide range of Internet services together with telecommunications services and/or high-value content. These firms can provide free access because they make profits from other sources. Along another path, independent ISPs that have survived in the market, are more inclined to target the business segment, offering value-added services and integrated solutions, which can be priced according to quality.

3. INTERNET SERVICES IN SWEDEN

3.1. Introduction

Sweden has the highest Internet penetration in Europe and the most advanced sectoral system of innovation in the Internet industry, both in terms of technological development and diffusion of new technology, services and applications. This means there is a well-developed demand for advanced services and the market is quite competitive for firms that are willing to respond to users' needs. The above-average GDP per capita, an equal distribution of wealth, a high PC penetration and a generally positive attitude towards the adoption of new technologies are the main explanatory variables for this phenomenon. Sweden has one of the most liberalized telecommunications markets in the world and this has been a major driver for the development of alternative networks to the one of the former incumbent operator Telia. Due to Sweden's advanced network infrastructure, value-added services such as video-conferencing, Web transactions, IP telephony and video-on-demand are emerging at a much faster rate than other European countries. This is impressive, considering the ISPs in the country have not adopted the free service model. Today there are many operators offering a wide range of telecommunications and broadcasting services and indeed the country already shows a very high cable penetration in Europe. A few big companies dominate the ISP market in Sweden, but it is likely that the competition will increase as new players for dial-up and broadband services emerge. In this respect, it is important to remember that, although it is still limited from a geographical point of view, broadband Internet access is offered via several technological solutions such as ADSL, cable networks and fibre-to-the-home.

The telecommunications market in Sweden was liberalized in 1993, well before most other European countries. The advanced infrastructure that characterizes the market consists of 69.6 fixed lines per 100 inhabitants, a mobile phone penetration of 60 per cent and a PC penetration of 66 per cent (EITO 2000). The process of liberalization and the consequent decrease in interconnection fees helped new companies enter the market. However, these operators had to make substantial investments in marketing in order to attract customers and compete with Telia, which was already benefiting from a large customer base. The unbundling of the local loop was achieved in March 2000. In the initial phases, Telia offered collocation but not line sharing and new entrants considered the price of interconnection too high to allow them to compete on an equal basis. The completion of local loop unbundling has been accomplished in the current year (2002).

Beyond the deregulation of the industry, the Swedish government is implementing a significant number of initiatives to stimulate the diffusion of broadband access in the country and is collaborating with commercial players in order to create an environment conducive to upgrading the Internet infrastructure. To ensure that the country remains a leader in the European Internet landscape, the government has appointed an ad hoc commission to build an infrastructure that will provide households a high-speed (5 Mbps) Internet access by 2005. This involvement is particularly important for the northern regions of Sweden, where a low density population could prevent the private sector from developing a broadband network profitably.

3.2 Technological Development at the Level of Backbone Providers

Although demand is playing an important role in developing the Swedish system of innovation in the Internet service industry, a major reason for the high rate of diffusion of Internet services is the technical advancement of the country's backbone infrastructure. All firms carry out substantial investments in their own network to meet existing demand for broadband by residential and business users and to develop service innovations that are appealing to Internet users. An important technological development in Sweden is represented by broadband access to the residential market. Telia and B2 have already started providing high-speed Internet access via fibre-to-the-building. The diffusion of cables in the country is high (available to around two million households in Sweden, with Telia providing services to 60 per cent of them) and this has stimulated cable operators to offer broadband cable connections.

All companies are upgrading their infrastructure to provide a system of communication that will facilitate cable Internet access. In a number of residential areas companies have installed networks that can simultaneously carry telephony and broadband services. This technological and market development may generate some problems at the regulatory level, as it may promote the creation of monopolies, since users are tied to a single provider for an entire package of services, making it impossible for other companies to compete. Fibre-to-the-building solutions are emerging in the country and are based on, for instance, a house installing a local area network connected to the fibre network. These solutions provide Internet access at very high speed for the users. Furthermore, Swedish users can also buy a one-way satellite service offering broadband content, although they still need a separate ISP. The ADSL development is still at an early stage and Telia is the only player offering this technology to residential users, although a number of companies are going to enter the market as soon as ADSL-based services are priced more competitively.

The incumbent Telia is the dominant backbone owner in Sweden, due to a monopoly the company enjoyed in providing telecommunication infrastructure services until 1993. Since the deregulation of the market, however, a significant number of players have entered the industry. Now Sweden has several national network providers and a group of companies owning a regional network, which previously belonged to other sectors, such as utilities and broadcasting firms. Regional networks include Vattenfall and Sydkraft, two electric utilities, and STOKAB, a firm owned by the City of Stockholm and the Stockholm County Council and charged with building a fibre network in the city to stimulate competitive telecommunications services. Telia is experimenting with Gigabit Ethernet solutions, which offer speeds of up to 100 Mbps. As mentioned, the incumbent leads in the market of ADSL services and is investing in 25 cities and towns to make broadband available to at least one million households in Sweden. At the same time, Tele2 has upgraded its network with wavelength division multiplexing (WDM) technology, and now provides backbone connections between the main cities of up to 20 Gbps. The company, as many other Telia competitors, is interested in offering ADSL services, but considers the price demanded by the incumbent for access to the local loop as too high. So far, only companies that focus on the business segment of the market have signed agreements to lease the last mile access from Telia.

If we look at the national backbone providers in Sweden, it is easy to see the extreme variety of the firms' core businesses. Beyond Telia and Utfors, a relatively new telecommunications company which started developing its national backbone in the summer of 1999, the other companies own quite different types of networks. Banverket is the national rail administration in Sweden and has a network of 13 000 km of fibre optics along the Swedish rail network. In addition to meeting the requirements of the rail network, the firm provides managed bandwidth to a substantial range of large and medium telecommunications operators. Svenska Kraftnaet operates the Swedish electricity infrastructure and has 1 800 km of fibre optics installed in the southern and central regions of the country. The firm leases back the fibres to the major Swedish ISPs and Tele2 is its largest customer. Teracom is a state-owned company whose primary business is the transmission of radio and TV programmes over its radio network, which can also be exploited by other telecommunications operators for its capacity to transfer voice and data. This is a particularly interesting development in Sweden's Internet market, since competencies of network management in different infrastructure providers are being integrated in the Internet market and allow the development of an advanced infrastructure that supports value-added services. Given that a high variety of competencies characterize the new entrants in the industry, a major issue for all operators will be how to combine their own critical assets to compete in the Internet market.

3.3. Technological and Market Opportunities for Swedish ISPs

Sweden's ISP market is competitive, although the country has already experienced a shakeout within the Internet services industry. There are 120 ISPs in the country, ten of which operate on a large scale and serve the large business community. Currently Telia, Tele1, Tele2 and Telenordia are the market leaders, although there are a number of specialized players covering the corporate sector, particularly in the main cities. However, none of the ISPs has a leading share in the portal market, which is dominated by Scandinavia Online and Microsoft. This means that the quality and variety of content is the most valuable benefit for frequent Internet users. The three largest players in the ISP market have seen a limited decline in their market share since the end of 1998, signalling the maturity of the sector in Sweden as compared to other countries.

In year 2000 Telia had 730 000 subscribers in Sweden and was the largest ISP in the Nordic region. The company accounts for a 40 per cent market share in terms of corporate subscriptions and a 32 per cent market share of the total Internet access market (compared to 34 per cent in 1999). It employs around 30 000 people and its network is present in 30 other countries. Competitors of Telia have chosen to target specific markets in order to gain market shares (with the exception of Tele1, most have a customer base of around 250 000 subscribers). As an example, Tele1 focuses mostly on medium and large businesses and offers fibre and digital subscriber line (DSL) services, exploiting its strong broadband position in the country. Tele2 provides Web hosting mainly to small and home businesses, although it also provides dial-up services to residential users. In providing Internet services, the company implements a strategy of aggressive price competition, which is similar to the one adopted in the telecommunication market.

In Sweden there are basically three types of pricing plans: no-subscription fee dial-up, subscription fee dial-up, or some form of fixed monthly payment for broadband services. This system is quite different from the Italian and British ones, whereby one of the most common pricing plans is the free service. Due to the sophisticated requirements of users in the country and to the related high diffusion of value-added Internet and telecommunications services, it is quite likely that choice between available pricing plans will be based upon specific needs for high-speed access. The subscription-free model was introduced in the country in 1998. It encouraged the growth of some smaller niche players, adding some complexity to the analysis of the ISP market. The problem is that many customers sign up for subscription-free access with different companies, but utilize just one of the services, although they remain a registered customer with all ISPs. Figure 7.2 shows the registered and active residential ISP subscribers. For a residential user choosing between various offerings, some fibre-to-the-home solutions are convenient on the basis of price/speed ratio compared, for example, to cable Internet access. This again reinforces the idea that the value of Internet services lies in content more than price.

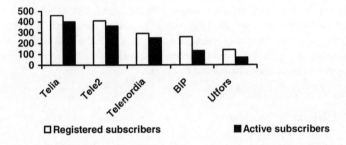

Figure 7.2: Registered and active residential ISP subscribers (thousands), March 2000

Source: Schroeder Salomon Smith Barney (2000).

As mentioned, major ISPs in Sweden do not offer much content to users, as attested by Telia, the leader in the ISP market, ranking fourth place in the portal market in terms of total users for its network. Telia's network is a collection of twelve different web domains with no general portal among them. If we look at once-a-month users among the top Swedish networks (considering all web properties), Microsoft appears to be the leader (with MSN network and Microsoft), followed by Scandinavia Online, Telia, AOL, Everyday WebGuide and others. When we consider the domains on a non-consolidated basis, the most accessed domain in Sweden is microsoft.com, the general web site for Microsoft, and it is quite likely that users access this web site to look for software products and technologies, and for using hotmail e-mail. The largest Swedish general portal is Passagen.se, which belongs to Scandinavia Online, while the Telia portal is at fourth place. However, companies such as

Everyday WebGuide and Spray Network lose their position in the ranking when domain level is concerned. This means that secondary domains drive the majority of Internet traffic for these two networks: therefore the characteristics of the web site that drive the overall traffic is important when evaluating the potential of the network for generating revenues.

Inhabitants of Nordic countries are generally very early adopters of new technologies, as illustrated by their rapid adoption of mobile phones, the Internet and WAP services. The high Internet penetration in Sweden has translated into strong demand for Internet applications as well as Internet-enabled enterprise solutions, especially customer relationship management, whose adoption in the country (and generally in the Nordic region) is higher than the European average. Furthermore, it is possible to say that one of the most important drivers of technological and market development in Sweden has been the high rate of diffusion of mobile phones, which, together with the adoption of WAP and the growth of the Internet may stimulate the take-off of mobile commerce. It is precisely in this area that Swedish service providers may take the lead within the European context, especially if one considers the proximity of the world's best mobile systems developers – Nokia and Ericsson.

REFERENCES

Assinform (2000), 'Report on Information Technology and Telecommunications', available: http://www.vormingsinstituut-wvl.be/projecten/Italian/Employment.htm.

Davies, A. (1996), 'Innovation in Large Technical Systems: The Case of Telecommunications', *Industrial and Corporate Change* **5** (4), 1143–80.

European Information Technology Observatory (2000), EITO, Frankfurt.

Federcomin (2001), *Osservatorio Federcomin sul Mercato ICT*, available: http://www.federcomin.it/osservatorio/osservatorio.htm.

Katz, C. (1996), 'Remarks on the Economic Implications of Convergence', *Industrial and Corporate Change* **5** (4), 1069–75.

Kavassalis, P., Solomon, R.J. and Benghozi, P.J. (1996), 'The Internet: A Paradigmatic Rupture in Cumulative Telecom Evolution', *Industrial and Corporate Change* **5** (4), 1097–126.

Lundvall, B.A. (ed.) (1993), *National Systems of Innovation*, London: Pinter.

Malerba, F. (2000), 'Sectoral Systems of Innovation and Production', Working Paper ESSY.

McKnight, L.W. and J. Bailey, (1998), *Internet Economics*, Cambridge (MA): MIT Press.

Merrill Lynch (1999), Internet/e-Commerce – The Quarterly Handbook: Q4 1999.

Mowery, D.C. (ed.) (1996), *The International Computer Software Industry*, New York: Oxford University Press.

Nelson, R. (ed.) (1993), *National Innovation Systems: A Comparative Study*, Oxford: Oxford University Press.

Nelson, R. and S. Winter, (1982), *An Evolutionary Theory of Economic Change*, Boston: Belknap Press of Harvard University Press.

OECD (2001), *Communications Outlook*, Paris: OECD.

OVUM (1998), Internet report, London: OVUM Ltd.

Schroeder Salomon Smith Barney (2000), 'The Internet in Sweden: A Market Overview'.

Shapiro, C. and H.R. Varian (1999), *Information Rules: A Strategic Guide to the Network Economy*, Boston: Harvard Business School Press.

Teece, D. and G. Pisano (1994), 'The Dynamic Capabilities of Firms: An Introduction', *Industrial and Corporate Change* **3**: 537–56.

Warburg Dillon Read (2000), *The Internet in Europe*, Paris: Warburg Dillon Read.

8. Policy Implications for the Future of the Sectoral System

Charles Edquist

1. INTRODUCTION

Policy implications for the Internet and mobile telecommunications will be discussed in this chapter. They are mainly based upon analyses in previous chapters, but also reflect the general policy implications of the systems of innovation approach briefly presented in chapter 1.

As mentioned in chapter 1 (section 2.2), institutional rules may be created, redesigned or abolished. Institutions that can be influenced by public agencies are public policy instruments. Similarly, institutions that are influenced by firms are firm strategy instruments. Further, organizations may be phased out, redesigned or created. If policy makers do this, these changes are also policy instruments. If firm managers do it they are firm strategy instruments.

2. FIXED INTERNET

Although several important inventions that served as bases for the development of the Internet did not emerge in the US – e.g., HTML and HTTP – the Internet developed commercially *first and fastest* in the US. The Internet was commercialized and diffused on a large scale in the US before anywhere else.

The US government was extremely important in the very early stages of the development of fixed data communications, when the sectoral system of innovation of fixed data communication was fragile and not well established. Government agencies were essential as financiers of research developing fixed data communications and they initiated public technology procurement of system elements. Other agencies required that organizations receiving public funding use the TCP/IP data communications protocol, which contributed to its diffusion and dominance. The state also increased dynamism in the telecommunications sector by pursuing deregulation.

State agencies were, however, ineffective in creating standards for the Internet in the US. This was instead a rather spontaneous process where private firms had great influence. The idea of 'open standards' or 'compatibility of standards' appears to have been the characteristic US strategy.

The relations among various organizations were crucial for the development of innovations in the sectoral system of innovation. These included the relations between public and private organizations – as in public research funding and in public technology procurement. Relations among different private organizations were also important, both in terms of competition and collaboration.

Early development and diffusion of the Internet in the US – with government support – gave that country's Internet equipment producers a 'headstart'. This is an important explanatory factor behind the fact that US Internet equipment-producing firms, such as Cisco, are still dominant globally. It is obviously very important for firm competitiveness in high-tech areas to be early movers in the sector and to be close to customers in these early stages.

3. MOBILE TELECOMMUNICATIONS

State-controlled organizations were very important in creating the first successful mobile telecommunications standard in Europe. Public telecommunications monopolies in the Nordic countries created the NMT 450 mobile telecommunications standard in collaboration with firms. The PTOs pushed the technical development of the standard and pulled national equipment-producing firms along their trajectory. They placed orders to firms and partly used the instrument of public technology procurement to create incentives for firms to develop equipment for NMT 450. NMT 450 provided the cradle for the development of mobile telecommunications in Europe. *Deregulation* of the telecommunications sector was also important in some European countries, such as Sweden and the UK. However, liberalization was not a key factor in Sweden's success with NMT and GSM. At most it aided the diffusion process that was already under way at the time of deregulation which began in 1993.

Relations among organizations were important in the process just described. So were relations between various kinds of institutions – like NMT 450 – and the firms and other organizations involved. Relations between operators – who were the main standard creators – and equipment producers were indispensable in making European equipment producers leaders at the global level. For firms like Nokia and Ericsson it was also important that mobile telecommunications got a 'headstart' in the Nordic countries and grew rapidly.

Most second-generation standards were developed with the potential to become de facto world standards through international adoption. The European GSM standard – which developed out of the NMT standard – more than fulfilled the expectation of wide international diffusion. Initially conceived as a pan-European standard, it became a world standard. No other second-generation standard achieved this. Deregulated operators (like Swedish Televerket/Telia) as well as firms (such as Ericsson and Nokia) were very active in the consortium that supported the development of the GSM standard. Hence, the close relations between users and producers continued. Over the long term, however, these close relations gradually became looser. The GSM success could not be ascribed only to the strategies of a few innovative organizations, but also to the collaborations of a variety of different organizations: PTOs, standard-setting organizations and research organizations as well as equipment producers.

The European Commission also had a leading role in the development of GSM. The EU was pushing one standard and it was developed *ex ante*. This was also a standard that was technologically advanced, operated well and therefore diffused rapidly outside Europe. In contrast, the US digital standards diffused internationally only to a limited extent and the single Japanese standard not at all. The European Commission pushed liberalization and competition in the (mobile) telecommunications sector.[1] But it did so within one single standard and did not care about letting standards compete – as in the US standards policy. The standard pushed by the EU was secured to serve all EU members, while the US digital standards were not completely compatible with one another. What the EU did across 13 European countries, the US did not manage to do for one (although large) country.

It proved to be a major policy mistake to have several standards in the US. This can be considered a serious policy failure for the US as well as a great success for the EU. The reasons for this are that it led to a slower diffusion of mobile telecommunications in the US than in Europe and that the strongest equipment producers emerged in Europe.

The US policy was calculated and consistent. The FCC was against *ex ante* standardization – which was preferred by ETSI – and advocated an open network architecture.[2] Arguments were that the open architecture was important for the creation of the Internet and that closing it could block further innovation. The FCC was passive in relation to the European invitation to participate in *ex ante* standardization in wireless services. The FCC also later blocked the route towards 3G convergence in the form of W-CDMA as a

---

[1] In 1996 the Commission decided that mobile services must be competitive, with multiple GSM licences in each member state.
[2] The FCC preferred market- and user-driven *ex post* standards.

global standard (supported by ETSI). This all happened in the latter half of the 1990s. One interpretation of this is that the FCC was tied by the fact that US participants in the 3G race represented different technological alternatives, and therefore the FCC remained 'neutral' in the standardization process. At the same time there is the line of thought that suggests 'the regulation of the new information infrastructure has gravitated toward a clearer recognition of market driven standards. As the world of mobile telecommunications and computer communication (The Internet) collide, the clear trend is for direct regulation to withdraw from the market' (Glimstedt 2001: 52).

Firms such as Ericsson and Nokia are also moving away from their original idea of a singular standard for 3G services and towards the position that the new mobile telecommunications services should be based on several different but compatible standards: 'a family of standards'. This is similar to the idea of open architecture in relation to the Internet which advocates that 'network architecture should be as open as possible, allowing user-led innovation and new combinations of radical technologies' (Glimstedt 2001: 52). At the same time, however, as we saw in Chapter 1 (section 4.3.2.2.B), the most important US mobile telecommunications access providers have, during the first years of the millennium, transferred to GSM. If the reason is to facilitate the transfer to W-CDMA, then *ex ante* standardization seems to be winning the game anyway. This may be because market sizes and economies of scale created by *ex ante* standardization lead actors into the dominant trajectory in the evolutionary process of standard creation.[3]

The promotion of one single standard was of great importance for European dominance in the production of equipment for the mobile telecommunications industry; for example, it allowed economies of scale to be exploited. The fact that the relations between users and producers were close also proved very important, primarily for the producers. The way GSM developed increased the leadership position of Nokia and Ericsson. This is all the more notable in light of the lack of European success – and US–Asian dominance – in most other ICT sectors. The mobile telecommunications market was growing rapidly and was a major job creator in Europe, until recently.

Europe has emerged as a clear leader in mobile telecommunications due to its success in defining good standards in mobile communications. Ericsson's and Nokia's dominance among equipment producers in mobile telecommunications is often traced to the early success of the NMT standard, and GSM is similarly regarded as the means by which early Nordic success was generalized to other EU countries in the second generation of mobile communications.

---

[3] In Chapter 1 it was argued that there has been an evolutionary process from NMT 450 over GSM to W-CDMA.

One reason for the relatively poor international performance of US-based second-generation mobile standards was the 'division' of the market between standards, none of which could match the subscriber base of GSM. These developments are considered to account for the subsequent loss of market share by US equipment manufacturers to European rivals during the second generation of mobile telecommunications. The slower transfer from first- to second-generation standards in the US was due to regulatory decisions that stressed the necessity of achieving 'backwards compatibility' with the existing analogue standards, rather than compatible digital standards. Decisions with regard to charges were another factor contributing to the low subscriber penetration rates; often the receiver has to pay for all or part of a mobile phone call.

The current 'crisis' of Ericsson is mainly caused by a drastic decrease in demand because of the slowdown in the international business cycle, and thereby in telecommunications system investments. It serves to conceal the fact that Ericsson is still dominant in base stations and switches (and has even conquered market shares), while Nokia strongly dominates global handset production.

In the 1990s we have experienced a convergence between traditional telecommunications, the Internet and mobile telecommunications. This has also been accompanied by a wave of mergers and acquisitions (and strategic alliances), both among equipment producers and among operators. A strategic decision for the equipment producers is whether they should select voice as their main business area and thus go for the growing mobile phone markets; concentrate on the rapidly growing Internet equipment market; or go for mobile Internet?

4. THE SECTORAL SYSTEM'S FUTURE IN EUROPE, THE US AND JAPAN

It is clear that Europe has had the initiative in mobile voice telephony. Whether this will continue during the third-generation UMTS standard is unclear. NTT DoCoMo's I-Mode now has 31 million subscribers and DoCoMo was also the first operator to enter 3G in October 2001. This means that the focus of the centre of experimentation may have moved from Europe to Japan. This can spur equipment producers since user/producer interaction has earlier proved to be important. In the US, some operators have transferred to GSM and they will be more standardized in 3G than they were in 2G. However, the US is a slow starter in third-generation mobile telecommunications (with regard to WLANs, see below). Although Europe will probably enter 3G earlier than the US, it is doing so at a slower pace than Japan. This might partly be because of the very high prices European operators had to pay in some countries for a 3G licence, i.e., it might partly be a consequence of public policy.

Currently 3G is developing quite slowly. However, telecommunications operators' revenue was growing by 10 per cent per year in 2001 and the immediately preceding years. This indicates that telecommunications operators are not subject to a structural crisis, but have been hit by the downturn of the business cycle during 2000 and 2001 – which is expected to take off again in 2002 or early 2003.

The most important obstacles to the diffusion of 3G are, in the short run, the availability of handsets and in the longer run the supply of attractive content suited for mobile Internet. This points to the crucial role of demand in the emergence of new sectoral systems. As far as equipment is concerned, the policy instrument of public technology procurement was used both with regard to the Internet (US) and mobile telecommunications (Scandinavia). When it comes to content in 3G mobile Internet, most of the demand has to be provided by final consumers – firms and individuals – outside the public sphere to the largest extent. The success of I-Mode in Japan indicates that this will happen,[4] but access providers and content providers will have to be innovative not only with regard to access and content proper, but also when it comes to charging systems and other innovations in the field of management and administration. It is also a matter of developing niche strategies adapted to the new medium: movies will never be watched best on a mobile phone!

Fixed Internet diffusion is proceeding and now about 70 per cent of households have access in the US. In other countries the degree of diffusion varies widely. The dominance of US equipment producers which was established early in the history of fixed Internet is likely to remain stable for some time. At the same time this sector may be entering a more mature stage of development – with slower growth and smaller profits.

If WLAN becomes a serious competitor or an alternative to third-generation mobile telecommunications, i.e., if the development is jumping the 3G 'step' and goes directly into 4G, this will probably benefit the US. The reasons are that 3G will not be implemented there in the near future, that there are already a number of WLAN installations and that the US is very strong in PCs and Palmtops. There seems to be a possibility for leapfrogging here. If WLAN (802.11) proves to be extremely successful, the Europeans and the Japanese may be left out.

---

[4] But the slow diffusion of WAP and GPRS in Europe and the US points in the opposite direction.

5. THE THREE MOST IMPORTANT POLICY ISSUES

Here follows a summary of the three most important policy issues with regard to fixed Internet and mobile telecommunications. They are presented in telegraphic form, and in no particular order.

The role of institutions has been crucial for policy. Standards have played a major role in innovation and the success of European mobile telecommunications, both in terms of diffusion of use and with regard to the success of equipment-producing companies. Deregulation has also played a role for the diffusion of the Internet and mobile telecommunications. Other important institutions are the structure and level of tariffs. Some institutions are national, some are sectoral and others are firm specific. An important firm strategy objective has been to influence institutions to the firm's benefit.

The relations between different organizations and between institutions and organizations are crucial for the functioning and performance of (sectoral) systems of innovation. Examples are the relations between private and public organizations in the form of research funding, standard setting or public technology procurement. Relations between different kinds of firms and other private organizations are also important, e.g., collaboration between users and producers. Organizations provoke institutional changes, and when the new institutions come into effect, they may greatly influence the same or other organizations.

It is of paramount importance that public policy intervention occurs early in the development of the sectoral system. Public technology procurement was crucial for the very early development of the Internet in the US and formulation of standards was crucial for the very early development of mobile telecommunications in the Nordic countries. This proved to be very important also for equipment producers in these fields. It is in the very early stage in the development of a sectoral system of innovation that uncertainty and risks are largest and private actors and markets therefore operate least efficiently and dynamically.[5] Therefore policy intervention in these nascent stages often means the difference between success and failure. Hence, policy resources – which are always scarce – should mainly be allocated to the very early stages of the development of new sectoral systems of innovation or new product areas.

---

[5] That public policy intervention in the field of innovation should be practised only in situations where private firms and markets fail to spontaneously achieve the wanted results is argued in Edquist (2001a; 2001b). This means that public policy action should not replace or duplicate markets and private actors.

REFERENCES

Edquist C. (2001a), 'Innovation Policy – A Systemic Approach', in D. Archibugi and B.-A. Lundvall (eds), *The Globalising Learning Economy: Major Socio-Economic Trends and European Innovation Policy*, Oxford: Oxford University Press.

Edquist, C. (2001b), 'Innovation Policy in the Systems of Innovation Approach: Some Basic Principles', in M.M. Fischer and J. Fröhlich (eds), *Knowledge Complexity and Innovation Systems*, Berlin: Springer Verlag.

Glimstedt, H. (2001), 'Competitive Dynamics of Technological Standardization: The Case of Third Generation Cellular Communications', *Industry and Innovation*, **8** (1), 49–78.

Abbreviations and Acronyms

3GPP Third Generation Partnership Project
ADSL Asymmetrical Digital Subscriber Line
AMPS Advanced Mobile Phone System
ARIB Association of Radio Industries and Businesses
ARPA Advanced Research Projects Administration
ATM Asynchronous Transfer Mode
B-ISDN Broadband Integrated Services Digital Network
BRAN Broadband Radio Access Network
BSS Base Station System
BT British Telecom
CCIR International Radio Consultative Committee
CDMA Code Division Multiple Access
CEPT Conference on European Post and Telecommunications
COMSAT Communications Satellite Corporation
COST Co-opération européenne dans le domaine de la recherche Scientifique et Technique
CPN Customer Premises Network
CTIA Cellular Telephone Industry Association
CWTS China Wireless Telecommunication Standards

D-AMPS Digital Advanced Mobile Phone System
DARPA Defense Advanced Research Projects Agency
DCC Digital Cellular Communications
DECT Digital European Cordless Telephony
DoD Department of Defense
DTH Direct-to-Home
DVB Digital Video Based
DVB-MHP Digital Video Based-Multimedia Home Platforms
DWDM Dense Wavelength Division Multiplexing
EDGE Enhanced Data Rates for GSM Evolution
EDTV Enhanced Definition TV
EMS Enhanced Messaging Service
ESA European Space Agency
ESSY European Sectoral Systems of Innovation
ETSI European Telecommunications Standards Institute
FCC Federal Communications Commission (US)
FDM Frequency Division Multiplexing
FDMA Frequency Division Multiple Access
FWA Fixed Wireless Access
GEO Geo-stationary Earth Orbit
GMSS Global Mobile Satellite System
GPRS General Packet Radio Service

GSM Global System for Mobile
Telecommunications
HDML Handheld Device Markup
Language
HDTV High Definition TV
HLR Home Location Register
HSCSD High-Speed Circuit-Switched
Data
HTML HyperText Markup Language
HTTP HyperText Transfer Protocol
IAB Internet Activities Board
IAP Internet Access Provider
ICCB Internet Configuration Control
Board
ICP Internet Content Provider
ICT Information and Communication
Technology
IETF Internet Engineering Task Force
IMP Interface Message Processor
IMT-2000 International Mobile
Telephone standard
IN Intelligent Network
INMARSAT International Maritime
Satellite Organisation
IP Internet Protocol
IPR Intellectual Property Rights
IRTF Internet Research Task Force
ISDN Integrated Services Digital
Network
ISP Internet Service Provider
IT Information Technology
ITU International Telecommunications
Union
ITU-R ITU Radio Communications Section
LAN Local Area Network
LDTV Low Definition TV
LEO Low Earth Orbit
MEO Medium Earth Orbit
MMS Multimedia Messaging Service
MoU Memorandum of Understanding

MPT Ministry of Posts and
Telecommunications (Japan)
MRP Market Representation Partner
MSC Mobile Service Centre
NMT Nordic Mobile Telephony
NRA National Regulatory Authority
NSF National Science Foundation
ONP Open Network Provision
PABX Private Automatic Branch
Exchanges
PAMR Public Access Mobile Radio
PAN Personal Area Network
PCN Personal Communications Network
PCS Personal Communications Service
PDA Personal Digital Assistant
PDC Pacific Digital Cellular
PMR Public Mobile Radio
PSTN Public Switched
Telecommunications Network
PTO Public Telephone Operator
PTT Post, Telephone and Telegraph
RAS Radio Access System
RNC Radio Network Controller
SDH/DWDM Synchronous Digital
Hierarchy/Dense Wavelength
Division Multiplexing
SDI Strategic Defense Initiative or
'Star Wars'
SDO Standards Development
Organization
SDTV Standard Definition TV
SES Société Européenne des Satellites
SI Systems of Innovation
SIG Special Interest Group
SIM Subscriber Identity Module
SMG Special Mobile Group
SMS Short Message Service
SONET/SDH Synchronous Optical
Network/Synchronous Digital
Hierarchy

SSI Sectoral Systems of Innovation
STM Synchronous Transfer Mode
TCP Transmission Control Protocol
TCP/IP Transmission Control
   Protocol/Internet Protocol
TD-CDMA Time Division-Code
   Division Multiple Access
TDMA Time Division Multiple
   Access
TETRA Trans-European Trunked Radio
TIA Telecommunications Industry
   Association
TTA Telecommunications Technology
   Association (South Korea)
TTC Telecommunications Technology
   Committee

UIPA UMTS Intellectual Property
   Rights Association
UMTS Universal Mobile
   Telecommunications System
UWCC Universal Wireless
   Communications Consortium
VHE Virtual Home Environment
VLR Visitor Location Register
W-CDMA Wireless Code Division
   Multiple Access
WAN Wide Area Network
WAP Wireless Applications Protocol
WARC World Administrative Radio
   Conference
WIM WAP Identity Module
WLAN Wireless Local Area Network

Author Index

Subject Index